DATE DUE

MAR 1 2 2002			
MAY 2 2 2002			
OCT 2 1 2003			

Nikki Giovanni

Twayne's United States Authors Series

Frank Day, Editor

Clemson University

TUSAS 613

NIKKI GIOVANNI

Frontispiece photograph of Nikki Giovanni by Bob Veltri.

Nikki Giovanni

Virginia C. Fowler

Virginia Polytechnic Institute & State University

Twayne Publishers

New York

Nikki Giovanni
Virginia C. Fowler

TWAYNE PUBLISHERS

1633 Broadway, New York, N.Y. 10019-6785

10 9 8 7 6

The paper used in this publication meets the minimum requirements of American National Standard for Information Sciences—Permanence of Paper for Printed Library Materials. ANSI Z39.48-1984.∞™

Printed and bound in the United States of America.

Library of Congress Cataloging-in-Publication Data

Fowler, Virginia C., 1948–
Nikki Giovanni / Virginia C. Fowler.
p. cm.—(Twayne's United States authors series ; TUSAS 613)
Includes bibliographical references and index.
ISBN 0-8057-3983-1 (alk. paper)
1. Giovanni, Nikki—Criticism and interpretation. 2. Afro-Americans in literature. I. Title. II. Series.
PS3557.I55Z66 1992
811′.54—dc20 92-16731
CIP

Dedicated to the memory of the grandmothers,
whose spirits live on in us:
my own,
Ruth Chambers Jacoby

and Nikki's,
Emma Louvenia Watson

Contents

Preface

Nikki Giovanni is quite possibly the most widely read living poet in the United States today. Her public lecture/poetry readings routinely attract large and unusually diverse audiences. Some of her individual poems are so frequently anthologized that they have become modern classics, and her books of poetry consistently remain in print. In a nation of people who prefer film and television to literature of any sort and who have never been enthusiastic readers of poetry, Giovanni's continuing appeal to readers young and old, black and white, educated and uneducated, is a remarkable phenomenon.

Equally remarkable is the relative neglect of her work by literary scholars and critics, those members of our society who act as the guardians and preservers of art, who determine what literature will be taught to future generations. Giovanni's race and gender perhaps explain her neglect by what continues to be a predominantly white, male literary establishment. Surprisingly, however, even the new scholarship by and about women, and by and about people of color, has had little to say about Giovanni's work, despite the fact that her poetry develops themes typically of interest to such scholarship.

My study of Giovanni's work has its origins in precisely these contradictions between Giovanni's widespread popularity with what I might call ordinary readers, on the one hand, and her neglect by literary critics and scholars, on the other. Initially, I thought to write perhaps a short essay on the insights into the critical and literary establishments that these contradictions seemed to provide; and, in fact, much is still to be said about the biases and pettiness that so frequently characterize literary scholarship and criticism.

Eventually, however, I became convinced that the critical neglect of Giovanni resulted from judgments derived from early reviews by her detractors and from extremely selective reading of her work itself. What was needed, I recognized, was a full-scale examination of her poetry and of her development as a poet. I did not, initially, give serious thought to tackling this project myself. After all, my previous criticism has focussed on fiction, not poetry. And certainly I was given pause by the admonishment Giovanni directed at white critics in "Nikki–Rosa." But I finally determined that, as Charles Gordone states in *No Place To Be Somebody*, "there's more to being black than meets the eye."

My primary purpose in this study is to initiate a serious dialogue about Giovanni's poetry by offering a critical and analytical overview of that work and by correcting misperceptions about her life as well as her work. I hope that this study will serve as a starting point for future consideration of Giovanni's individual volumes of poetry as well as of her overall development.

In the study that follows, I situate Giovanni's development as a poet within the biographical, social, and political contexts that helped shape her identity as a human being. In particular, I argue that gender becomes an increasingly critical and problematic issue in her poetry. I also attempt to show the relationship of her poetry to the black musical traditions of the spirituals, the blues, and, in her most recent volume, jazz. The study considers the orality of Giovanni's poetry, which is one of its most important features, and connects this orality to her ideas about the purposes of poetry and the poet. Giovanni is without question a political poet, although not an ideological one; she is also a spiritual poet, although not a religious one.

This study has been immeasurably enhanced by the fact that Nikki Giovanni has been my colleague at Virginia Tech for the past five years. Not only has she graciously answered innumerable questions, but she has made available to me material that would have otherwise been difficult, often impossible, for me to obtain. She also allowed me to conduct a long, formal interview for inclusion in the Appendix to this study, an interview in which she addresses many of the topics my study explores. Without question, this study has been made far richer by her personal generosity and cooperation.

Limitations on space have obliged me to focus in this study exclusively on Giovanni's poetry for adult readers. While I have also dealt peripherally with her autobiography and many of her essays, I have had to ignore her children's poetry.

Finally, I would like to say a word or two about my uses of the terms *black* and *Afro-American*. Because Giovanni herself has a decided preference for and most consistently employs *black* rather than *Afro-American* as an adjective, I have by and large followed her practice. Although I occasionally use *Afro-American*, I have, out of respect for Giovanni's preferences, completely refrained from using *African-American*, which is currently the preferred choice of many.

Acknowledgments

I wish to thank Karen Swenson for reading and talking with me about the manuscript throughout the process of its composition. For their moral support and encouragement, I am indebted to many friends, but especially to the members of my whist group, David, Karen, Maple, Nikki, and Roberta. For keeping me in the here and now, I must certainly acknowledge all 18 pounds of Wendy.

Dr. Howard B. Gotlieb, director of Mugar Memorial Library's Special Collections, facilitated my access to Nikki Giovanni's papers; for his assistance, I am most appreciative. My visit to Mugar Memorial Library to conduct research essential to this book was made possible by a Travel to Collections Grant from the National Endowment for the Humanities. Completion of the project would not have been possible without the research leave granted me by Virginia Polytechnic Institute and State University. Finally, the professional support staff of my department has provided invaluable assistance on this project; I wish especially to thank Rebecca Cox, Tamera Shepherd, and Terri Whaling.

Permission to quote at length from the following material protected by copyright has been granted by Nikki Giovanni, author: *A Dialogue: James Baldwin and Nikki Giovanni,* J. B. Lippincott (1973); *A Poetic Equation: Conversations Between Nikki Giovanni and Margaret Walker*, Howard University Press (1974); *Black Feeling, Black Talk/Black Judgement*, William Morrow (1970); *Cotton Candy on a Rainy Day*, William Morrow (1978); *Gemini: An Extended Autobiographical Statement on My First Twenty-Five Years of Being A Black Poet*, Bobbs-Merrill (1971), Viking (1973), and Penguin (1976); *My House,* William Morrow (1972), *Re: Creation*, Broadside Press (1970); *Sacred Cows . . . And Other Edibles*, William Morrow (1988); *Those Who Ride The Night Winds*, William Morrow (1983); and *The Women and the Men*, William Morrow (1975).

Chronology

1943 Yolande Cornelia Giovanni, Jr., born June 7 in Knoxville, Tennessee, second child of Yolande and Jones Giovanni; family moves to Cincinnati, Ohio, in August.

1957 Moves to Knoxville to live with maternal grandparents, Emma Louvenia and John Brown Watson; attends Austin High School.

1960 Enrolls as an early entrant in Fisk University, Nashville, Tennessee.

1961–1963 Grandfather Watson dies; dismissed from Fisk University in February; returns to Cincinnati; works at Walgreen's and takes occasional classes at University of Cincinnati.

1964 Reenters Fisk University.

1965 Reestablishes the Student Nonviolent Coordinating Committee (SNCC) Chapter at Fisk University.

1966 Assistant in John O. Killens's writers' workshop at Fisk University.

1967 Receives bachelor of arts, Fisk University; Grandmother Watson dies; organizes first Cincinnati Black Arts Festival; managing editor of *Conversation*; attends Detroit Conference of Unity and Art; enters University of Pennsylvania's School of Social Work with a Ford Foundation fellowship.

1968 Attends funeral of Martin Luther King, Jr.; moves to New York City; receives grant from National Foundation of the Arts to attend Columbia University's School of Fine Arts; publishes *Black Feeling, Black Talk.*

1969 Publishes *Black Judgement* with grant received from Harlem Council of the Arts; gives birth to son, Thomas Watson Giovanni, on August 31; teaches at Queens College and at Rutgers University.

1970 Establishes NikTom, Ltd., a communications company; edits and publishes *Night Comes Softly*, an anthology of poetry by black women; publishes *Black Feeling, Black Talk/Black Judgement, Re: Creation*, and "Poem of Angela Yvonne Davis."

1971 *Truth Is On Its Way* (record) released; receives Highest Achievement Award from *Mademoiselle* magazine; travels in Europe and Africa; tapes video with James Baldwin in London; publishes *Gemini* (autobiographical essays) and *Spin A Soft Black Song* (children's poetry).

1972–1980 Helps finance, serves as editorial consultant to, and writes regularly for *Encore American & Worldwide News*; gives frequent lectures/poetry readings throughout the country, in some years, as many as 200.

1972 *Truth* receives NATRA's (National Association of Radio and Television Announcers) Award for Best Spoken Word Album; interviews Margaret Walker in Jackson, Mississippi; gives poetry recital at Lincoln Center; publishes *My House* and *A Dialogue: James Baldwin and Nikki Giovanni.*

1973 Gives poetry recital at New York's Philharmonic Hall; receives one of eight Women of the Year awards from the *Ladies' Home Journal* at Washington's Kennedy Center; visits Africa on a lecture tour sponsored by the Department of State; *My House* receives commendation from the American Library Association as one of the best books of 1973; is given Life Membership and Scroll by The National Council of Negro Women; publishes *Ego Tripping and Other Poems for Young Readers*; releases *Like A Ripple On A Pond* (record).

1974 Publishes *A Poetic Equation: Conversations Between Nikki Giovanni and Margaret Walker*; receives honorary doctorate of humanities from Wilberforce University, Wilberforce, Ohio.

1975 Publishes *The Women and the Men*; releases *The Way I Feel* (record).

1976 Receives Honorary Doctorate of Literature from Ripon University, Ripon, Wisconsin; releases *Legacies* and *The Reason I Like Chocolate* (records).

1977 Receives honorary doctorate of literature from the University of Maryland, Princess Anne Campus.

1978 Publishes *Cotton Candy on a Rainy Day*; releases record of *Cotton Candy on a Rainy Day*; receives honorary doctorate of literature from Smith College, Northampton, Massachusetts; father has a stroke; moves with son back to Cincinnati.

1978–1987 Makes her home with her parents; shoulders extensive domestic and financial responsibilities for her family.

1979 Publishes *Vacation Time* (children's poetry); named an honorary commissioner for the President's Commission on the International Year of the Child.

1982 Father dies.

1983 Publishes *Those Who Ride The Night Winds*; named YWCA Woman of the Year (Cincinnati Chapter).

1984–1985 Visiting Professor of English, Ohio State University, Columbus; her opposition to boycott of South Africa leads to her being blacklisted by TransAfrica and subsequently to bomb and death threats.

1985–1987 Professor of Creative Writing, College of Mount Saint Joseph on-the-Ohio.

1985 Receives honorary doctorate of human letters from the College of Mount Saint Joseph; named to the Ohio Women's Hall of Fame; named Outstanding Woman of Tennessee; makes European lecture tour for USIA (United States Information Agency).

1986 Receives the Post-Corbett Award (Cincinnati *Post*); Detroit City Council gives her its Distinguished Recognition Award; serves as Duncanson Artist-in-Residence at the Taft Museum of Cincinnati.

1987–1989 Commonwealth Visiting Professor of English, Virginia Polytechnic Institute and State University, Blacksburg.

1987 *Spirit To Spirit: The Poetry of Nikki Giovanni* (PBS film); performs *A Signal in the Land* with the Johnson City Symphony Orchestra; serves as judge for the Robert F. Kennedy Memorial Book Award; appointed to a three-year term on the Ohio Humanities Council.

1988 Publishes *Sacred Cows . . . And Other Edibles* (essays); named a Cincinnati bi-Centennial honoree; *Spirit To Spirit* receives Silver Apple Award from Oakland Museum Film Festival; *Sacred Cows* receives the Ohioana Library Award; *Vacation Time* receives the Children's Reading Roundtable of Chicago Award; receives honorary doctorate of humanities from Fisk University.

1989 Accepts permanent position as Professor of English, Virginia Polytechnic Institute and State University.

1991 Receives honorary doctorate of humane letters from Indiana University, Gary Campus.

1992 Receives honorary doctorate of humane letters from Otterbein College, Westerville, Ohio.

Chapter One
An Introduction to the Life of Nikki Giovanni

"Childhood remembrances are always a drag / if you're Black."[1] Thus begins Nikki Giovanni's most famous poem, "Nikki–Rosa," written in 1968 and included in her second volume of poetry, *Black Judgement.* What makes memories of childhood "a drag," the poem goes on to explain, is the likelihood that biographers—in particular, white biographers—will seize on the tangible, objective facts, falsely confident of the subjective reality to which such facts point. Like Daniel Moynihan, whose 1965 report, *The Negro Family: The Case for National Action,* outraged Giovanni[2] and other black Americans, white biographers will "probably talk about my hard childhood / and never understand that / all the while I was quite happy" (*BF*, 58).

Chief among the subjective realities apt to be missed by white biographers is the truth that "Black love is Black wealth"—the most famous line in this signature poem[3] and one of the central ideas in Giovanni's work. Frequently quoted, these five words may indeed have "stated to the world a new commitment,"[4] but their implications, which Giovanni explores in each subsequent volume of poetry, have often been missed by those reviewers and critics puzzled or disappointed by what they perceive to be a change in her commitment to "the revolution." In fact, however, "Nikki–Rosa" immediately precedes "The Great Pax Whitie" in *Black Judgement*, just as "Detroit Conference of Unity and Art," a love poem, is the first poem in *Black Feeling, Black Talk.* In "Nikki–Rosa," Giovanni both lays claim to her exclusive right to determine the meaning of her life and inscribes the centrality of family and love in that life. As she was to write in her autobiography, *Gemini*, "I was trained intellectually and spiritually to respect myself and the people who respected me. I was emotionally trained to love those who love me. If such a thing can be, I was trained to be in power—that is, to learn and act upon necessary emotions which will grant me more control over my life."[5]

400 Mulvaney Street

Although Giovanni's parents established their home in Cincinnati, Ohio, when Nikki was a mere infant, her spiritual home and most important roots are found in Knoxville, Tennessee, the small southern city where she was born and the home of her maternal grandparents, John Brown and Emma Louvenia Watson. Their house on 400 Mulvaney Street—poignantly remembered in *Gemini*—was where young Nikki, her sister Gary, and their cousins spent summer vacations and many holidays.

John Brown Watson, nicknamed *Book* because he was a Latin teacher and scholar, was some 20 years older than Louvenia Terrell, his second wife. A graduate of Fisk University, he was a schoolteacher in Albany, Georgia, where he and Louvenia lived during the first years of their marriage. His young wife's outspoken assertion of her rights—perhaps the very quality to which the conservative teacher was attracted—soon necessitated their unexpected flight from Georgia, where lynchings of black people were frequent. After an altercation with a white merchant, in which Louvenia refused to be appropriately intimidated by bullying threats, the Watson and Terrell families agreed that the couple must flee. So, under cover of night, they set out with their first child, Yolande Cornelia, the poet's mother.

Although their original intention had been to travel as far north as Washington or Philadelphia, they soon decided that they were unable to make such a long journey; instead, they stopped in Knoxville. Here they purchased the house at 400 Mulvaney Street, where, over the next three years, baby Yolande acquired two sisters, Anne ("Anto") and Agnes.

The Watson family enjoyed a respected position in the Knoxville black community. John Brown, who had graduated from Fisk University in 1905, taught Latin at Austin High School and was brilliant with numbers. He held responsible positions in their church, Mt. Zion Baptist, serving, for example, as head of the Church Building Fund, and impressing everyone with financial reports given directly from memory—he carried every figure in his head. Scholarly, quiet, and conservative, he seemed in every way the exact opposite of his young wife Louvenia, who had herself attended Albany Normal School. Even with three children and a house to care for, Louvenia was a tireless volunteer. A civil rights activist, she worked in such organizations as the National Association for the Advancement of Colored People (NAACP), the Colored Women's Federated Club (which later became Women United, the founding basis of the National Council of Negro Women), the Court of Calanthy, and of course, Mt. Zion Baptist Church. Unlike her husband, who was a staunch Republican, Louvenia was a Democrat who helped in such endeavors as the voter registration drives. Louvenia's activism was a frequent source of unhappiness to John Brown; she would attend, for example, conferences at the controversial Highlander Folk School, which white people suspected of being communist because it was interracial.

Possessed of a strong, committed, assertive, and sometimes controlling personality, Louvenia Watson was one of those pillars of the black community without whose efforts the civil rights movement could never have been successful. She was to become one of the most important influences on Nikki Giovanni's life; along with several other women like her whom the poet encountered as she was growing up, Louvenia embodied those qualities and values that Giovanni most respects: Louvenia devoted her energies and talents to a future that would be better for her people; she insisted on her rights as an individual, even though she was a black woman in a racist and sexist society; she provided a home for her children that was nurturing yet disciplined; together with her husband, she made certain that their daughters received college educations; whatever she and hers had was always generously shared with others. It was her spirit that gave her granddaughter a sense of belonging in the world. In *Gemini*, Giovanni describes her first visit to Knoxville after Louvenia's death; her description of her visit—as a newly famous young poet—is charged with the emotion generated by her memories of her grandmother and of 400 Mulvaney Street, which her grandmother had seen destroyed by urban renewal and "progress":

So they took me up what would have been Vine Street past what would have been Mulvaney and I thought there may be a reason we lack a collective historical memory. And I was taken out to the beautiful homes on Brooks Road where we considered the folks "so swell, don't cha know." And I was exhausted but feeling quite high from being once again in a place where no matter what I belong. And Knoxville belongs to me. I was born there in Old Knoxville General and I am buried there with Louvenia. And as the time neared for me to speak I had no idea where I would start. I was nervous and afraid because I just wanted to quote Gwen Brooks and say, "This is the urgency—Live!" And they gave me a standing ovation and I wanted to say, "Thank you," but that was hardly sufficient. Mommy's old bridge club, Les Pas Si Betes, gave me beads, and that's the kind of thing that happens in small towns where people aren't afraid to be warm. And I looked out and saw Miss Delaney in her blue furs. And was reminded life continues. And I saw the young brothers and sisters who never even knew me or my family and I saw my grandmother's friends who shouldn't even have been out that late at night. And they had come to say *Welcome Home*. And I thought Tommy, my son, must know about this. He must know we come from somewhere. That we belong. (*GE*, 12)

Like Louvenia before her, Giovanni in this passage determines to provide her son a sense of his roots, of the fact that he belongs somewhere; her motivation in writing *Gemini* and in setting down her memories of her grandparents is in fact to give her son this sense of his roots. Significantly, white "progress" has succeeded in destroying black people's "collective historical memory" by razing their homes, but it has not been able to destroy their love and support of each other—the spirit that made their houses homes. What Giovanni acknowledges in the passage is the imperative to communicate to her son the particular meaning in her own life—and therefore in his—of "Black love is Black wealth."

The Man with an Exotic Name

The oldest Watson daughter, Yolande, was attending Knoxville College when she "ran into a shiny-head Negro with a pretty suit on. He, being warm and friendly and definitely looking for a city girl to roost with, introduced himself. I have always thought that if his name hadn't been exotic she would never have given him a second thought" (*GE*, 29).

Unlike his young wife-to-be, Jones Giovanni, nicknamed "Gus," had never enjoyed a 400 Mulvaney Street or the sense of self and belonging it could engender. Gus was born five years earlier than Yolande, in 1914, in the small town of Berbena, Alabama, long since swallowed by Mobile. Little is known of his father, Thomas, who seems simply to have disappeared when Gus was very young. There were two other children, both older than Gus, a brother or half-brother, William, and a sister, Fannie. Their mother, Mattie Jones Giovanni, decided to move north when Gus was still a child; she took William and Gus with her to Cincinnati (it is unclear what happened to Fannie at this point, although she, too, later lived in Cincinnati). Apparently unable to provide for herself and her children in Cincinnati, Mattie moved with William to Detroit, where she was eventually able to buy a house.

Young Gus, who was perhaps eight or nine years old at this point, was left with a relative, Fannie Brown, who lived in the small town of Zenia just outside Cincinnati. Fannie Brown became a mother to Gus, who grew up in Zenia with his cousin, William Atkinson. It seems likely that Gus never saw Mattie again.

Like most people during the depression years, Fannie Brown was poor, but she had a farm that provided subsistence for herself and the two boys. Hardworking, intelligent, and personable, Gus won an athletic scholarship to attend Morris Brown, a junior college in Tennessee. After completing his studies there—which were actually comparable to high school courses—Gus returned for a time to Cincinnati. There he met Lee Render, a Knoxville College graduate through whose efforts Gus received a scholarship to attend Knoxville College. Like other scholarship students, Gus worked while he went to school, putting him a year behind the pretty young Yolande Watson. A charming individual, Gus soon won the approval of Louvenia, but was less successful with John Brown, who refused to attend his first-born's wedding.

Gus Giovanni and Yolande Watson were married on 3 July 1939, just after her graduation. He continued to work for the Tennessee Valley Authority (TVA) during the following year, stoking furnaces at night and attending classes during the day. He graduated from Knoxville College in June 1940, and the couple's first daughter, Gary Ann, was born that August.

While a college degree in 1940 was a ticket to a good job or professional position for most white men, it was virtually worthless for a black man in the South. Thus, despite his hard struggle to obtain a college education, and despite his intelligence and ability, Gus was able, after his graduation, to find only menial, low-paying jobs. Stoking furnaces for TVA and working as a bellhop at local hotels defined the limits of his career opportunities. Added to these limitations were the insulting and oppressive conditions for blacks living in the segregated, Jim Crow South. And though the pain and humiliation engendered by those conditions might be bearable for oneself, to see one's children confronting them was far more difficult. When the film *Snow White* was being widely promoted in Knoxville, young Gary of course wanted to go see it; though Gus and Yolande realized the futility of taking their daughter to the theater, they nevertheless tried. In segregated Knoxville, the outcome was inevitable, but their being refused admittance constituted a final straw for Gus. He determined to return to the North.

Through the efforts of his old mentor, Lee Render, Gus was able to secure a position as houseparent at Glenview School, a home for black boys in Cincinnati. Because Yolande was pregnant with Nikki, Gus was able to defer moving to Cincinnati until after his second daughter's birth. The poet was born on 7 June 1943, and in August, Gus, Yolande, and their two children moved to Cincinnati.

Childhood in Cincinnati

Glenview School made a wise decision in allowing Gus Giovanni to defer acceptance of his position as houseparent, because when he came to work he brought his wife with him. Clearly an asset to him, Yolande herself was as much and as fine a houseparent as he, even though they drew only one salary. Both of them enjoyed working with the boys in the school, but the pay was inadequate to support a family of four. Eventually, Gus was able to obtain a teaching position at South Woodlawn School, and the family moved to Woodlawn, a northern suburb of Cincinnati. Here they lived in a house with no running water—the house that Giovanni was later to write about in "Nikki–Rosa." Because Woodlawn had no school for black children, Gary was sent to live with Bill and Gladys Atkinson in Columbus, where she attended second grade.

The following year, Gus and Yolande were able to find an apartment in neighboring Wyoming, where Nikki and Gary both attended Oak Avenue School. Nikki began kindergarten here and attended first, second, and third grades. After third grade, she entered St. Simon's, an all black, Episcopal school where her mother had taken a position the previous year teaching third grade. St. Simon's proved to be a very positive experience for the young Nikki; always something of a homebody and a mamma's girl, Nikki found familiar faces at St. Simon's: in addition to her mother, an old friend of the family, Flora Alexander, taught there, as did a young nun who became Nikki's first real friend "of her own," Sister Althea.

The family's financial position began to improve during the years Nikki attended St. Simon's. Her father, who always worked at least two jobs and sometimes three, stopped teaching to become a probation officer in the Hamilton County Juvenile Detention Office. After he began working in this position, Gus was able to help Yolande obtain a job working for the Hamilton County Welfare Department, which paid considerably more than the $100 a month she made at St. Simon's. These improvements in their financial circumstances enabled the parents to move their children to the black community of Lincoln Heights.

As these details indicate, the young Nikki Giovanni grew up in relative poverty, but her parents clearly instilled in their children the notion that poverty does not necessarily exclude the possibilities of education and self-determination. The poet is fond of introducing readings of "Nikki-Rosa" with anecdotes that illustrate the values she absorbed from her parents. Though the house in Woodlawn had no inside plumbing, for example, it contained hundreds of books as well as a piano. Moreover, Gus always made his children feel that whatever they had was the best. One Christmas, all the neighborhood children, except Gary and Nikki, received bicycles. All Gus and Yolande had been able to afford for their girls were roller skates. "Just look at those poor children," Gus lamented. "Isn't it terrible that their parents gave them bicycles when it's so cold. They won't be able to ride until spring." As Giovanni tells the story today, she and her sister ended up feeling terribly sorry for all their friends whose parents had so thoughtlessly given them bicycles for Christmas. Thus did Gary and Nikki learn not just contentment but happiness with what they had.

In *Gemini*, Giovanni writes humorously about her childhood, in particular, about her older sister, Gary. Three years her senior, Gary greatly enjoyed playing the all-knowing big sister to an admiring Nikki, who always felt that nobody was as perfect as *her* big sister. It was Gary, in fact, who dubbed the poet "Nikki–Rosa"; no one knows exactly how the three-year-old Gary came up with this nickname, but it stuck, though as Giovanni grew up, it was shortened to "Nikki." Most readers and even many of Giovanni's acquaintances are unaware that her actual name is Yolande Cornelia Giovanni, Jr., and countless fans have in fact named their infant daughters *Nikki* in honor of the poet.

As Giovanni tells it in *Gemini*, she envisioned herself, ironically, as her big sister's protector, fighting her fights for her so that Gary's piano-playing hands would not be marred. Although little sisters are not normally expected to take care of big sisters, Giovanni's humorous image of her younger self in this role corresponds accurately to the strong feelings of familial responsibility she developed as an adult.

A quick and cheerful child who enjoyed spending time by herself, Giovanni excelled in school. Given to frequent illness, she filled her long and lonely hours at home with reading and then writing. When she was about 12 or 13, her mother had her put through a battery of tests because she seemed to have odd behavioral patterns. On the one hand, she was extremely bright and performed well at intellectual tasks; on the other, she could be sent on an errand and return, mission unaccomplished, having totally forgotten the purpose for which she was sent. The test results indicated that she possessed no manual dexterity whatever; but they also registered her intelligence at the level of genius.

Although her father struggled successfully to provide for his family and to contribute to the community through his work, that struggle was difficult and painful, as indeed it was for virtually every black American of his generation. As Giovanni writes in *Gemini*, "My family on my father's side are survivors" (*GE*, 33). But the emotional cost of Gus's struggle for his own and his family's survival seems to have been paid in part by the wife and children he cared the most about. He became, at any rate, an abusive man. Though unafraid of him, Giovanni found herself, on the eve of beginning high school, unable any longer to tolerate the tensions that erupted so frequently between her parents. Even at age 14, she possessed a strong sense of independence and self-determination and, with characteristic decisiveness, called her grandmother Watson, asked if she could come to Knoxville for the summer, and, once there, asked her grandparents to let her stay.

Radicalization of an Adolescent Intellectual

The adolescent Giovanni's decision to get away from the tensions at home by living with Louvenia and John Brown Watson proved fortuitous not just for her emotional well-being but for her intellectual growth as well. The three years she spent at 400 Mulvaney Street (1957–60) strengthened her bond with her grandmother, who was one of the most important people in her life. Young Nikki became the first person anyone had ever known to be able to hold her own with Louvenia, who was accustomed to maintaining almost imperialistic control over anyone living under her roof. Between the strongminded, determined Louvenia and the equally strongminded and independent Nikki, developed the kind of mutual love and respect often possible between grandparents and grandchildren and equally rare between parents and children.

As granddaughter-in-residence, Nikki was expected to help Louvenia not just with domestic chores but with Louvenia's many charitable, social, and political activities. When bodies were needed to demonstrate against segregated dining facilities at Rich's department store in downtown Knoxville, Louvenia cheerfully volunteered her granddaughter—then took a cab downtown with her husband to give Nikki moral support (neither Louvenia nor John Brown could drive). Similarly, Nikki would be sent to take food from Sunday's dinner to shut-ins or folk who were ill.

From countless activities such as these, the girl developed a strong sense of responsibility and commitment to her community—a sense of the importance of "giving something back." She likewise grew in awareness of America's racism and of the need to fight against what is morally wrong. Louvenia instilled in her a belief in the importance of individual action, of the moral imperative to "stand up and be counted" whether your side wins or not.

At Austin High School, which she attended for ninth, tenth, and eleventh grades, Giovanni encountered another grandmotherly woman who was to exercise an important influence on her, Miss Alfredda Delaney. Giovanni's high school English teacher in all three grades, Miss Delaney recognized the intelligence and talent behind the bored and "hip" façade that Nikki was apt to present at school. Realizing that her young pupil needed to be challenged, Miss Delaney launched her on a course of reading Afro-American writers and required her to write about what she read. Such projects gave Giovanni, who as a high school student entertained the ambition of becoming a lawyer, the opportunity to think about what it might mean to be a writer; as the following excerpt from her report on Gwendolyn Brooks shows, she was beginning, however crudely, to think about the issues that in a few short years she would address in such publications as *Negro Digest*: "She [Brooks], of course, writes of Negroes; but not 'of course' as many other Negroes do. She writes, as I see her, as a woman would write, which is an incoherent statement. What I mean is, she writes poetry as a mother might—with understanding, love, and a gentle sense of humor. She and Langston Hughes, the Negro, can read without feeling the chains of slavery hanging heavily on his back."[6] Miss Delaney encouraged Nikki to pursue writing herself, and, with Nikki's French teacher, Miss Emma Stokes, helped her pupil apply for early admittance to Fisk University. Thus, Giovanni left Austin High School at the end of eleventh grade and entered Fisk shortly after her seventeenth birthday.

Although Fisk had recognized Giovanni's intellectual capability by accepting her into its Early Entrants Program, it was not prepared to recognize the extent of individual autonomy she was accustomed to exercising. It was perhaps predictable that her values would come into conflict with those of virtually any institution; and, given her inexperience, it was inevitable that she would lose in any conflict with the then dean of women, Ann Cheatam. A stickler for rules, Dean Cheatam was outraged that Giovanni went to Knoxville to visit her grandparents over Thanksgiving without having obtained the necessary permission. In February, when her first semester at Fisk had ended, Giovanni was "'released from the school,'" she explains in *Gemini*, "because my 'attitudes did not fit those of a Fisk woman'" (*GE*, 8). Expulsion from Fisk was perhaps a high price to pay for the conviction that she did not need anyone's "permission to go home" (*GE*, 7), but, given that her grandfather died in April, Giovanni remained convinced that she had done the right thing. In fact, expulsion from Fisk gave her the time and independence she needed to sort out her own personal goals and her relationship to the different struggles being made by her fellow black Americans to wrest their rights as American citizens from a bigoted but weakening white majority.

Years of Germination

After dismissal from Fisk University in February 1961, Giovanni moved back home with her parents, where she stayed until 1964. During the years she had lived in Knoxville, her sister, Gary, had graduated from high school, done a brief stint at Central State University, married, had a son, been divorced, and was soon to remarry. Gary's son, Christopher, was living with Gus and Yolande, and when Nikki returned home it fell to her to take care of him. She soon became very attached to the two-year-old Chris, nicknamed Peppe; in fact, when Peppe left to join his mother and her new husband in New Jersey, Nikki broke out in hives all over her body for three days. Throughout his childhood, she remained a doting aunt, spending long days with him at the Cincinnati zoo and eventually dedicating poems to him, including one of her most famous poems, "The True Import of Present Dialogue, Black vs. Negro (For Peppe, Who Will Ultimately Judge Our Efforts)."

She found a job at Walgreen's drug store and began taking classes at the University of Cincinnati. She also spent a good deal of time working with children whose parents were clients of Yolande, now a social worker. The spring and summer of 1961 witnessed a key link in the long chain of events that resulted in the passing of civil rights legislation; on 4 May, 13 Freedom Riders began their historic bus trip through the Deep South. Although Giovanni was not a participant in any of the major demonstrations that ensued, her consciousness and sense of self developed simultaneously with them.

In 1964, she decided to visit Nashville and explore the possibility of being readmitted to Fisk. Recognizing that the dean of women was the person with whom she needed to cooperate, she went first to that office.

To her amazement, Dean Cheatam had been replaced by a middle-aged Oklahoman, Blanche McConnell Cowan ("Jackie"). A Fiskite herself and a former social worker, Dean Cowan pulled and read the file on Giovanni accumulated in one short semester by former Dean Cheatam and promptly recognized the pettiness and injustice of the complaints in it. She not only purged the file but urged Giovanni to return to Fisk and finish her undergraduate degree. The young woman and the older one struck responsive chords in one another; Dean Cowan was to become the most important figure in Giovanni's life at Fisk and to remain a close friend until Cowan's death in 1986. Like the poet's grandmother and Miss Delaney, Cowan offered nurturance and interest rather than criticism and disapproval; she was unperturbed by the fact that Giovanni was a serious-minded, intense young woman who was looking for something in life other than marriage and a family. Her impact on Giovanni can be readily seen in the poems dedicated to her in *Black Feeling, Black Talk.*

When Giovanni returned to Fisk in the fall of 1964, she threw herself into both literary and political activities. Majoring in history, she also edited a student literary / political journal and reestablished the chapter of the Student Nonviolent Coordinating Committee (SNCC), which the school's administration had banned several years earlier. Arguing that it had as much right on campus as other student organizations, Giovanni persuaded the new administration to recognize it as a legitimate and official student group. Although clearly political, Giovanni did not advocate violence; indeed, she refused to allow her fellow SNCC members to bring Stokely Carmichael to campus, knowing that such an event would bring the Nashville police to campus as well—and an eruption of violence. After she graduated from Fisk, SNCC did bring Carmichael to campus with precisely the results she had predicted.

During her years at Fisk, Giovanni became more serious about her writing. She had the opportunity to work with the distinguished novelist and essayist, John O. Killens, who was writer-in-residence at Fisk and an important figure in the Black Arts Movement. At his writers' workshop in April 1966, Giovanni had the opportunity to hear LeRoi Jones (later Imamu Amiri Baraka), the leading figure among the "new black poets" and prophet of the cultural nationalists, read his groundbreaking "Up Against the Wall Motherfucker, This Is A Stickup."

Giovanni finished the requirements of her degree in December 1966 and moved back to Cincinnati, this time to her own apartment. The following year was one of the most important and productive of her life. In April, just two months after her graduation from Fisk, her grandmother died. As she was to write in the poignant first chapter of *Gemini*, her grandmother, having lost her home on Mulvaney to "progress," no longer had a desire to live; she had wanted to live long enough to see her favorite granddaughter graduate from Fisk, and, that accomplished, was ready to die.

After her death, Giovanni took refuge from her grief in work. Most of the poems of her first volume, *Black Feeling, Black Talk*, were written during the remaining months of 1967. In addition to her writing, she became the editor of *Conversation*, a local black revolutionary publication. And she continued her volunteer work in a neighborhood center in the black suburb of Avondale. She organized Cincinnati's first Black Arts Festival, which took place that June. The centerpiece of the festival was a dramatic adaptation, written and directed by Giovanni, of Virginia Hamilton's *Zeely*. The primary goal of the production was to demonstrate to Cincinnati's white theatrical community that there were, in fact, talented black actors in Cincinnati. The highly successful, all-white theater group of Playhouse in the Park had for years claimed no black people were in their company because no black actors were available. Giovanni's production of *Zeely* refuted that claim; it also gave birth to a black theatrical company, The New Theatre. When Giovanni left in the fall for graduate school, Charles Holman took over as director of The New Theatre, which in subsequent productions continued to demonstrate that in the Cincinnati community were black talent and audiences for black plays. Playhouse in the Park eventually invited The New Theatre to join it, and the two companies merged.

Giovanni's work in putting together this first Black Arts Festival was to become typical of her strategies for fighting the racist exclusion of black people in American society. In May 1967, she attended the Detroit Conference of Unity and Art, where she met H. Rap Brown, who replaced Stokely Carmichael as the head of SNCC. From this point forward, she was closely involved with many of the key figures of the Black Arts Movement and the black power movement. Giovanni, however, always maintained an independent position in relationship to the leaders of the movements and to the ideologies they preached. A festival celebrating black art and artists was always to remain her conception of "revolution"; though she occasionally tried out the rhetoric of black power in her poems or essays, she never confused rhetoric with action, and she remained convinced that progress at the cost of human lives was not progress at all.

The Big Move East

Influenced no doubt by the fact that her beloved Dean Cowan had attended the University of Pennsylvania's School of Social Work, Giovanni began studies there with the aid of a fellowship from the Ford Foundation in September 1967. Housing being considerably cheaper in Wilmington, Delaware, than in Philadelphia, she took an apartment there. As a part of her graduate program, she worked at the People's Settlement House, and she continued to work there after her studies at the university came to a premature close. One semester of social work school was sufficient for the young poet to realize that she lacked the personality necessary for a successful career as a social worker.

She left school and continued to work at the People's Settlement House. She was living in Wilmington when Dr. Martin Luther King, Jr., was killed on 4 April 1968, and she managed to leave the city before the National Guard, prepared for riots, sealed it. She drove all night to get to Atlanta for King's funeral. Throughout the spring and summer, she continued to write at a prodigious rate, producing most of the poems that were to comprise her second volume, *Black Judgement*, including "Nikki–Rosa."

In the summer, she moved to New York City, where she would live for the next 10 years. In the fall, by means of a grant from the National Foundation of the Arts, she entered Columbia University's School of Fine Arts. Her intention was to earn an M.F.A. in creative writing, but, angered by the conservative white literary critics she encountered at Columbia, who tried to tell her she could not write, she rejected the validation of a degree and resigned from the program. By the end of the year, she had borrowed the money to publish her first volume, *Black Feeling, Black Talk*. From that point on, her publications sufficed as testimony of her poetic abilities, and her remarkable career was launched.

Controversial Stardom

Over the course of the next 10 years, Giovanni achieved a national prominence and popularity unheard of for a poet, especially a black poet or a black woman poet. Her initial volumes, which were combined and published by the commercial press, William Morrow, in 1970, were applauded by such Black Cultural Nationalists as Don L. Lee (later Haki R. Madhubuti) and LeRoi Jones, largely because of the handful of "revolutionary" poems they contained. By the time *My House* was published, however, these same individuals, and others like them, were writing scathing reviews and making vicious personal attacks on the poet. Simultaneously, she developed a huge popular following and was in great demand for personal appearances. This division in the responses to her work by the black literary avant-garde (which eventually became the black literary establishment) on the one hand and by ordinary readers on the other continues even today. How do we account for this?

The reasons are to be found in her life, rather than in her poetry itself. In the only thoughtful and substantive analysis of this phenomenon to date, Margaret B. McDowell, surveying the reviews of Giovanni's work between 1969 and 1974, convincingly demonstrates that "critics have allowed personal and political attitudes not merely to affect their judgment but to dominate it."[7] As McDowell shows, reviewers and critics from the outset gave disproportionate attention to Giovanni's political poems, even though these were outnumbered by poems about love and other personal subjects. Thus, when Giovanni stopped using "revolutionary" rhetoric and exploring "revolutionary" ideology, her critics believed there had been a major change in the focus and purpose of her poetry. Having inaccurately defined her as their kind of radical, or revolutionary, they subsequently criticized her for having "sold out" because she refused to write didactic poetry on behalf of the revolution.

Like many organized efforts for change, the Black Arts Movement and the black power movement had quickly become rigid, dogmatic, and prescriptive. The Black Arts Movement must itself be an instrument of the black revolution, many argued, and "there is no place for nonrevolutionary art during a period of revolution."[8] But anyone who knew Giovanni at all would have had to realize that she would never allow her poetry or her life to be dictated by others or by any ideology. As she was to say many years later in an interview, "I don't see why I should live in hostage to other people's idea of me."[9]

Giovanni's refusal to follow the prescriptions of Black Arts leaders such as Lee and Jones might not have drawn their disapproval had it not been for two things: she was a woman and she was enormously successful. The movement was, like its white counterpart, the new left of the 1960s and early 1970s, male controlled. Giovanni, moreover, not only refused to acknowledge the superior wisdom of its male leaders or their right to dictate her art; she also, in 1969, had a son whose father she refused to identify, and she even went so far as to triumphantly tell the world that she was an unwed mother because she could afford to be. Not surprisingly, then, criticism of her work soon became criticism of her personal life. The problem, one reviewer of *My House* wrote, was that Giovanni could not get a man: "I betcha Nikki wanted to be married."[10]

Giovanni's success without the help of the Black Arts Movement's male leaders angered them even more. Although Jones and other proponents of a "black aesthetic" had argued that the new black poetry should be accessible to ordinary people and had themselves given oral presentations of their poetry to enthusiastic audiences, they were outstripped by Giovanni, whose gift for speaking and charismatic personality combined with the essential orality of her poetry to propel her into a kind of stardom. Her frequent appearances on the television program *Soul!* brought her national attention and led her to consider a mixed media presentation of her poetry. She teamed with the New York Community Choir, directed by Benny Diggs, to produce a recording of her poetry against the background of gospel music. Entitled *Truth Is On Its Way*, the album was introduced at a free concert performed at Harlem's Canaan Baptist Church in the summer of 1971 before a crowd of 1,500. As Giovanni explained, "I'm spiritual and I believe that God is black. I was baptized in a Baptist church and my poetry springs partly from this source. What could be more appropriate than having a church for your stage with gospel and poetry together?"[11] The album was a phenomenal success, staying for weeks on the hit charts and receiving the National Association of Television and Radio Announcers (NATRA) award for the Best Spoken Word Album the following year.

Honors, awards, and increasing popularity continued for Giovanni throughout the 1970s, and her life took on an almost impossible pace. She was following the philosophy of the Black Arts Movement that the poet should "take his [*sic*] work where his people are: Harlem, Watts, Philadelphia, Chicago and the rural South,"[12] and she was quick to acknowledge that "the people" were responsible for her success: "I believe firmly in the power of the people. . . . If it wasn't for the people where would I be? I wasn't made by TV or magazines but by the people who came out to see me" ("Princess," 17). Her success went beyond what has traditionally been regarded as acceptable for a "serious" writer; even those writers who had advocated taking poetry to "the people" had not really envisioned the degree of popularity with the people that Giovanni's poetry quickly achieved. It was perhaps predictable and inevitable, then, that Giovanni's very success led to attacks that failure would never have prompted. One reviewer of *Truth Is On Its Way*, for example, suggested that Giovanni was exploiting black people: "It is the responsibility of black artists to be Seekers-of-the-Truth in the tradition of Douglass and

Dubois and not to become moneychangers in the Temple of black people's future."[13] Others, disappointed by her refusal to continue to write polemical poems for the revolution, accused her of "ego-tripping" and warned that she was compromising her integrity.[14] The ultimate symbol of this compromised integrity, as they saw it, was her acceptance—on national television—of a Woman of the Year award from the *Ladies' Home Journal*. The ceremony, which took place at the Kennedy Center in Washington, honored eight women for distinguished achievement in different categories; Giovanni, who was honored for youth leadership, was in illustrious company: Virginia Apgar, Shirley Chisholm, Katherine Graham, LaDonna Harris, Helen Hayes, Mary Lasker, and Ellen Straus were the other winners. Not only did some black leaders believe Giovanni should not have accepted this award from a white organization, but they were outraged by her joining the other winners in singing "God Bless America" at the end of the ceremonies. By contrast, Giovanni regarded her selection for the award as indicative of progress: "If this award had been presented three years ago there never would have been a black woman involved. But it would be very small of us not to rejoice."[15] And, as Jeanne Noble points out, Giovanni did "not shun confrontation or even violence if whites provoke it."[16]

Giovanni herself remained relatively unperturbed by such attacks. More remarkable, perhaps, is the fact that she also refused to be overly influenced by her success. "Any artist who thinks his audience is applauding him is crazy," she stated in a 1974 interview. "The audience is applauding itself and you just happen to be the focal point of that particular applause. If you fail to understand that, then you will not survive, let alone do anything further. You are simply a personification of the desires of the people at that particular time."[17]

In reality, Giovanni had committed herself to making a career as a writer and a speaker. Once she had a child to support, she approached that career as a source of income and a vehicle for making a future for her family and especially her son. Honors and awards were certainly not meaningless; as she wrote in *Gemini*, "I think I wanted to be famous because my mother deserves to make the world notice her existence. And my family has worked too hard to be ignored. I don't think I would have much cared if it weren't for them. But they deserve more. Other people put a lot of time and energy into me and they too deserve something" (*GE*, 149). Achieving success by "taking her poetry to the people" was not a simple matter. Writing poetry or essays was not enough, because "the people"—black and white—have never been in the habit of buying or reading books of poetry. For Giovanni during the 1970s, success came from speaking and reading her poetry in little towns and large cities, in churches and on campuses, to young people and old people, throughout the country. It came from sleeping in airports or not sleeping at all as she made in excess of 100 appearances a year—in some years, in fact, she had 200 speaking engagements.

In addition to the volumes of poetry she continued to publish during the 1970s, she also became a regular columnist for the black news magazine, *Encore American & Worldwide News*, which was launched by her friend Ida Lewis, a former editor at *Essence*. Giovanni's contributions to *Encore* were not just literary; she also invested thousands of dollars in this journalistic venture and hundreds of hours trying to solicit advertising support for it. Intended to be a "magazine not just of so-called 'black news,' but of all the news of the world reported from a black perspective,"[18] *Encore* was an upscale magazine that tried "to tread the line between stridency and complacency, advocacy and disinterest" (*Time*, 85). A laudable enterprise with talented writers, *Encore* never seems to have had effective management; that it survived as long as it did was undoubtedly the result of Lewis's determination and Giovanni's dollars. When it went under, those dollars went with it. Throughout the 1970s, it was a major drain on the poet's financial resources, most of which were generated by the physically exhausting speaking schedule she maintained. Her involvement in it provides one of the most striking illustrations of Giovanni's loyalty to friends, a loyalty that sometimes, as in this instance, proved self-destructive.

The 1970s were also years of travel abroad for Giovanni. She visited Africa several times and made numerous trips to Europe, nearly always with her son. Magazine and newspaper articles from the period consistently emphasize the presence of her son in her life, and, in fact, young Tommy was and still is, in her mind, the poet's most important claim on the future.

New York City Star Comes Home

The prodigious rate at which Giovanni produced during the first decade of her career could not have continued indefinitely. In 1978, just 10 years after her first volume of poetry appeared, her twelfth book, *Cotton Candy on a Rainy Day*, was published. During that 10-year period she had also released five record albums in addition to the award-winning *Truth*, performed at New York's Philharmonic Hall, and received four honorary doctorate degrees. Such a pace would have had to slow eventually or there would doubtless have been increasingly frequent occasions on which she collapsed from exhaustion, as she did in 1971.

As it turned out, however, her father, Gus, had a stroke in 1978, and was subsequently diagnosed with cancer. Her mother needed help taking care of him, so she and Thomas packed their bags and moved to Cincinnati. The pace of her life slowed, but her responsibilities multiplied. Her parents were financially devastated by Gus's unexpected illness, for he had no medical or mortgage insurance. The family home in Lincoln Heights, which had taken her parents so long to acquire, badly needed to be renovated and redesigned to accommodate the wheelchair necessitated by Gus's stroke.

Characteristically, Giovanni never protested the responsibilities that now fell on her. She and Thomas moved in with her parents, and for the next five years she was mother, nurse, and head of household. Away from New York, she was obliged to continue her career without the advantages that center provided. Her responsibilities at home naturally reduced the amount of traveling she could do, although she continued to conduct a speaking schedule that would daunt many. And she continued to write, but at a slower rate.

After her father's death in 1982, she remained with her mother and began to think about what new directions she might want to pursue. Then, in 1984, her critics once again struck out at her for refusing to follow the correct ideology. This time, the issue was the boycott of South Africa, which she had opposed because she did not see it as an effective strategy. Always more concerned about addressing the problems she encountered in America than those elsewhere, Giovanni had never been sympathetic to pan-Africanism. She also had little patience with Americans who wanted to offer solutions to the South African situation even though they had no firsthand experience of South Africa themselves. Furthermore, as she stated in a 1985 interview, "We are facing the resegregation of America, and we are asking abroad for freedoms that are not secure at home. Black America has its own problems, and Black America ought to be looking at what we can do to save ourselves because we are in trouble."[19] Thus, when she was asked by Artists and Athletes Against Apartheid to support a boycott of South Africa, she refused: "As both a black American and an artist, I feel a presence is more significant than an absence."[20]

With characteristic fearlessness where a principle is at stake, Giovanni also publicly defended the rights of artists to perform in South Africa and protested the blacklisting of individuals such as Ray Charles, Tina Turner, and Millie Jackson who had performed there.[21] Retaliation was swift and ugly. Giovanni was soon being falsely accused of having herself performed in South Africa, rumors were circulated that her name was on the International Dishonor Roll, and she began receiving threats on her life. Eventually the reports of her performing in South Africa were acknowledged for the lies they were, but her life and her career had already been damaged. Indeed, even *before* the 1984–85 crisis, Amiri and Amina Baraka had excluded her poetry from their 1983 anthology, *Confirmation: An Anthology of African American Women*; the exclusion was explained in a footnote as action taken because she had traveled in South Africa in 1982. In actuality, her "travel" had been as a speaker on a United States Information Agency tour of Africa; it had taken place in 1973; and it had consisted of a required "courtesy stop" in Johannesburg.[22]

What was at stake, Giovanni eventually recognized, was not truth but the right to individual thought: "There's no room right now in the black community for dissent on any number of issues" (Reynolds, 1985, 11A). Just as her independence of thought and action had led to scathingly personal attacks at the beginning of her career, it was again the real target of these more recent ones. If Giovanni today remains remarkably free of bitterness, it is surely because she has never lost the support of her most important audience: ordinary people. Though she is far from humble, Giovanni is nevertheless quite modest. But in reviewing some of her public correspondence from the last several years, I discovered that her audiences are consistently enthusiastic; repeatedly, these letters speak of the positive impact she and her poetry have had. The following comment, by the dean of a California college, is typical: "You helped launch the Library Associates 1991 Author Series. You also drew the largest audience, over 400. We are still receiving outstanding comments about your appearance from outside as well as inside the University community. Because you gave so generously and shared so much in your dialogue and in your readings, we have been encouraged to make the series an annual event."[23]

From the outset of her career, Giovanni aimed at reaching ordinary people. And as she wrote in a 1978 review article, "always poems are written because . . . the heart explodes with the necessity to bare itself in the hope that others might see. . . . Poetry at its best is not busy refining questions that are never raised, but defining the life or lack of life we are experiencing."[24] Without question, Giovanni's ability to define the lives we experience has kept her volumes of poetry consistently in print—in an age that has little use for poetry—and made her the most widely read of our living poets.

Chapter Two
The Early Volumes

In a recent interview, Nikki Giovanni explained the difference between the poetry she wrote at the beginning of her career and the poetry she writes today as the difference between photography and painting. "As a photographer," she says of herself in the late 1960s, "I was trying to capture the moment because we as a people did not have a voice. And during that period we didn't have that many people to explain what we were feeling and the rightness of that desire. In the '80s we really are a capable people. Now I don't have the obligation to speak for anyone. There is a multitude of voices out there and there should be. Painters get to paint what they see, what they believe, as distinguished from a photographer, who can only photograph what is there."[1]

The photographic quality of Giovanni's poetry in her first several volumes is both readily apparent and yet, at our distance of more than two decades, not always easily grasped. The identification and significance of the photograph's details may elude even those who were there to see the flash of the camera. Considerable knowledge of the intellectual, literary, social, and political contexts within which Giovanni first began writing poetry is essential to even a rudimentary grasp of that poetry as well as to an understanding of the directions her later poetry was to take.

The Emergence of a New Black Renaissance

The flourishing of black writers and artists of which Giovanni was a part in the late 1960s has frequently been compared to the Harlem Renaissance. Although there are many similarities between the writers of the 1920s and those of the 1960s,[2] the historical events of the intervening 40 years led to several important differences: the writers of the "new" renaissance wrote to and for a black audience; their writing offered an affirmation of black identity rather than simply a protest against white racism; and they consciously viewed their art as an instrument of social change. These differences all point to a new concept of literary and cultural separatism—a deliberate effort to break with the Western literary tradition—which the writers saw as the counterpart of the kind of social and political separatism urged by Malcolm X.

Countee Cullen, one of the most important poets of the Harlem Renaissance, had posed the dilemma confronting every generation of black writers in America, in his famous sonnet, "Yet Do I Marvel": "Yet do I marvel at this curious thing: / To make a poet black, and bid him sing!" Living in a country that has not only relegated black people to second-class citizenship but also placed small value on literature and writing, Afro-American writers before the 1960s had been caught in the defensive position of insisting on their own humanness and protesting the inhumanity of their predominantly white audience. The crippling effects of such a defensive position[3] are unwittingly revealed in a review written by Louis Simpson of one of Gwendolyn Brooks's books: "I am not sure it is possible for a Negro to write well without making us aware he is a Negro. On the other hand, if being a Negro is the only subject, the writing is not important."[4] Such a definition of literary excellence ensured that no black writer could be admitted to the canon of great Western literature.

Notwithstanding these conditions, the writers after the Harlem Renaissance continued, in various ways, to struggle with the dilemma initially defined by W. E. B. DuBois and later applied to the artist in Countee Cullen's poem. DuBois had argued, in *The Souls of Black Folk*, that black Americans suffer from a "double-consciousness," a "sense of always looking at one's self through the eyes of others, of measuring one's soul by the tape of a world that looks on in amused contempt and pity."[5] One of the primary goals and achievements of the new renaissance writers of the sixties was to move beyond the impasse this double-consciousness created by destroying it (Neal, 647).

Quite clearly, however, the new renaissance writers were simply giving artistic expression to the social and political phenomena around them—they were, as Giovanni said, photographers. After the landmark decision in the *Brown vs. Board of Education* case and the retaliatory murder of Emmett Till, the 1950s witnessed the emergence of a new civil rights movement under the leadership of Dr. Martin Luther King, Jr. In February 1960, the year Nikki Giovanni first entered Fisk University, four college students in Greensboro, North Carolina, began the sit-in movement, which quickly spread throughout the South. From the outset of the sit-in demonstrations, white Americans countered nonviolence with violence. For several years, however, black Americans remained hopeful that the country would recognize the moral legitimacy and justice of integration. Instead, violent opposition to the black struggle for civil rights intensified. When the largest civil rights demonstration in history—the August 1963 March on Washington—was followed by the bombing of the 16th Street Baptist Church in Birmingham, Alabama, and, two months later, by the assassination of President John F. Kennedy in Dallas, Texas, the long-deferred dream exploded.

In the summer of 1964, the year Dr. King received the Nobel Peace Prize, race riots broke out in cities across the country, initiating a pattern that became increasingly horrifying as the decade progressed. Dr. King's nonviolent efforts to achieve integration began to be viewed—especially by younger black Americans—as futile. This change was reflected in the black intellectual and literary world by a call for the rejection of the Western tradition and the establishment of a new separatist black aesthetic. Finding expression in a host of little magazines that sprang up throughout the 1960s—beginning with *Negro Digest* in 1961—the angry young intellectuals, writers, and artists began to shape what came to be known as the Black Arts Movement.[6]

The Black Arts Movement

On 6 June 1966, an assassination attempt was made on James Meredith, whose federally supported integration of the University of Mississippi in 1962 was a key event in the civil rights movement. During the march to Jackson that the assassination attempt sparked, Stokely Carmichael, chairman of SNCC, launched the black power movement, thus marking a strategic change in the struggle for civil rights. "Most Black Power advocates," explains historian Lerone Bennett, Jr., "denounced the integration orientation of the old civil rights coalition and called for a new strategy based on black control of the organizations, institutions and resources of the black community. . . . Despite different emphases and different strategies, most members of the new movement stressed black pride, black dignity and black self-determination."[7] Just four months after the launching of the black power movement, its most visible group, the Black Panther Party, was established by Huey Newton and Bobby Seale in Oakland, California.

Although the Black Arts Movement had actually begun to emerge before the black power movement, the latter had an increasing impact and influence on the former. As Larry Neal, the cofounder of the Black Arts Repertory Theater and a major leader of the Black Arts Movement, explained, "Black Art is the aesthetic and spiritual sister of the Black Power concept. As such, it envisions an art that speaks directly to the needs and aspirations of Black America. In order to perform this task, the Black Arts Movement proposes a radical reordering of the western cultural aesthetic."[8] Exactly what this "radical reordering" might mean was the focus of essays in journals such as *Negro Digest* throughout the second half of the 1960s, and by the early 1970s the new concept of a "black aesthetic" began to be explored by many writers. Underlying the new work produced by Black Arts writers and artists was the plethora of ideas associated with black nationalism. In a January 1971 essay in *Black World* (formerly *Negro Digest*), James Turner identifies "the central significance of Black Nationalism" as "the emergence of Black group-consciousness, self-assertion, and cultural identity."[9] "One of the two main trends among Black people in America," the other being integrationism, black nationalism can be defined, Turner says, by five features:

1. The desire of Black people to determine their own destiny through formation, preservation, and control of their own political, social, economic, and cultural institutions.
2. The determination of Black people to unite as a group, as a people in common community, opposing white supremacy by striving for independence from white control.
3. The resistance of Black people to subordinate status and the demand for political freedom, social justice, and economic equality.
4. The development of ethnic self-interest, racial pride, group consciousness, and opposition to and rejection of the dominant ideas of white-defined society perceived to be incompatible with this objective.
5. The re-evaluation of self and of the Black man's relationship with the social system in general. (Turner, 9)

Participants in the Black Arts Movement sought to "control" their "cultural institutions" by establishing their own journals and magazines, presses and publishing houses, and television and radio programs. Many of the writers who later achieved national and international fame first had their work published by the new black magazines and presses. The oldest and most significant of the presses for poetry was Broadside Press, established and directed by Dudley Randall, which distributed Giovanni's first two volumes of poetry and published her third.

Although considerable disagreement arose among the writers of the Black Arts Movement about such issues as the function of art and the relationship between form and content, most of them would have agreed with Baraka's 1983 assessment:

> We wanted an art that would actually reflect black life and its history and legacy of resistance and struggle!
> We wanted an art that was as black as our music. A blues poetry (à la Langston and Sterling); a jazz poetry; a funky verse full of exploding antiracist weapons. A bebop and new music poetry that would scream and taunt and rhythm—attack the enemy into submission.
> An art that would educate and unify black people in our attack on an anti-black racist America.
> We wanted a *mass art*, an art that could "Monkey" out the libraries and "Boogaloo" down the street in tune with popular revolution. A poetry the people could sing as they beat Faubus and Wallace and Bull Connor to death![10]

"Poetry for the people" meant, among other things, the use of the language and the rhythms of black speech and music; music in particular was reclaimed in "poetry for the people" because of the recognition that "black music is our most advanced form of black art."[11] "Our music," Neal wrote, "has always been the most dominant manifestation of what we are and feel, literature was just an afterthought, the step taken by the Negro bourgeoisie who desired acceptance on the white man's terms" (Neal, 1968, 654).

The sheer number of young black people who began writing poetry and organizing arts festivals during the last five years of the 1960s is eloquent testimony of the liberating power of the Black Arts Movement. The emphasis on breaking with Western tradition freed writers from the necessity of "mastering the master's tongue"[12] and allowed them to shape their art from their own rich—but often maligned—speech. As has often been the case in literary history, the decision to write literature using the vernacular led indeed to a "new" renaissance of black poetry.

Because the Black Arts writers were committed to applying the ideas underlying the black power movement to art, conflict and disagreement were—from the beginning—inevitable. Some of the notions underlying black nationalism, for example, were not so easily transferred into the arts. Of these, the emphasis on group identity, the suppression of individuality, would ultimately constitute stifling conditions for many writers, including Giovanni. Similarly constricting was the codification of the idea that poetry *could* advance the revolution into the prescription that "all art must reflect and support the Black Revolution, and any art that does not discuss and contribute to the revolution is invalid, no matter how many lines and spaces are produced in proportion and symmetry and no matter how many sounds are boxed in or blown out and called music."[13] No writer wishing to maintain her integrity could long allow her art to be controlled by this sort of ideological prescriptiveness; and certainly no one as insistent on the right of the individual to make her or his own decisions as Giovanni was and is would be likely to submit to such control. Nevertheless, the spirit that gave birth to the Black Arts Movement—which was the spirit of the 1960s—is very evident in her first volumes of poetry.

Publishing History of the Early Work

Although several women writers emerged during the Black Arts Movement, it was, like other movements during the 1960s, dominated by men—among the poets, LeRoi Jones and Don Lee were beyond question the most famous and influential. Sonia Sanchez was, of the women, the only poet routinely acknowledged and accorded respect by the male leaders and spokesmen. When Nikki Giovanni began publishing poems and essays in the little magazines, the Black Arts Movement was well-established, and she was just one more "new kid on the block." She had met Dudley Randall, director of Broadside Press, at Killens's writers' workshop at Fisk, but he showed no real interest in publishing her in his Broadside Poets series.

Feeling that if she were going to establish herself as a poet she would be obliged to do so without help from the established writers, Giovanni borrowed money from family and friends, had *Black Feeling, Black Talk* privately printed (in 1968), and distributed it herself. As she said in an interview, she decided against submitting her book to a publisher because "I couldn't stand the possibility of rejection. I decided to take my poetry to the people, and if they rejected it, that would be that."[14] The people, however, did not reject it. On the contrary, sales of *Black Feeling, Black Talk* were sufficiently strong that she was able in 1969 to take the money generated and put it into a private printing of *Black Judgement*; in fact, whereas *Black Feeling, Black Talk* had been printed as cheaply as possible, *Black Judgement* was a handsome volume, printed on fine quality paper with a cover designed by an artist. Both volumes sold well and brought a good deal of attention to the poet, and Randall showed an interest in having Broadside serve as distributor for them and as publisher of Giovanni's next volume, *Re: Creation*, which came out in 1970. Meanwhile, William Morrow had approached her about publishing future volumes; because Broadside did not own either *Black Feeling, Black Talk* or *Black Judgement*, she was able to publish them as one volume with Morrow. Five years later, she incorporated the poems she liked best from *Re: Creation* (which Broadside did own) into *The Women and the Men*.

This brief publication history can serve to correct the criticism (frequently made in the early stage of her career) that, after using a black press to launch her career, Giovanni signed on with a white publisher. In fact, *Re: Creation* and *Black Feeling, Black Talk/Black Judgement* were both published in 1970, Morrow having approached Giovanni after she had made an agreement with Broadside for the publication of *Re: Creation*.

Black Feeling, Black Talk

One of the charges frequently made by Giovanni's detractors is that, after she achieved success with her early volumes, she abandoned black revolutionary concerns and wrote about personal issues only. Quite aside from the aesthetic assumptions underlying this charge—assumptions with which Giovanni in fact would and did disagree—the charge itself reveals how selectively her early volumes were read.[15] Of the 26 poems in *Black Feeling, Black Talk*, fewer than one-half could be considered purely revolutionary or ideological poems. Many of the poems address personal subjects, express personal emotion, or evoke a mood; several are dedicated to women who had been important to the poet (most notably, Blanche McConnell Cowan) or with whom the poet had worked; and a few are dedicated to some of the black leaders she had met (Rap Brown, Don Lee, Dudley Randall).

The very first poem in the volume expresses a tension between political causes and private concerns, and its resolution should have served to communicate to early readers that Nikki Giovanni was not just another young writer willing to be a poet for the revolutionary cause. "Detroit Conference of Unity and Art (For HRB)," like many of Giovanni's titles, establishes an expectation that the poem itself reverses:

> We went there to confer
> On the possibility of
> Blackness

And the inevitability of
Revolution

We talked about
Black leaders
And
Black Love

We talked about
Women
And Black men

No doubt many important
Resolutions
Were passed
As we climbed Malcolm's ladder

But the most
Valid of them
All was that
Rap chose me (*BF*, 3).

Although the Detroit Conference is intended to result in revolutionary action, it is itself given over (as conferences usually are) to "conferring" about "possibilities" and "inevitabilities," to endless "talking" about abstractions such as "Black Love" and relationships between men and women. The speaker does not in the first three stanzas criticize the conference, but her language draws our attention to its rhetorical emphasis; and in the fourth stanza, the passive voice reinforces the sense of boredom and deadness evoked by "many important / Resolutions." The final line of the stanza gently mocks the conference participants' self-conscious efforts to model themselves after Malcolm X.

The concrete action of the final stanza thus strikingly contrasts with the mere rhetoric that dominates the conference. It also particularizes and gives meaning to the abstractions of the earlier stanzas—"Valid" "Resolutions" about "Black leaders," "Black Love," and "Women / And Black men" are unlikely; validity comes when one black leader chooses one black woman. Far from "frivolous," as this poem has been described,[16] "Detroit Conference" makes an important philosophical statement about the poet's hierarchy of values; it unhesitatingly asserts the precedence of the individual over ideology, one of the most consistent and important themes throughout Giovanni's work.

As other poems in the volume show, however, revolutionary times threaten to disrupt the individual's desire for individual identity and to destroy those fragile connections between individuals that give life meaning. Like the male speaker of "On Hearing 'The Girl With the Flaxen Hair,'" who is too "tired and beat" from picking cotton all day to "sing pretty" for his "woman with hair of gray" (*BF*, 4), the poet finds herself in a world where love is regarded as—and becomes—a luxury. In the ironically titled "Black Separatism," for example, a couple's impending divorce prevents any meaningful communication between them; estranged from one another, they nevertheless sign their "letters / YOURS FOR FREEDOM" (*BF*, 15). The revolutionary ideologies of the time call into question the legitimacy not only of individual love but of any emotion, as "Letter to a Bourgeois Friend Whom Once I Loved (And Maybe Still Do If Love Is Valid)" makes clear:

> maybe I just
> developed a bad case of paranoia which in the next
> thousand years may be understood by all the people
> everywhere who can understand how it feels to be
> lonely and afraid when there is no place for emotion (*BF*, 31).

Although Giovanni rejects the notion that individual feelings have no significance in revolutionary times, she does not suggest that revolutionary struggle should cease. The "naziboots" of white racists have taken over,

> They already got Malcolm
> They already got LeRoi
> They already strapped a harness on Rap
> They already pulled Stokely's teeth (*BF*, 24).

It is too late to think of not becoming involved in the revolution, because the white backlash against it is overpowering:

> If you hear properly
> negroes
> Tomorrow was too late to properly arm yourself
> See can you do an improper job now
> See can you do now something, anything, but move now
> negro
> If the Black Revolution passes you bye it's for

damned sure
the whi-te reaction to it won't (*BF*, 25).

Throughout *Black Feeling, Black Talk* we find Giovanni caught in an inescapable dilemma that is in part a result of the historical moment in which she finds herself. This dilemma is articulated in one of the early poems in the book, "Poem (For TW)," which recounts an afternoon spent in the home of Thelma Watson, the poet's French professor at Fisk:

You gave me a small coke
And some large talk about being Black
And an individual
You had tried to fight the fight I'm fighting (*BF*, 6).

Denial of a black American's individuality—and hence, humanness—is at the core of white racism. The struggle against racism is a struggle to be treated as an individual. Yet the black revolution of the 1960s—in both the black power and the Black Arts Movements—seemed to require a denial of individuality as well. As is clear in *Black Feeling, Black Talk* and in each of her subsequent books, this denial of individuality from both white America and black revolutionaries constituted an intolerable situation for Giovanni: although the motivation for such denial was different in each instance, the effects were the same.

In some poems in *Black Feeling, Black Talk*, then, we see Giovanni looking exclusively at either a political situation or a personal situation.[17] In only a few poems does she bring the two together, and when she does, she is most apt to assert the greater value of the personal by satirizing or mocking the excesses or style of those involved in political struggle. We saw this strategy at work in "Detroit Conference of Unity and Art," and it is even more successfully employed in "Seduction." Giovanni's ever-present sense of humor is at its most effective in this poem, which presents the black revolutionary male as being so preoccupied with talking ideology that he remains oblivious to the female speaker's slow undressing of both herself and him. When he finally realizes that he is naked, the speaker fantasizes, he will probably "just say / 'Nikki, / isn't this counterrevolutionary . . . ?'" (*BF*, 38). The delightful humor of the poem, which is especially effective in Giovanni's oral presentations, eases but does not erase the painful reality of its theme: the schism between black men and women created by the male devotion to ideology, and the absurdity of an ideology that denies the validity of human connection.

In most of the poems in *Black Feeling, Black Talk*, Giovanni thus chooses not to bring personal and political situations together because she has not found a way to resolve her revolutionary desire to change the social and political realities of her world, on the one hand, and the impact that revolutionary struggle inevitably has on the individual and individual needs, on the other. Many of the poems of this first volume that became well-known are poems that focus exclusively on political subjects and that seem to present a poet for whom social and political issues are of greater importance than personal needs and desires. Thus, it is doubly important as one reads these poems to remember that they constitute only half the story told by *Black Feeling, Black Talk*.

In the political poems, Giovanni enters the dialogue of the 1960s about black identity. Addressed to a black audience, these poems urge that audience to stop looking at themselves as white America looks at them, to recognize that white America seeks their destruction, and to seek power through uniting with each other. "The True Import of Present Dialogue, Black vs. Negro"—one of Giovanni's best-known poems—offers the poet's own interpretation of the logical implications of the "dialogue" to which the title alludes. That dialogue, an inevitable by-product of the civil rights movement and a crucial component of the black power movement, centered on the idea that the act of naming is central to power. Historically, of course, Africans brought as slaves to America had no power or control over their names; they were stripped of their African names and given whatever name their masters desired. In the slave narratives, this assertion of the right to name oneself became a critical step in the slave's journey to freedom. Malcolm X and others in the 1960s argued that freedom is an internal condition as well as an external one—or, as Giovanni herself states in *Black Judgement*, "the last bastion of white supremacy is in the Black man's mind" (*BF*, 46).

In the 1960s, naming assumed enormous importance as a source of identity and power. As Sarah Webster Fabio wrote in a 1968 essay in *Negro Digest*, "Scratch a Negro and you will find a nigger and a potential black man; scratch a black man and you may find a nigger and the remnants of a Negro. Negro is a psychological, sociological, and economical fabrication to justify the status quo in America. Nigger is the tension created by a black man's attempt to accommodate himself to become a Negro in order to survive in a racist country. Black is the selfhood and soul of anyone with one drop of black blood, in America, who does not deny himself."[18]

Several of Giovanni's poems in the politically titled *Black Feeling, Black Talk* draw on these distinctions between *nigger, Negro,* and *Black*. In "The True Import of Present Dialogue, Black vs. Negro," Giovanni juxtaposes *nigger* to *black*, and although *black* is clearly a preferable identity to *nigger*, both are positive in relation to *Negro*, which she actually uses only in the poem's title. In using *nigger* repeatedly in the poem, she was, she has said, trying to demythologize and take the venom injected by white people out of it.[19] The poem's short, staccato lines, repetition of phrases, and use of the vernacular make it one of Giovanni's first effective efforts in oral poetry; they also combine with the poem's subject matter to create a powerful, often shocking effect:

> Nigger
> Can you kill
> Can you kill
> Can a nigger kill
> Can a nigger kill a honkie
> Can a nigger kill the Man
> Can you kill nigger
> Huh? nigger can you
> kill (*BF*, 19).

To Giovanni, the logical question that the revolutionary struggle posed was the question of one's willingness to kill: "It bugged me to always hear talk of going out to die for our rights. . . . That's not the hardest thing to do. It's harder to go out and kill for your rights. I wrote the poem as a protest against that attitude" (Bailey, 50). The poem's argument is that, having killed for America in its many wars, having killed

> for UN & NATO & SEATO & US
> And everywhere for all alphabet but
> BLACK
> Can we learn to kill WHITE for BLACK
> Learn to kill niggers
> Learn to be Black men (*BF*, 20).

Learning "to be Black men" involves killing "the nigger in you": "Can you make your nigger mind / die / Can you kill your nigger mind" (*BF*, 20). This poem rightly helped earn Giovanni the title "revolutionary poet," for its central point requires a revolution in the way black people think about and behave in the racist world they inhabit: "We ain't got to prove we can die / We got to prove we can kill" (*BF*, 20). Nonetheless, the poem cannot be read in isolation from Giovanni's other work nor taken as evidence that she encouraged or attempted to incite killing; as she said in a 1977 interview, "In the middle '60s, because I was fascinated by ideologies, I spent a great deal of time in my writing exploring ideologies and where this could lead and what it could do if we followed the philosophy of A."[20] I would argue, in fact, that, recognizing the violence required to revolutionize a racist America, she would find herself unable to commit to the revolution. The question posed by "The True Import" was a question she herself had to confront and, ultimately, to answer negatively. To her credit, she did not take refuge in the relatively comfortable position of being willing to die for the revolution. Nor was she willing to allow others to kill on her behalf. The question was, could she herself kill? And if the answer was "no," then how could she support "the revolution"? And yet without a revolution, how would white America ever change?

The poems in both *Black Feeling, Black Talk* and *Black Judgement* show Giovanni approaching the dilemma created by such questions and then backing away from it, choosing to deal more frequently with serious issues but not ultimate ones. Thus we have poems that satirically attack "negroes," who are obstacles to change of any sort, let alone revolutionary change. "Wilmington Delaware" is one such "funni negro," "a cute little gingerbread man" (*BF*, 26). Written about the head of People's Settlement in Wilmington (where she worked), this poem attacks both Wilmington the "funni negro" and Wilmington the city, home of more corporations than any city in the United States because of the advantageous tax situation it offers. In the poem, one of Wilmington's largest corporations, DuPont, becomes a symbol of white hypocrisy and destructiveness. Wilmington is "A GOOD BOY / AND TRIES HARD" to please his white benefactors; in fact, "he's up for the coloredman-of-the-year / award" (*BF*, 26). Though Wilmington "can really order some colored people around," he is unable to "stop wetting on himself each and / everytime he / meets a Due-pontee" (*BF*, 27, 26). Wilmington, in fact, thrives on the "banquits" supported by DuPont money, even though "The last one they replaced jello with / jellied gas" (*BF*, 28), a reference, of course, to the napalm DuPont produced throughout the Vietnam War.

One of the finest poems in *Black Feeling, Black Talk* is "Black Power

(For All the Beautiful Black Panthers East)," which elegantly but simply reveals the racist assumptions underlying white people's behavior toward blacks, assumptions that render black behavior inexplicable to white people. As Margaret Reid has shown, the poem employs the indirection and circumlocution characteristic of the African tradition in language use.[21]

Of all the poems dealing with political themes, however, "Love Poem (For Real)" is perhaps the most poignant. Written in December 1968, just one month before the inauguration of Richard M. Nixon, the poem mourns the many deaths of the 1960s, most recently, of course, the assassinations of Dr. Martin Luther King, Jr., and Robert F. Kennedy:

> it's so hard to love
> people
> who will die soon
>
> the sixties have been one
> long funeral day
> the flag flew at half-mast
> so frequently
> seeing it up
> i wondered what was wrong (*BF*, 33).

With the election of Richard Nixon, moreover, "united quakers and crackers / for death, inc. / are back in the driver's seat" (*BF*, 34). Given America's apparent dedication to death, especially to the death and destruction of black Americans, the speaker concludes that

> it's masochistic
> (derived from colored
> meaning sick to kiss massa)
> to love honkies,

even such "honkies" as John F. Kennedy:

> riderless horses
> backward boots
> the eternal flame of the flammable
> Black Man
> who does not plan to screw
> honkies to death (*BF*, 34).

Entitled "Love Poem," the poem is, in fact, about power, which is what makes love possible. A slave had no choice about whom to love, the poem implies, but black people today must recognize the self-destructiveness of choosing to love white people; black people "must not die / with america," but must instead celebrate that death, when it comes, as "our first international holiday" (*BF*, 34). For ultimately,

> it's a question of power
> which we must wield
> if it is not
> to be wielded
> against
> us (*BF*, 34).

The success of *Black Feeling, Black Talk* was something of a phenomenon for a privately printed and independently distributed volume of poetry—roughly 2,000 copies were sold during the first year. That success must be attributed to the fact that the young poet was writing honestly and freshly about subjects that were daily realities to her audience. As I have tried to indicate, the poems reflect the conflicts and complexities generated in the poet by the revolutionary times in which she came of age. Although technically the poems often betray the inexperience of their creator and although they show the poet in the process of seeking a voice that is comfortable and effective, they nevertheless constitute a strong and promising first volume.

Black Judgement

Published just one year after *Black Feeling, Black Talk*, in 1969, *Black Judgement* is a pivotal volume in Giovanni's development as a poet. In it, more than in any other volume, we find the rage against white America that was largely responsible for earning her the label of "revolutionary poet"; we also find, however, increasing conflict between her identification with revolution and her identity as a black woman. The voice in many of the political poems is often the voice of an outsider, of an individual who would in some ways like to be a revolutionary but is somehow prevented. The rage is an impotent and ineffective rage; the apparent endorsement of violence as the only solution is rarely convincing.

As we read through the volume, Giovanni's struggle to find a comfortable voice as a "black female poet" (*BF*, 95) becomes increasingly apparent. Interestingly, the whole notion of "poet" is called into question by events that seem to demand the sword, not the pen, as the speaker of the powerful "For Saundra" discovers. Because "revolution doesn't lend / itself to be-bopping," the speaker speculates that

> maybe i shouldn't write
> at all
> but clean my gun
> and check my kerosene supply (*BF*, 89–90).

Although "For Saundra" concludes that "perhaps these are not poetic / times / at all" (*BF*, 90), other poems in the volume accord music and musicians a poetic kind of role and significance. Perhaps because musicians—especially popular songwriters and singers—were not working within a highly self-conscious movement such as the Black Arts Movement, they were more able to be instruments of the revolution than was the poet, who was aware of the expectations upon her. At any rate, *Black Judgement* is pervaded by allusions to the music of the day, and many of the most successful poems themselves employ devices characteristic of black music.[22]

The poems comprising *Black Judgement* were, with one exception, all written between March and November 1968, and they are quite clearly responsive to the tragic events that mark 1968 as one of America's most infamous years. In February, the Kerner Commission Report had identified white racism as the insidious cause of the riots taking place across the country and had concluded that America was "moving toward two societies, one black, one white—separate and unequal" (Bennet, 581). White determination to hasten that movement was made sickeningly clear by the assassination of Dr. Martin Luther King, Jr., in April, followed by the assassination of Robert F. Kennedy in June, and the election of Richard M. Nixon in November. The hopes and ideals of a decade were shattered.

Giovanni's poems during this period mark the destruction of the ideals symbolized by King and Kennedy as the end of childhood—the poet's own as well as the nation's. Several poems focus specifically on memories of childhood, including "Nikki-Rosa," which was, in fact, written just eight days after King's assassination. The thematic centrality of childhood's end to the volume as a whole is evident in the arrangement of the poems: among the 27 poems in *Black Judgement*, "Adulthood" is positioned in the exact middle.

"Adulthood" (*BF*, 68–70) traces the speaker's stages of growth, from the time "when i was a little girl in indianapolis" to the present, when she is "a for real Black person who must now feel / and inflict / pain." As a little girl, she "was meaningless / and i wondered if life / would give me a chance to mean." The only option available to girls seemed to be going to church and being a debutante; even the "catatonic emotions and time wasting sex games" of adolescence left her "recognizing the basic powerlessness of me."

In college, she discovered that there were "things approaching reality" in which she could become involved and "possibly have a life." And after graduation, her success as a writer and her activity in the movement generated happiness and made her begin "to believe all good people could get / together and win without bloodshed." The complete destruction of this naive belief is reflected in the short, staccato lines that document the long list of deaths, beginning with Dag Hammarskjold's and ending with Robert Kennedy's. The finality of childhood's end, and of the innocence and ideals associated with it, is underscored by the repetition of the simple syntactic structure ("and lumumba was killed / and diem was killed / and kennedy was killed / and malcolm was killed," etc.). The horror of murder renders the rewards of her own human development dubious at best:

> and i sometimes wonder why i didn't become a
> debutante
> sitting on porches, going to church all the time,
> wondering
> is my eye make-up on straight
> or a withdrawn discoursing on the stars and moon
> instead of a for real Black person who must now feel
> and inflict
> pain

"Adulthood" not only is positioned at the center of *Black Judgement* but also serves as a kind of emotional climax for the volume. It is prepared for by two poems dealing specifically with the poet's childhood, "Nikki–Rosa" and "Knoxville, Tennessee." The latter, one of her finest poems, offers a lyrical expression of the irretrievability of childhood, here imaged as the "summer" of life when the positive value of being "warm" happened "all the time / not only when you go to bed / and sleep" (*BF*, 65).

Significantly, most of the "revolutionary" poems of anger in *Black Judgement* precede "Adulthood"; the few political poems that follow it use satire as a way of distancing the speaker from the anger that threatens to consume her in the first half of the volume. The first four poems in the volume, which were written before King's assassination, show the poet struggling with the necessity for revolution and following revolutionary ideology through to its logical imperatives. Of these, the finest is unquestionably the poignant "Poem for Black Boys (With Special Love to James)," which considers the sort of future that will be faced by children. Giovanni's satiric powers are most effective here, as she envisions the kinds of games little black boys should be playing in order to prepare themselves for the future:

> Also a company called Revolution has just issued
> a special kit for little boys
> called Burn Baby
> I'm told it has full instructions on how to siphon gas
> and fill a bottle (*BF*, 51).

The poem makes clear that the poet's quarrel with the revolution and revolutionaries is about the senseless violence revolution seems to require, the meaningless deaths—especially of young black men—it exacts.

Even in "Poem for Black Boys," however, revolution remains something of a debatable conception or idea, an ideology and program of action connected to specific leaders such as Rap Brown. With King's assassination and the ensuing riots, revolution is no longer a controlled course of action but becomes instead a visceral, life-preserving response from all black Americans; it no longer has to do with ideology, because King's assassination "is an act of war," as Giovanni writes in "Reflections on April 4, 1968" (*BF*, 54). In this piece, written in prose, "the collapse of poetic structure parallels the collapse of everything."[23] Because King's assassination "is an act of war," the only intelligent response is the destruction of America—this is the assumption on which "Reflections" is based. If the evil that America has become must be destroyed, the question confronting each individual is, how: "What can I, a poor Black woman, do to destroy america? This is a question, with appropriate variations, being asked in every Black heart. There is one answer—I can kill. There is one compromise—I can protect those who kill. There is one cop-out—I can encourage others to kill. There are no other ways" (*BF*, 54).

In other poems from the first half of *Black Judgement*, Giovanni reiterates the necessity to kill. "A Litany for Peppe," for example, concludes with this inversion of Christ's beatitudes: "Blessed is he who kills / For he shall control this earth" (*BF*, 57). And "Records," written just after Robert Kennedy's assassination, speaks of the poet's desire

> to record
> the feeling of shame
> that we Black people
> haven't yet
> committed a
> major assassination,

and concludes that

> this country must be
> destroyed
> if we are to live
> must be destroyed if we are to live
> must be destroyed if we are to live (*BF*, 66–67).

By far the most poetically effective of the poems responding to the assassination of King is "The Great Pax Whitie" (*BF*, 60–62), one of the best poems in Giovanni's entire oeuvre. Again employing ironic biblical allusions, Giovanni also patterns this poem after the structures common to black music. Included on Giovanni's award-winning *Truth Is On Its Way*, where it is read against the choir's singing of "Peace, Be Still," the poem has a call-response pattern common to the spirituals and blues; as one critic has noted, it becomes, when it is read "as a poem in which a congregation of voices speaks, a brilliant literary approximation of the kind of collective dialogue which has been going on underground in the black community at least since the nineteenth century and of which the blues in its various forms was an important part."[24]

Thematically, the poem views history as one long record of white antagonism against black people, an antagonism that has repeatedly led to the destruction of black people. The Judeo-Christian tradition itself began with a dedication to death:

In the beginning was the word
And the word was
Death
And the word was nigger
And the word was death to all niggers
And the word was death to all life
And the word was death to all
   peace be still

"Peace be still," the first of three refrains that alternate in the poem, concludes the first two stanzas; in the third stanza a new refrain is introduced:

In the name of peace
They waged the wars
   ain't they got no shame

In the name of peace
Lot's wife is now a product of the Morton company
   nah, they ain't got no shame

"Peace be still" alternates with "nah, they ain't got no shame" as the refrains of the next four stanzas, which carry us through a biting history of the Western world, culminating with the establishment of America, "Where war became peace / And genocide patriotism / And honor is a happy slave." As this indictment of the essential hypocrisy and brutality of white people moves to events of the twentieth century, a new refrain is introduced, "ain't we never gonna see the light." The next stanza interrupts the refrain pattern established in the poem by ending with the answer, "Only the torch can show the way."

The poem's concluding stanzas bring all three refrains together, but with a significant variation on the refrain, "nah, they ain't got no shame":

So the great white prince
Was shot like a nigger in texas
And our Black shining prince was murdered
like that thug in his cathedral
While our nigger in memphis
was shot like their prince in dallas
And my lord
ain't we never gonna see the light

The rumblings of this peace must be stilled
  be stilled be still

ahh Black people
ain't we got no pride?

The recital of black deaths throughout history is here brought to a stunning climax with the assassinations of John Kennedy, Malcolm X, and Dr. Martin Luther King, Jr. His own people make a "nigger" out of Kennedy, linking him (as Giovanni does elsewhere with both John and Robert Kennedy) to black leaders; similarly, "our Black shining prince," Malcolm X, is linked to Thomas à Beckett, for both of them are killed because of their own growth as individuals. Finally, the similar murders of King ("our nigger") and Kennedy ("their prince") provoke the speaker into the expostulatory pleading of the poem's final lines, which make a significant variation on "ain't got no shame": the question instead becomes, "Black people / ain't we got no pride?"

The poem leaves this question unanswered, as it does the more important question of how that pride would be demonstrated or acted upon. The poet does not, in fact, offer a solution to the problem, which may be one reason "The Great Pax Whitie" is one of her best poems. The poem's purpose seems to lie in its impact on the reader, that is, in the arousal and purgation of the reader's (or listener's) anger. Moreover, because of the poem's call-response pattern, it simulates a collective experience and thus functions to bring the individual reader into a community; and the vision of the poem is given authority precisely because it expresses a collective experience. Ultimately, "The Great Pax Whitie" does not so much *mean* something as it *expresses* something; like the blues, it reflects "an impulse to keep the painful details and episodes of a brutal experience alive in one's aching consciousness, to finger its jagged grain, and to transcend it, not by the consolation of philosophy, but by squeezing from it a near-tragic . . . lyricism."[25]

It seems appropriate that Giovanni's finest "revolutionary" poem is so rooted in and reflective of black music. Although the music of black Americans may have some of its roots in Africa, the spirituals, out of which the blues and jazz grew, are uniquely American, reflecting the struggle of an oppressed people to order and thus make tolerable and meaningful the conditions of life imposed on them. Similarly, in the sequence of poems we have been examining, Giovanni turns to the forms and patterns offered by music as a way of containing the rage engendered by King's assassination. Increasingly, in the second half of *Black Judgement* and in her subsequent volumes, she writes poems that either offer an experience similar to the experience of music or comment on and quote music and musicians.

One of the best examples of this kind of poem is "Revolutionary Music" (*BF*, 75–76), which takes the music and musicians of the late 1960s as its subject. The poem not only is about the music and musicians but it draws on countless song titles or lines for its own construction. The poem's argument, and its simultaneous revelation, is that musicians of the day are employing coded language in much the same way as we find in black music and black speech, from slavery until today. As an enslaved and later an oppressed minority living constantly under the scrutiny of the white majority, black Americans in their speech and music have been obliged to use oblique and elliptical expressions whose real import is unlikely to be grasped by the majority culture. "Revolutionary Music" celebrates the popular music and musicians of the day, whose lyrics have served the revolution by communicating positive messages to black listeners and coded revolutionary messages to white listeners. Giovanni concludes her own virtuoso performance in this poem by applauding the names taken by black groups:

> even our names—le roi has said—are together
> impressions
> temptations
> supremes
> delfonics
> miracles
> intruders (i mean intruders?)
> not beatles and animals and white bad things like
> young rascals and shit
> we be digging all
> our revolutionary music consciously or un
> cause sam cooke said "a change is gonna come" (*BF*, 76).

The reference in the final line to Sam Cooke's hit song "A Change Is Gonna Come" actually provides the central theme of the poem. Stephen Henderson has cited this poem, in fact, as an excellent example of "the use of tonal memory as poetic structure" in much black poetry. By "tonal memory," Henderson means "the practice, with considerable variety, of forcing the reader to incorporate into the structure of the poem his memory of a specific song, or passage of a song, or even of a specific delivery technique. Without this specific memory the poem cannot properly be realized" (Henderson, 53–54).

"Revolutionary Music" marks a minor turning point in *Black Judgement*, for it shows Giovanni moving away from writing poems expressive of the rage that was erupting into riots throughout the country to writing poems expressive of pride, humor, love, and a range of other emotions—poems such as "Balances," "For a Poet I Know," and "For Theresa."

As I stated earlier, most of the angry poems in *Black Judgement* are placed in the first half of the volume, that is, before the climactic "Adulthood." Although the theme of white racism and destructiveness continues to appear in some of the poems after "Adulthood," Giovanni, with the exception of "Ugly Honkies, or The Election Game and How to Win It," treats that theme with more emotional restraint. One reason for this restraint may perhaps be found in the options she defined in "Reflections on April 4, 1968," for, if one finds oneself unable to kill, urging others to do so is a "cop-out." Equally important, the level of rage expressed in some of the poems I have discussed could not continue indefinitely. Rhetorically, its usefulness diminishes with repetition; and the real emotion to which the rhetoric points ultimately would prove self-destructive.

Many poems in *Black Judgement* suggest an additional reason for Giovanni's movement away from angry or revolutionary poetry: her gender really sets her apart from the black revolutionary leaders. When she envisions the revolutionary imperatives that the children she knows will confront—as she does in "Poem for Black Boys" and "A Litany for Peppe"—those children are always male, never female. Though a dangerous and uncertain future may await these male children, it nonetheless seems more meaningful than that of the debutante in "Adulthood."

The limitations imposed by gender are explored in three poems that follow "Adulthood." The first of these, "Dreams," takes music as its subject and is in some ways a companion piece to "Revolutionary Music," which it directly precedes:

> in my younger years
> before i learned
> black people aren't
> suppose to dream
> i wanted to be
> a raelet

and say "dr o wn d in my youn tears"
or "tal kin bout tal kin bout"
or marjorie hendricks and grind
all up against the mic
and scream
"baaaaaby nightandday
baaaaaby nightandday"
then as i grew and matured
i became more sensible
and decided i would
settle down
and just become
a sweet inspiration (*BF*, 74).

Although the poem makes specific reference to the restrictions imposed on the speaker because she is black, the restrictions imposed by her gender, which are not explicitly stated, are in fact equally important. Before she learned "black people aren't / suppose to dream," she dreamed of singing with Ray Charles, of being either one of the Raelets or, even better, Marjorie Hendricks, having the microphone all to herself, if only for a few minutes at the end of a song. The requirements of adulthood, however, force her to become "more sensible," to "settle down" and "become / a sweet inspiration." The first part of the poem establishes youth as a time when the speaker did not understand the limitations imposed on her future because she was black; the expectation established is that adulthood will involve accepting those limitations. But the language used to describe her identity as an adult clearly suggests that her gender, not her race, is responsible for the restrictions on her choices. The double entendre of the poem's final line renders maturity not simply a change in style but also an acceptance of a more passive role in life. The Raelets with whom Marjorie Hendricks was associated were often thought to be "wild" because of the way they sang, but the primary point of difference between them and the Sweet Inspirations is that they sang the blues while the Sweet Inspirations sang three-part harmony. *Sweet inspiration* also suggests, however, a role women are often expected to play in the lives of men, especially of artists. Just as the Sweet Inspirations provided harmonic back-up for singers such as Aretha Franklin, so too are women often the background for men's important action. As a female "revolutionary poet," Giovanni was in fact usurping a role that was claimed exclusively by the male leaders of the day.

Female identity is explored most fully in the second of the three poems, the frequently anthologized "Woman Poem" (*BF*, 78–80). Here, Giovanni presents a female speaker

> whose whole life is tied
> up to unhappiness
> cause it's the only
> for real thing
> i
> know

One of the first poems in which Giovanni focusses on relationships between men and women, "Woman Poem" reveals the destruction of trust and of a capacity for intimacy that results from the rigid and reductive ways black men view black women:

> it's a sex object if you're pretty
> and no love
> or love and no sex if you're fat
> get back fat black woman be a mother
> grandmother strong thing but not woman
>
> gameswoman romantic woman love needer
> man seeker dick eater sweat getter
> fuck needing love seeking woman

As subsequent stanzas make clear, the black woman's only value lies in the strength and sacrifices she can offer to others; eventually, playing this role renders her incapable of allowing herself to find "someone to hold." Because she herself "ain't shit," she looks at anyone reaching out to her as "lower / than that to care." Her only "joy is finding a pregnant roach / and squashing it," just as unhappiness has become a mode of being "cause it's the only / for real thing / i / know."

The self-loathing expressed by the speaker of "Woman Poem" is made all the more horrifying by the placement of this poem immediately after the celebratory rap of "Beautiful Black Men" (*BF*, 77). The whole "Black is Beautiful" perspective on the world has given black men a new pride, put a new strut in their walk, made them irresistibly sexy and wonderful: "and i scream and stamp and shout / for more beautiful beautiful beautiful / black men with outasight afros." Similar joy and pride and strut have not, apparently, come to the black woman, at least not to the speaker of "Woman Poem," who wishes she "knew how it would feel / to be free."

The third and final poem that deals with female identity is "My Poem," the penultimate poem in *Black Judgement* (*BF*, 95–97). On first reading, this poem seems to be about the idea that the revolution is larger than any single individual, and therefore not dependent on the actions of any single individual. In some ways a logical thematic companion to "Reflections on April 4, 1968," "My Poem" emphasizes that "a change is gonna come" because "the revolution / is in the streets." The repetition of the same refrain in every stanza until the final one reinforces this notion that "the revolution" has taken on a life of its own and cannot be controlled; regardless of what the speaker (Giovanni herself in this instance) does, or fails to do, "it won't stop / the revolution."

Other details in this poem suggest that it is something more than a simple affirmation of the inevitability of the revolution. Especially when it is read within the context of the pressures exerted on the artist to put her talents in the service of the revolution, "My Poem" is an assertion of the poet's right to create the kind of art she chooses and to live her life as she wants. Just because she "wrote a poem asking / nigger can you kill," she asserts that even "if they kill me / it won't stop / the revolution." "My Poem" is thus a disclaimer of responsibility for the success or failure of the revolution. At the same time, it presents the realization that the ideological positions and prescriptions of so-called revolutionaries have nothing to do with the revolution:

> if i hate all black
> people
> and all negroes
> it won't stop
> the revolution

I have connected "My Poem" to "Dreams" and "Woman Poem" because I think it is also concerned with female identity, even though that theme may be subordinate to the poem's larger concerns. For ultimately, Giovanni's refusal to be controlled by the leaders of either the Black Arts Movement or the black power movement was a refusal to be controlled by the men to whom both these movements seemed to belong. Support for this line of interpretation may be found outside the poem as well as within it. As early as 1966 (two years before composing "My Poem"), in an essay published in *Negro Digest*, Giovanni had expressed her concern about the basic sexism in the movement: "Is it necessary that I cease being a Black woman so that he can be a man," she asked in "First Steps Toward A True Revolution."[26] And six months after "My Poem" was written, she observed that "it sometimes seems that the only thing that culturalists care about is assuring themselves and the various communities that they are the vanguard of the Black revolution. They have made Black women the new jews while they remain the same old niggers."[27]

The opening lines of "My Poem" assert the poet's own female identity: "i am 25 years old / black female poet." In the stanzas that follow, Giovanni unequivocally insists that she will not be a "new jew" to the black men who seek to dictate how she should live and what she should write.

Though the male artists and critics of the day would soon find such insistence on her independence anathema, with the publication of *Black Judgement*, Giovanni struck responsive chords in an amazingly large audience. Within six months of publication—and with limited distribution—*Black Judgement* had sold 6,000 copies, which was nothing short of miraculous in a market where publishers feel a volume of poetry is doing well to sell 2,500 copies a year (Dusky, 81). Giovanni's career was launched, and she herself was soon to achieve a kind of "star" status rarely experienced by poets.

Re: Creation

The question of female identity addressed in only a few poems of *Black Judgement* is a central theme of *Re: Creation*, which was published by Broadside Press in 1970. The 42 poems[28] of this volume were written between June 1969 and July 1970, that is, during the final months of Giovanni's pregnancy and the first months of her son's life. Few of the poems are overtly political or employ the explosive language of the poems in the first half of *Black Judgement*, which no doubt explains the complaint expressed in a review published in *Black World* that Giovanni had been "transformed (re-created?) into an almost declawed, tamed Panther with bad teeth."[29] As we have seen, the attentive reader would have noticed that Giovanni was a poet of many facets, which were evident from the outset.

Re: Creation reflects a growth in the young Giovanni's abilities as a poet, especially with regard to her increased facility with lyric and her experimentation with blues. In theme and mood, it moves away from the rage and despair so frequent in the first two volumes; in subject, it focusses much more on the particular and concrete. The poetic voice is stronger and more self-confident, continuing the assertion of independence expressed in "My Poem." The title itself, suggesting a memorandum from Nikki Giovanni about the subject of creation, is more individualistic than the deliberately political titles of the first two volumes. The year in which she was writing the poems was without question one of the most significant in her life, for the birth of her son became a central organizing principle not simply of daily living but of her vision of and commitment to the future.

Giovanni did not suddenly become unaware of or indifferent to the death and destruction being waged against black Americans. But, as we have seen, she did reach a realization of her own impotence to stop that death and destruction or alter its course; the central insight achieved in "My Poem" necessitated that she find her own direction, her own poetic voice, her own identity. The conditions of her existence were clear—"i am 25 years old / black female poet"—but her responses to those conditions, at the end of *Black Judgement*, were not. The year following the composition of the poems in *Black Judgement* witnessed her defiance of the limitations those conditions so often dictate. Because the creation of life was preferable to its destruction, she chose to have a child. But she also chose not to marry[30] and to make her own decisions regarding the kind of writer she would be. She responded to the criticism she received on both counts in poems in *Re: Creation*. "Poem for Unwed Mothers (to be sung to 'The Old F. U. Spirit')" asserts that "it was good for the virgin mary / its good enough for me."[31] And "Yeah . . . But . . . ," takes on those who criticized Diana Ross because she "don't sing / like she used to." The speaker understands how painful to the fans such changes can be, because she herself experienced pain when Dionne Warwick "didn't sing for me and my love / no more." But the artist must be allowed to grow and develop—to change—and the speaker suggests that

> maybe we can
> remember
> we don't poet like that
> no more either (*RC*, 44).

The poem stands as a gentle but firm assertion of Giovanni's intention to determine her own artistic direction.

Thus, although *Re: Creation* contains some poems that explicitly address white racism and the black revolution, the majority of its poems focus on more personal subjects and strike a reflective, rather than incendiary, chord. Central to the volume is Giovanni's concern with black female identity, a concern explored not only in private lyric poems but also in poems about other women. The poem of dedication at the beginning of the volume announces the personal revolution wrought in the poet's life by the birth of her son:

> to tommy who:
> eats chocolate cookies and lamb chops
> climbs stairs and cries when i change his diaper
> lets me hold him only on his schedule
> defined my nature
> and gave me a new name (mommy)
> which supersedes all others
> controls my life
> and makes me glad
> that he does (*RC*, 3).

Giovanni not only embraces her new role of motherhood but asserts its primacy in her sense of who she is; her son has "defined my nature" and given "me a new name . . . /which supersedes all others." The poem conceives of motherhood as a liberating force, not the stifling and restrictive force it so often became in the work of white women writers of the period.[32]

Motherhood thus enables the poet to discover and express an essential part of her being—the most essential part, perhaps. It is a more liberating and revolutionary activity than being a political activist or spokesperson; indeed, the whole concept of "revolutionary" must be redefined, as Giovanni indicates in "Revolutionary Dreams":

> i used to dream militant
> dreams of taking
> over america to show
> these white folks how it should be
> done
> i used to dream radical dreams
> of blowing everyone away with my perceptive powers
> of correct analysis
> i even used to think i'd be the one
> to stop the riot and negotiate the peace

then i awoke and dug
that if i dreamed natural
dreams of being a natural
woman doing what a woman
does when she's natural
i would have a revolution (*RC*, 20).

This poem occupies a central place not only in *Re: Creation* but in Giovanni's entire oeuvre, for it expresses what increasingly became a dominant theme in her poetry: the necessity—and the difficulty—of individuality and individual integrity. As the last third of the poem indicates, revolution results from "being a natural woman" and "doing what a woman / does when she's natural." The earlier dreams of being a revolutionary leader were the dreams of a sleeping person, and therefore expressive of a distorted vision. They are replaced by "natural dreams," consciously chosen by the waking self ("then i awoke and dug") and expressive of a more accurate perception of reality.

Her "militant dreams" cast the poet as a key leader in the larger, public arena. But, as we saw in *Black Judgement*, such a role was not actually available to her because of her gender. "Revolutionary Dreams" juxtaposes that role to the role of "a natural woman," and it also implicitly juxtaposes the "revolution" pursued by men to the "revolution" created by "a natural / woman doing what a woman / does when she's natural."[33] Although the poem does not particularize the activities of a "natural woman," it does suggest that her revolution is somehow superior to the revolution envisioned by men. What makes it superior is, in fact, that it does not have an ideology that others must follow. The poem leaves "natural woman" undefined because its meaning must be determined by each individual woman.

As with other poems in this volume, "Revolutionary Dreams" alludes to a popular song of the period, Carole King's "(You Make Me Feel Like A) Natural Woman," which was one of Aretha Franklin's biggest hits. Giovanni's readers at the time would undoubtedly have made the association with the song. Giovanni draws on the song, but changes it significantly. In the song, the woman "*feels like* a natural woman" (my emphasis), but her feeling is dependent upon the man who has rescued her, as the song's title makes clear. In Giovanni's poem, by contrast, the speaker "dreams of *being* a natural woman" (my emphasis). Not feeling but a state of being is her dream—and it is *her* dream, that is, it is self-generated. Giovanni's changes in the conception of woman that underlies the song serve to reinforce the statement the poem is making.

The poem's equation of individual integrity with revolution does not diminish the difficulties in effecting such a revolution; though the familiarity of the phrase "natural woman" might lead us to think this "revolutionary dream" would be easy to realize, nothing could be less true, as other poems in *Re: Creation* and in Giovanni's subsequent volumes make clear. Individual integrity exacts a high price, as we see in "The Lion in Daniel's Den (for Paul Robeson, Sr.)." This poem inverts our ordinary understanding of the biblical story of Daniel in the den of lions by asking us to recognize that the lions—symbols of majesty and nobility—are as doomed to slaughter as Daniel would have been, were it not for his faith in God. The object of our fear should not be the lion or Daniel but the people who trapped and encaged them both. As Giovanni says in *Gemini*, "We have all been lions in a den of Daniels" (*Gemini*, 90). The poem makes an eloquent statement about the courage of Paul Robeson, whose insistence on identifying himself with his people seriously damaged his career.[34]

A similar theme is developed in "Poem for A Lady Whose Voice I Like," which delineates the kinds of attacks to which the successful and independent black woman is made subject by the black man. Written for Lena Horne, the poem also undoubtedly reveals experiences that Giovanni herself was beginning to face:

so he said: you ain't got no talent
    if you didn't have a face
    you wouldn't be nobody

and she said: god created heaven and earth
    and all that's Black within them

so he said: you ain't really no hot shit
    they tell me plenty sisters
    take care better business than you

and she said: on the third day he made chitterlings
    and all good things to eat
    and said: "that's good"

so he said: if the white folks hadn't been under
    yo skirt and been giving you the big play

> you'd a had to come on uptown like everybody
> else
>
> and she replied: then he took a big Black greasy rib
> from adam and said we will call this woeman and
> her
> name will be sapphire and she will divide into
> four parts
> that simone may sing a song
>
> and he said: you pretty full of yourself ain't chu
>
> so she replied: show me someone not full of herself
> and i'll show you a hungry person (*RC*, 45).

The male voice in the poem attributes the female's success to everything except her talent, launching attacks derived specifically from her gender. As Giovanni says in her essay on Lena Horne in *Gemini*, "Lena Horne has been singing a long time not to have a singing voice. I mean, she has a voice—*they* don't understand the melody" (*Gemini*, 87). What he most despises is her refusal to be destroyed by his attacks—"you pretty full of yourself ain't chu." Her self-confidence about who she is prompts this predictable accusation of arrogance. But as her response in the final lines of the poem indicates, such self-confidence, far from indicating excess, is necessary to her survival: "show me someone not full of herself / and i'll show you a hungry person."

Other poems in *Re: Creation* confirm women's need to find sustenance within themselves because the world in which they live provides no nurturance, if, in fact, it is not actively destructive. Giovanni shows particular sensitivity in this volume to the variety of forces that threaten women artists, such as Lena Horne, who have achieved a high level of success—forces with which the poet was herself beginning to contend as she suddenly found herself a kind of "star." With the exception of the poem "For Gwendolyn Brooks," all of these artists are singers: Lena Horne, Diana Ross, Dionne Warwick, Nina Simone, and Aretha Franklin. The lovely, blueslike poem "The Geni in the Jar (For Nina Simone)" draws on female characters from fairy tales to express the dangers that threaten the woman who sings "a Black song our Black song / from the Black loom / singing to me" (*RC*, 24). And "Poem for Aretha" speaks of the way "we eat up artists like there's going to be a famine" and asserts that, despite the enormous impact and influence Aretha has had, "she's more important than her music" (*RC*, 18).

Giovanni pays tribute not only to the famous women of her generation but also to ordinary and apparently unremarkable women whose lives nevertheless have something to teach us. "Poem for Flora," for example, points to the need that every woman has to be "full of herself" if she's not to be "hungry." The little girl in the poem would go to Sunday school where she learned

> how god was neither north
> nor south east or west
> with no color but all
> she remembered was that
> Sheba was Black and comely
> and she would think
> i want to be
> like that (*RC*, 42).

Two other poems dramatize the poet-speaker's almost mystical and certainly highly significant encounters with older women. "For a Lady of Pleasure now Retired" invokes the spirit of the poet's grandmother to remind her that

> there are so many new mistakes
> for a lady of pleasure
> that can be made it shouldn't be
> necessary to repeat the old
> ones (*RC*, 30).

Like virtually all of Giovanni's poems about elderly women, this one reaffirms the poet's commitment to life:

> and it was cold
> on the elevator that morning
> when i spoke to her and foolishly asked
>   how are you
> she smiled and tilted her head
>   at least, i said, the sun is
>   shining
> and her eyes smiled   yes
> and i was glad to be
> there to say through spirits
>   there is a new creation
> to her (*RC*, 30–31).

Similarly, "Alabama Poem" uses trees as a metaphor for old people, whose wisdom is superior to the knowledge acquired from schools and books. The speaker of the poem encounters first an old man, then an old woman, both of whom make the same kind of comment. But whereas the speaker walks "on down the dusty road" after her encounter with the old man, she goes "back to the porch" of the old woman to learn what she might "read" in the old woman's feet (*RC*, 33). Secure in who she is and in the value of what she knows, the old woman offers to let the speaker learn from her:

> "i say gal" she called down
> "you a student at the institute?
> better come here and study
> these feet
> i'm gonna cut a bunion off
> soons i gets up"
>   i looked at her
>   she laughed at me
> if trees would talk
>   wonder what they'd tell me (*RC*, 33).

Two poems in *Re: Creation*—"All I Gotta Do" and "Ego Tripping"—might almost be considered companion poems for their sharply contrasting conceptions of female identity. The first of these, "All I Gotta Do," is another blueslike poem in which the speaker's frustration is reflected in the repetition of the line, "sit and wait" (*RC*, 25). The first stanza identifies sitting and waiting as "all i gotta do" for "it" to "find" me. In the second stanza, the reason for this passive and patient sitting and waiting is identified as the speaker's gender:

> what i need to do
> is sit and wait
> cause i'm a woman
> sit and wait
> what i gotta do
> is sit and wait
> cause i'm a woman
> it'll find me (*RC*, 25).

The third stanza states that "you get yours" and therefore "i want mine," because "i gotta get it / cause i need to get it / if i learn how." Although "it" is never identified, in the fourth stanza the speaker humorously describes her unsuccessful efforts to find "it" by calling on the phone and going to the store; nor does asking the "you" of the poem for "it" work, because "you didn't have it / so i'm sitting" (*RC*, 26). The final stanza changes the pattern of "all i gotta do" in order to reveal the speaker's realization:

> all i know
> is sitting and waiting
> waiting and sitting
> cause i'm a woman
> all i know
> is sitting and waiting
> cause i gotta wait
> wait for it to find
> me (*RC*, 26).

Like the blues, this poem does not offer a solution to the unhappy reality it delineates; rather, it simply inscribes the existential situation of the speaker, which is grounded in her female identity.[35] That situation locates the source of life's meaning and significance outside the speaker's purview and control.[36] Presumably, the "you" of the poem has succeeded in getting "it" because he is male. But the speaker, because she is female, must learn both stillness and patience, in the hopes that, if she learns them well enough, "its gonna find me."

The conception of female identity underlying the poem is also at work in "Master Charge Blues," where the speaker is "all alone / sitting with myself / waiting for the telephone" (*RC*, 28). The speaker of this funny/sad poem is, however, "a modern woman baby," and as such, she has developed a strategy for coping with the loneliness of "sitting and waiting":

> i'm a modern woman
> ain't gonna let this get me down
> gonna take my master charge
> and get everything in town (*RC*, 28).

The poem offers a telling insight into the relationship between powerlessness and money, revealing the action of which the speaker is capable to be as destructive for her as simply "sitting and waiting."

Against this socially constructed and imposed female identity, the expansive and delightful "Ego Tripping (there may be a reason why)" poses a wholly different way for women to look at themselves. A poem that has been compared to Langston Hughes's "The Negro Looks At Rivers" (Harris, 227), "Ego Tripping" is not simply the crowning poem of *Re: Creation* but a signature poem in Giovanni's oeuvre. As the poet frequently explains when she reads the poem, it "was really written for a little girl. I almost hate that because little boys like it. I really got tired of hearing all of the little girls' games, such as Little Sally Walker" (Reynolds, 1988, 94). Building on one hyperbolic claim after another, "Ego Tripping" identifies woman as the creator of the world and all its treasures as well as the shaper of every significant accomplishment of civilization. It celebrates woman's ability to create herself, to shape for herself whatever identity she wants. As the poem builds to its concluding assertion of the speaker's divine identity, the reader—and even more, the listener—is filled with ungrudging admiration and assent:

> I am so perfect so divine so ethereal so surreal
> I cannot be comprehended
>   except by my permission
>
> I mean . . . I . . . can fly
>   like a bird in the sky. . . . (*RC*, 38).

It is difficult to imagine a more resounding affirmation of women, and indeed "Ego Tripping" remains unequalled in its claims for women, for their power and infinite possibilities. It was—and is—Giovanni's memorandum to the world about creation.

Chapter Three

Defying Categories: *My House* and *The Women and the Men*

Although only two years separated the publications of *Re: Creation* and *My House*, they were profoundly significant years in Giovanni's development as a poet. Not only did Giovanni travel abroad extensively for the first time in her life, but she also discovered the power of performance and the attention to her poetry's oral qualities that performance necessitated. By the time Giovanni was writing the poems that became *My House*, she had also begun to respond to the increasingly hostile rebukes of both the black intellectual community and the literary establishment. The poems in *My House*, as the title itself suggests, constitute Giovanni's emphatic statement to the world about her identity as a black woman and a poet, about her values, and about her intention to live the kind of life and write the kind of poetry she wished. As she recently stated, *My House* completes what *Re: Creation* started,[1] but her experiences during the two-year interval between the books lent a different tone and a more consistent confidence to the voice of that completion.

Poetry as "the Culture of a People"

In 1971, Giovanni for the first time in her life had the opportunity to travel to both Europe and Africa; her first visit to Africa was without question the more significant, for it helped sharpen the focus of her vision of Afro-Americans.

Giovanni's travels in Africa represented only one of many important events of her twenty-eighth year. For several years, her friends had urged her to consider taping her poetry, but her lack of confidence about the sound of her recorded voice had made her reluctant. "Finally," she explained, "I decided to try it with gospel music, since I really dig the music. I first did 'Peace Be Still' with the Victory Choral Ensemble of

Philadelphia just to see if it would work" (Bailey, 52). With the help of Ellis Haizlip, on whose television show, *Soul!*, Giovanni had made several appearances, she teamed up with the New York Community Choir to produce her first album, *Truth Is On Its Way.* Released in July 1971 while she was traveling in Africa, *Truth* rather quickly and quite unexpectedly became a phenomenal success.

The results of *Truth* were many and far-reaching. The recognition it brought Giovanni had, and continues to have, a bittersweet taste. The literary establishment, both black and white, tends to prefer a writer whose work can be appreciated and understood by only a few—otherwise, the literary critic is out of a job.[2] While one might have expected the other "new black poets" to applaud Giovanni's successful execution of the black aesthetic principle of "taking the poetry to the people," such was not the case. Reviews of her work from *My House* forward have betrayed the anger and the envy of the reviewers. Ironically, Giovanni herself had identified the black artistic community's disinclination to approve the success of black artists in one of her earliest published essays, "Black Poems, Poseurs and Power." First published in 1969 in *Negro Digest* and subsequently included in *Gemini*, the essay exposes the reasons "that the black community is withdrawing from involvement with the black artist" (*GE*, 109). "It would sometimes appear," Giovanni asserts, "some elements of the black artistic community are against popular success unless it's theirs. Sidney Poitier has moved into the area where we have said we want actors to go—only we didn't mean and make money, I guess" (*GE*, 109).

Like Poitier, Giovanni began to find herself scorned for her very success. To many in the literary establishment, her popularity among ordinary people has been sufficient evidence that her work is second-rate. To many black writers in the early 1970s—especially poets—the material success she began to enjoy was sufficient evidence that she had "sold out." While white critics breathed an almost audible sigh of relief at the "universality" they found in the poems of *My House*, that same vague and ambiguous quality was sufficient reason for black critics to question her racial integrity.[3]

It is thus not surprising that in both *Gemini*, published late in 1971, and *My House*, which came out a year later, Giovanni voiced her objections to the kinds of attacks to which she was beginning to be subjected. In her essay in *Gemini* on Angela Davis, for example, Giovanni states that Davis "needs our defense because she involved herself in black action. This is the tragedy, this is the national shame of black people. If you move to black rhythms even your own people will turn against you" (*GE*, 82). Several pages later in the essay, she argues against the defensive posture human beings attempt to impose on each other: "The more you love someone the more he wants from you and the less you have to give since you've already given him your love. And he says, 'Prove it,' with the same arrogance we show when we say, 'Be Black'" (*GE*, 85).

Similar kinds of statements appear in Giovanni's dialogue with James Baldwin, which is based on the videotape made in London in November 1971 and aired on *Soul!* the following month. The book version, *A Dialogue: James Baldwin and Nikki Giovanni*, appeared in 1972; it reflects Giovanni's concerns about the individual in relation to society, about the relations between black men and black women, and about the responsibilities thrust—wrongly—on the black writer. At one point she asserts that because "there is no such thing as the individual" allowed any more, "the movement" is being killed.[4] Similarly, she complains that "there's a whole movement or something that says we have to write only about black people" (*AD*, 73).[5]

If the leaders of the "movement" were critical of Giovanni's refusal to follow any dictates but her own, however, "the people," to whom *Truth* made her poetry even more accessible, were increasingly enthusiastic. Giovanni had established public recognition before *Truth* appeared, but its unexpected success placed her in even greater demand for poetry readings and other public appearances, including an appearance on the *Tonight Show* on 14 June 1972, on which she read her poetry and was interviewed by Flip Wilson. The album allowed her to expand her audience in ways that were important to her sense of the purpose of poetry: "I wanted something my grandmother could listen to and I knew if gospel music was included, she would listen. I have really been gratified with the response of older people, who usually feel that black poets hate them and everything they have stood for. The record demonstrates that this isn't so. You know, it's funny but you practically never see militants with their mothers. You'd think they were hatched or something, so it's really outasight when they bring their parents and introduce them to me at one of the concerts" (Bailey, 52).

Rejecting both the elitist claims often made by white poets and the ideological prescriptions imposed by the new black poets, Giovanni dramatized in *Truth Is On Its Way*, explained in *Gemini*, and illustrated in *My House* her own theory that "poetry is the culture of a people" (*GE*, 95). This claim was increasingly validated by the frequency with which Giovanni read her poetry to large and diverse audiences across the country and abroad. Radically different from the traditional poetry reading in which the poet dazzles the audience with his or her virtuosity, a Giovanni reading unites the poet with her audience as a spiritual community. McDowell argues that Giovanni fulfills her conception of poetry as "the culture of a people" through her oral presentations: "As a poet of the people, Giovanni renews the tradition of the bard, prophet, or witness who sings or chants to inform the people, to subvert tyranny, and to bring an audience together as a community to celebrate a cause or person or a heritage, or to establish a basis for sympathy and understanding of one another's suffering or problems. For Giovanni's audience participation at a poetry reading can be as much a part of the aesthetic experience as congregational expression may be part of worship experience" (McDowell, 153).

Thus, although reviewers and critics became sharply critical of Giovanni's work from *My House* forward, audiences recognized her as, indeed, "a poet of the people." By the time *My House* was published, many of its poems were already familiar to those who had attended Giovanni's performance at Lincoln Center's Alice Tully Hall on 25 July 1972. Reading once again with the New York Community Choir to a capacity crowd of 1,096, Giovanni "controlled the reading with her presence and her reading gave the evening its character of . . . joyousness."[6]

It is not surprising, then, that initial sales of *My House* outstripped those of the poet's earlier volumes. Nor is there any question that *My House* is a pivotal work in the poet's career, for in it Giovanni established a consistently secure, confident, and mature voice that was to remain one of the most distinguishing features of her subsequent work. The volume's title itself—unique in all of Giovanni's work for its inclusion of a personal pronoun—lays claim to a poetic space governed by the poet alone. With the exception of two poems written in 1970, the poems of *My House* were composed between January 1971 and June 1972 and are organized into two sections, "The Rooms Inside" and "The Rooms Outside."

My House: "The Rooms Inside"

Of the 36 poems comprising *My House*, 23 are in the volume's first section, "The Rooms Inside." *My House* as a whole may be read as a poetic autobiography in which Giovanni assesses the first three decades of her life. Writing as she neared her thirtieth birthday, she seems in this volume to have been taking the sort of survey of her life commonly made as we reach certain milestones.

The poems in "The Rooms Inside" chart the speaker's personal life, viewing it sometimes against a traditional norm and revealing the speaker's values and their sources. Arranged to reflect the poet-speaker's own aging process, the poems show her development from childhood to adulthood and beyond. The very first poem, "Legacies," presents a childhood experience from a third-person point of view. It describes a grandmother's unsuccessful efforts to provide her granddaughter a legacy; her efforts are unsuccessful because the legacy she wants to give is not the legacy the granddaughter wants to take. Proud of the rolls she makes, the grandmother wants to teach her granddaughter the secrets of making them, but the granddaughter "don't want to know how to make no rolls" because she knows "even if she couldn't say it that / that would mean when the old one died she would be less / dependent on her spirit."[7] Though they have a common desire, the grandmother and granddaughter are unable to communicate this to each other; as the speaker concludes, "neither of them ever / said what they meant / and i guess nobody ever does" (*MH*, 5).

Clearly looking back on her own younger self, the adult speaker of the poem finds the meaning of the childhood experience only from the perspective provided by adult recollection. The failed communication is a frequent occurrence in Giovanni's poetry; but through memory, an understanding of the experience can be achieved—whether that memory be personal, as in this poem, or collective. "Legacies" thus establishes a connection to and continuity with the past as a critical element in identity, a theme that we see frequently in Giovanni's work, and especially in her loving depictions of older people. As she had stated in *Gemini*, "We should always talk with old people because they know so much. Even the jivest old person, in line with his collective historical need, can give a history of some movement or maybe just his block and the people on it" (*GE*, 97).

The placement of "Legacies" at the beginning of *My House* establishes the past and the people who embody it as a cornerstone of the house Giovanni is building. Not surprisingly, the second poem in the volume, "Mothers," continues to develop this theme, making clear that the poet's connections to the past are through women. Well in advance of many feminist writers, Giovanni's poetry celebrated women, especially mothers and grandmothers. At a time when many of her contemporaries, especially the revolutionaries, wanted to reject the older generations and their strategies for negotiating a racist world, Giovanni's insistence on claiming and valuing the mothers and grandmothers was one more instance of her individuality.

In "Conversation," Giovanni humorously presents her encounter with an older woman whom she attempted to stereotype. Another "Alabama Poem," "Conversation" also depicts the bright young poet from the city as a naif inclined to take herself and the world very seriously. Ironically, the old woman is more in touch with the significance of current events than the young poet. "Packing her jaw / with *bruton* snuff," she does not yearn for the past but is excited by the adventures of the present—"peoples be going to the moon and all . . . ain't that / wonderful" (*MH*, 11). By contrast, the only stars the young poet thinks of are the black singers she sees "at madison square garden." She shows her sophistication, she thinks, through her cultivated contempt for what she was supposed to have gained from her earlier visit:

> she clapped her hands and smiled
> "you been here before"
> and i said "yes ma'am but would you tell me just one
> thing
> what did i learn"
> and she spat out her juice
> "honey if you don't know how can i" (*MH*, 12).

The climax of the poem develops from the poet's self-absorption, which makes her unable to recognize when her leg is being pulled:

> "tell you this," she said
> "keep yo dress up and yo pants down and you'll be
> all right"
> and i said impatiently "old lady you got it all
> wrong"
> "honey, ain't never been wrong yet
> you better get back to the city cause you one of
> them
> technical niggers and you'll have problems here" (*MH*, 12).

Other poems in "The Rooms Inside" trace the poet-speaker's development in terms of her relationships with men. Despite several love lyrics—such as "Winter Poem," "The Butterfly," and "When I Nap"—her life is not anchored to the patterns typical of women's lives. In

"Rituals," for example, she satirically reveals that her friends cannot think of her in terms of marriage, even as a participant in *their* marriages:

> wedding rituals have always intrigued me
> and i'd swear to friends i wouldn't say goddamn not
> even
> once no matter what neither would i give a power
> sign but would even comb my hair severely
> back and put that blue shit under my eyes
> i swear i wanted to be in a wedding (*MH*, 13).

Similarly, "The Only Song I'm Singing," a blues poem, mocks the idea that a woman's most important mission—despite whatever she may achieve as a public figure—is to learn how to love her man. And in "Mixed Media," the poet has replaced her habitually tired, drunk lover with his picture because she has become "tired of bathing and oiling / and waiting for you" and has realized that it was his "smile / that turned me on" (*MH*, 24).

Although tender love poems are included in this volume, they take on a nostalgic tone as we move through "The Rooms Inside." Giovanni had written in *Gemini* that she began to realize as she grew older that a profound division between the sexes makes permanent, lasting relationships impossible: "around twenty-five or thirty you say, maybe men and women aren't meant to live with each other. Maybe they have a different sort of thing going where they come together during mating season and produce beautiful, useless animals who then go on to love, you hope, each of you . . . but living together there are too many games to be gotten through. And the intimacies still seem to be left to his best friend and yours" (*GE*, 137).

In "[Untitled]," Giovanni describes the pain of seeing

> someone
> you used to love and enjoyed
> loving and want
> to love again
> though you know you can't (*MH*, 27).

As a woman, the "hunger" the speaker feels for the former lover remains unsatisfied because of the demands placed upon her by "the real world," which is

made up of baby
clothes *to be washed*
food *to be cooked*
lullabies *to be sung*
smiles *to be glowed*
hair *to be plaited*
ribbons *to be bowed*
coffee *to be drunk*
books *to be read*
tears *to be cried*
loneliness *to be borne* (*MH*, 27).

Moreover, this "real world" also "says you are a strong woman / and anyway he never thought you'd really miss him" (*MH*, 27). Clearly, not only is the world of women different from that of men, but the woman is perceived to be unaffected by the man's behavior.

The next poem in "The Rooms Inside" makes explicit the superhuman capacity expected of the poet because of her gender. "The Wonder Woman (A New Dream—for Stevie Wonder)" marks yet another stage in the poet's life. As we saw, in "Dreams" (*BJ*, 74) the poet marked her maturity by her willingness to become "a sweet inspiration." In "Revolutionary Dreams" (*RC*, 20), she replaced "militant" and "radical" dreams with

natural
dreams of being a natural
woman doing what a woman
does when she's natural

Now, in "Wonder Woman," she finds a new challenge:

dreams have a way
of tossing and turning themselves
around and the times
make requirements that we dream
real dreams for example
i wanted to be
a sweet inspiration in my dreams
of my people but the times
require that i give
myself willingly and become
a wonder woman (*MH*, 28).

Once again, as in the earlier poems, Giovanni bases her figure on the name of a musical group; Stevie Wonder's group was called Wonderlove, but Giovanni always thought of it as wonderwomen.[8] This poem, which is in the last fourth of "The Rooms Inside," describes the unending responsibilities borne—and borne without help—by a woman who is also a mother, a poet, and a public figure. The speaker does not suggest, however, that she is unequal to these "requirements" of the "time." But the remaining poems in the volume do indicate that if she is required to be a wonder woman, then she ought at least to claim control over her own "house," her own life.

The five poems that follow "The Wonder Woman" and complete the section of "The Rooms Inside" are among the most serious in this sequence of poems tracing the poet's development from childhood into adulthood. As a group, these five poems represent a transition of sorts to the more public subject matter of "The Rooms Outside." The first poem, "Categories," culminates a line of thought that we have traced from Giovanni's first volume. There is an inevitability to this poem, in the sense that Giovanni's impatience with prescriptiveness of any sort and her insistence on her right to her own individuality eventually required a poem like "Categories." Because people look at each other so exclusively in terms of categories, the poem argues, intimacy, or even just connection, becomes impossible. Moving from the categories placed on Giovanni herself—unwed mother, famous person—to the larger category of race, the poem emphasizes that human empathy is the major victim of categories. By placing others in preconceived categories, we eliminate the possibility of seeing their lives from their perspective; thus, we also eliminate the capacity for empathy, without which we can forge no bonds or connections with each other.

"Straight Talk," which follows "Categories," explores other categories human beings use to structure their lives and continues the analysis of the effects of such thinking. Titled after a 1970s television talk show hosted by a black woman and a white woman, the poem calls into question language itself as an effective means of bringing people together:

> i'm giving up
> on language
> my next book will be blank
> pages of various textures and hues (*MH*, 31).

The satirical tone and word play of "Straight Talk" give way to wistful melancholy in "Scrapbooks," a poem which, like "The Rooms Inside" as a whole, traces the speaker's growth from childhood to adulthood. Although the particulars of the speaker's situation in the present are limited to the sensual world, she has for whatever reason found herself at a low point, in which the meaning of her life has somehow been put into question:

> it's funny that smells and sounds return
> so all alone uncalled unneeded
> on a sweaty night as i sit armed
> with coffee and cigarettes waiting
>
> sometimes it seems
> my life is a scrapbook (*MH*, 33).

As in "Legacies," recollection of the past infuses meaning and hope into the present. Her early reading was of romantic books that excluded her because they were about a white world and white experiences; she remembers that she nevertheless found a way to take something from them. She learned that being misunderstood does not necessarily mean that one is wrong:

> never understanding my exclusion
> but knowing quite clearly the hero
> is always misunderstood
> though always right in the end (*MH*, 33).

The speaker looks through the scrapbooks in which her past has been distilled, from the faded flowers and dance cards of adolescence to the crisis of her first year at Fisk to the current "black leather book filled / efficiently by a clipping service" (*MH*, 35). These records of her life and of her accomplishments give her hope that, whatever the unhappiness of the present, the future will be meaningful:

> and i sit at dawn sometimes
> listening to *something cool* sometimes
> hearing *tears on my pillow*
> and know there must be other books
> filled with failures and family and friends
> that perhaps one day i can unfold
> for my grandchildren (*MH*, 35).

Each of the last two poems of "The Rooms Inside" offers a final assessment of the poet's life. In both, the speaker presents what she hopes will be remembered of her after her death. The first of these, "When I Die," expresses the poet's rage at the many people who have attacked her because she wanted to live her own life. These people, she makes clear in the first stanza, include many whom she "probably tried / to love" (*MH*, 36). In fact, as the poem continues we see that her rage has been triggered by the betrayal of those from whom she might have expected support: the "black man who said it was / negative of me to want him to be a man," the "white folk" who were frightened by her success, and the "black ones" who were made "truly mad" by it (*MH*, 36–37). The final stanzas of the poem constitute a kind of credo:

> but i do hope someone tells my son
> his mother liked little old ladies with
> their blue dresses and hats and gloves that sitting
>   by the window
> to watch the dawn come up is valid that smiling at
>   an old man
> and petting a dog don't detract from manhood
> do
> somebody please
> tell him i knew all along that what would be
> is what will be but i wanted to be a new person
> and my rebirth was stifled not by the master
> but the slave
>
> and if ever i touched a life i hope that life knows
> that i know that touching was and still is and
>   will always be the true
> revolution (*MH*, 37).

As these lines make clear, the person in whose memory she wants to live is her son, and she wants him to understand exactly what values were significant to his mother: caring about "little old ladies" and responding to the wonder and beauty of the natural world. Giovanni's preoccupation with black male identity during these years of her life is also evident in the poem; she is concerned that her son not repress his gentleness toward and connection to others out of some false conception of masculinity. She wants him as well to understand that one's growth can be hampered by those with whom one is supposed to share significant bonds—that "the slave" "stifled" her rebirth, not "the master."

Although the final lines of the poem are frequently quoted, they are nearly always quoted out of context, diminishing their impact and diluting their power. Within the context of the poem as a whole, however, they are a throwing down of the gauntlet. They insist on the poet's absolute conviction of the truth about human life and social change: human connection, which is always individual, is "the true revolution," not social or political movements. Giovanni had expressed a very similar idea in *Gemini*, where she remarked that "in listening to Smokey and the Miracles sing their *Greatest Hits* recently, I became aware again of the revolutionary quality of 'You Can Depend On Me'" (*GE*, 106). The poetic rendering of the idea, however, especially because of the context provided by the poem as a whole, is much more emphatic and powerful.

The final poem in "The Rooms Inside," an untitled poem for Margaret Danner, a Chicago poet, is one of Giovanni's finest efforts to shape language like a blues song. The poem's theme is expressed in the line, "one ounce of truth benefits like a ripple / on a pond," which came from a letter to Giovanni written by Danner.[9] The poem's repetition with variation of the refrain "as things change remember my smile" emphasizes the importance of memory and of the past, ideas central to the volume as a whole. A radical change in tone, if not altogether in theme, from "When I Die," this poem restores a sense of peace and creates a sense of closure for "The Rooms Inside." The speaker here is beyond the reach of those who would harm her because she is confident, in a sense, that "all is well with [her] soul." Like "When I Die," this poem expresses a relationship with others after the speaker's death, but the need for vengeance in the earlier poem has disappeared:

> remember i smiled when i'm gone
> remember i smiled when i'm gone
> sing a good song when i'm gone
> we ain't got long to stay (*MH*, 39).

My House: "The Rooms Outside"

If in "The Rooms Inside" Giovanni traces her personal development, in "The Rooms Outside" she places that personal self within the larger contexts of Afro-American culture and history. The 13 poems in this section of *My House*, with the exception of the final, title poem, all refer to subjects and events directly related to the lives and consciousness of black Americans. In these poems, Giovanni presents herself as a poet "of the people," who has a truthtelling responsibility to those people. Some of the poems celebrate blackness and black women, while others sharply criticize individual black people or particular black behavior.

Central to "The Rooms Outside" are three poems on Africa, or, more precisely, on the black American's experience of Africa. Written during and shortly after Giovanni's first visit to Africa, all three poems deal with the complex relationship between the black American and Africa. In "Africa I," the poet self-consciously measures the idea of Africa against its reality as a way of presaging the inevitability of that process. Flying high above Africa, the speaker fantasizes a lioness whose cubs are waving at the plane; when her companion points out that "there are no lions / in this part of africa," the speaker mumbles "it's my dream dammit" (*MH*, 47).

The sudden appearance of Giovanni's grandmother in the next stanza suggests that the exchange the poet has just had with her companion is in some ways serious and prototypical:

> but my grandmother stood up
> from her rocker just then
> and said you call it
> like you see it
> john brown and i are with you (*MH*, 47).

"Calling it like you see it" is the imperative facing the poet, but it is an imperative that may produce conflict with others, who will assert the greater authority of their vision of Africa. At the end of this first poem, the speaker glimpses the complexity of her relationship to the home of her ancestors:

> we landed in accra and the people
> clapped and i almost cried wake up
> we're home
> and something in me said shout
> and something else said quietly
> your mother may be glad to see you
> but she may also remember why
> you went away (*MH*, 47–48).

The final lines suggest that Africa's pleasure in seeing her long-lost American children may well be qualified by her awareness of her complicity in their fate. "Africa II" makes clear, however, that it is not Africa, "your mother," who will remember; on the contrary, Africa has repressed or denied all memory of the thousands of children she sold into slavery. The poem's setting is Cape Coast Castle on the coast of Ghana, which was one of the holding places for slaves who were to be shipped to the New World. The speaker's African guide recites his tourist information about Cape Coast Castle, saying, " 'are you afro-american / cape coast castle holds a lot for your people' " (*MH*, 49). He clearly sees no relation between himself and "your people," nor does he grasp what the castle might "hold" for *his* people. He is oblivious of the participation of his own people in the history of this castle, as his horrifying pun, of which he seems unaware, betrays. Instead, he boasts about the eighteenth-century lock on the dungeon, evidence that a British major was once in charge of the fort. The climax of his guided tour reveals how completely he has denied the history of which he speaks:

> "and there is one African buried
> here   we are proud of him" he said
> and i screamed NO there are thousands
> but my voice was lost in the room
> of the women with the secret passageway
> leading to the governor's quarters (*MH*, 49–50).

The controlling metaphor for Africa is "a young man bathing," against whose innocence and beauty Giovanni juxtaposes the slave women held in the castle, whose bodies were used by the white governors of the castle before they were shipped to the New World to be used and abused by still other white men. The young man bathing is beautiful and desirable, but he cannot be clean until he acknowledges his relationship to the Afro-American woman. The final stanza of the poem reveals the intense ambivalence of the speaker's feelings toward Africa:

> and africa is a baby to be
> tossed about and disciplined and loved
> and neglected and bitten on its bottom
> as i wanted to
> sink my teeth into his thigh
> and tell him he would never be
> clean until he can
> possess me (*MH*, 50).

Although Africa may be as beautiful and naive and innocent as a baby, his adult body renders those qualities unnatural. Though he may bathe his splendid body endlessly, it will remain defiled until he rejects his perverse innocence and "possesses me." This final verb of the poem elegantly suggests the complex facets of Africa's relationship to Afro-Americans: Africa's initial rejection of its relationship to its children resulted in their becoming "possessions" of other human beings; the only way Africa can redeem this transgression whereby white people became "owners" of Africa's children is by Africa's "owning," in the sense of claiming, them as its children; and finally, acknowledgment of this kinship is imaged as copulation, symbolic of the closest possible intimacy.

The last poem of the series takes its title and first line from "Africa I," thereby establishing a contrast between the anticipation of the Afro-American visitors before they had seen Africa and their disillusionment at the end of their visit. "They Clapped" records the cumulative effect on the Afro-American tourists of experiencing their dream of Africa called into question by its reality. The insight gained from their long-anticipated journey to their "mother land" is their recognition that "they are strangers all over / and love is only and always about the lover not the beloved" (*MH*, 52).[10] Having come to Africa with the expectation that they were coming "home," these Afro-Americans (including, of course, the poet-speaker) discover that they have no home, are "strangers" everywhere.

The final lines of the poem qualify this idea by suggesting that "home" for Afro-Americans is America, not Africa: "they clapped when they took off / for home despite the dead / dream they saw a free future" (*MH*, 52). The "free future" of the final line would seem to refer to a future free of the kind of double consciousness of which DuBois had written (DuBois, 364). The dual heritage implicit in the very name, *Afro-American*, need not be the source of anguish DuBois and others had thought it. For Giovanni, at least, the firsthand experience of Africa resolved this particular issue about the identity of black Americans.

These three poems about Africa help explain Giovanni's consistent refusal to find in Africa a solution to the black American's problems or to locate her identity as a black American in Afrocentrism. Her position is grounded in the concrete experiences described in these poems: no bond of kinship can exist, let alone be meaningful, if a "mother" refuses to acknowledge or claim her "child." Giovanni's perception of the real absence of relationship between black Americans and Africa also partially explains her preference for the term *Black American* to describe herself and her people rather than *Afro-American* or *African American.*[11]

Other poems in "The Rooms Outside" insist that race will not be allowed to prevent black Americans from claiming the world—not just Africa—as their own. As Giovanni writes in "Poem (For Nina)," if skin color is regarded as something that imprisons black people, they are nonetheless free to create of that prison a "castle," the boundaries of which can be coextensive with the world's. And black people can create within those boundaries whatever world they wish; as the speaker says, she can "color my world Black Gold" (*MH*, 46). The final lines of the poem reiterate the idea that black people have the power to claim and define the world:

> if i am imprisoned in my skin let it be a dark world
> with a deep bass walking a witch doctor to me for
>   spiritual
> consultation
> let my world be defined by my skin and the skin of
>   my people
> for we   spirit to spirit   will embrace
> this world (*MH*, 46).

If in "Ego Tripping" Giovanni lays claim to the black woman's ability to create herself, to make herself into whatever she wishes, in "My Tower," the first poem of "The Rooms Outside," she celebrates the black woman as the creator of beautiful new life. Few poets have described the experience of giving birth more beautifully than Giovanni does in this poem. Although the black female speaker of the poem has foolishly invested herself in fantasies ("wings of a spider") and "daydreams"; although she has constructed her dreams "on the love of a man" who has no answers; and although she has "built my castle by the shore," this time her castle has miraculously become more substantial than sandcastles normally are because, hardly noticing it, she has conceived, carried, and birthed new life:

> i was an oyster clammed shut forever
> when this tiny grain i hardly noticed
> crept inside and i spit around
> and spit around and spun a universe inside
> with a black pearl of immeasurable worth
> that only i could spin around
>
> i have borne a nation on my heart
> and my strength shall not be my undoing

cause this castle didn't crumble
and losing my pearl made me gain
and the dove flew with the olive branch by
    harriet's route
to my breast and nestled close and said
    "you are mine"
and i was full and complete while emptying
    my wombs
and the sea ebbed ohhhhhhhh
what a pretty little baby (*MH*, 45).

Such celebrations of blackness and of the black woman are juxtaposed in "The Rooms Outside" to poems that sharply criticize the actions of particular black people. In "Atrocities," for example, Giovanni scathingly indicts the boxer Joe Frazier for his decision to fight Muhammed Ali before Ali had had sufficient time to prepare for the fight. This poem is a good example of the topicality so characteristic of many of Giovanni's poems. An important aspect of the poet's function, as Giovanni sees and practices it, is to comment on events as they are happening; as truthteller, the poet has a responsibility to address topics of immediate concern to her people. The resulting particularity of poems such as "Atrocities" has made Giovanni vulnerable to critical charges that her poetry is not "universal." Frequently, however, such charges betray an unwillingness on the part of the critic to understand the topical allusions of a poem and then examine what insights into human behavior Giovanni finds in the particular event. For her, quite clearly, the universal must be found as it is manifest in the particular.

"Atrocities" consists of a long enumeration of the many horrors that occurred in the 1960s, from America's napalming of Vietnamese children, to the assassinations of so many of our leaders, to the corruption of the presidency. All these atrocities build to the poem's concluding climax: in a nation and an age such as ours, which has witnessed and perpetrated so many atrocities, "it is only natural that joe frazier / would emerge" (*MH*, 55). The poem assumes the reader's knowledge of Joe Frazier, whose behavior is being viewed as comparable to some of the most horrifying and shameful events of a decade; the intensity of the poet's feeling is clear, however, even if the reader does not know what Joe Frazier did to evoke that feeling. But a knowledge of what he did is necessary if the reader is to understand Giovanni's criticism—and importantly, Giovanni could assume such knowledge in the audience she most wanted to reach, even though that audience may not include the typical literary critic.

Joe Frazier acquired the heavyweight boxing championship through a series of events that resulted from Muhammad Ali's having been stripped of the title in 1967, for refusing, on religious grounds, to be drafted into the United States Army. In addition to being stripped of the title, Ali was barred from the boxing ring for four years. In 1970, a court order overturned the suspension, and Ali began training for a comeback. Frazier agreed to defend his title against Ali in 1971, well before Ali had had adequate time to regain the physical shape demanded by championship fighting. Quite predictably, Frazier won, although Ali regained the heavyweight title in 1974 (from George Foreman, who had taken it from Frazier the year before) and successfully defended it against Frazier in a subsequent fight.

Muhammed Ali had long been a popular figure in the black community for his charismatic personality as well as for his athletic prowess. His outspoken attacks on racism in the United States and his refusal to fight in Vietnam made him a hero to black Americans. Frazier, who many believed would never have gained the heavyweight title had Ali not been unfairly stripped of it, allowed himself to be used by the boxing world in agreeing to fight Ali so soon after Ali was allowed back in the ring. His doing so was regarded by many as a betrayal not simply of Ali but of the ideals for which Ali stood and had been punished. Thus, when we examine and understand the particulars of this poem, we discover that Giovanni locates in them a universal truth about betrayal. The failure to be "my brother's keeper" is certainly a pervasive theme in literature, which would seem to suggest that Giovanni's poetry is as "universal" as any critic might want.

"Atrocities," which was written shortly after Frazier's fight with Ali in 1971, records Giovanni's own outrage at Frazier's behavior, but it gives expression to the outrage of many other black Americans as well. It is a good example of Giovanni's role as poet-bard of the people. Several other poems in "The Rooms Outside" similarly criticize specific black individuals for specific actions. Together, they establish Giovanni's claim to speak about public events that are also a part of her world.

The final poem of "The Rooms Outside" and of the volume as a whole is, appropriately, "My House." After having established her personal identity in "The Rooms Inside" and her public role as a poet in "The Rooms Outside," Giovanni announces in "My House" her right to make herself at home in the world, to claim it and order it as she wishes.

Ironically, the poem is constructed of images and metaphors drawn from a female world that is often experienced as limiting and constricting—cooking, quilting, caring for others. Indeed, "My House" opens like a typical love poem, projecting a rather traditional female speaker:

> i only want to
> be there to kiss you
> as you want to be kissed
> when you need to be kissed
> where i want to kiss you
> cause it's my house
> and i plan to live in it
>
> i really need to hug you
> when i want to hug you
> as you like to hug me
> does this sound like a silly poem (*MH*, 67).

Although the opening lines seem at first reading to carry none of "the imaginative extensions of figurative language" (Juhasz, 171), the repetition of words and phrases alerts us to the fact that more is at stake here than the literal statements might suggest. "As you want," "when you need," "where i want," "when i want"—these phrases seem to suggest the speaker's desire to create a space in which she and her lover are free to act as they wish. The final line of the second stanza, by drawing our attention to the fact that we are reading a poem, intensifies our growing sense of the figurative import of the apparently simple and matter-of-fact statements (Juhasz, 172).

The next two stanzas of the poem detail conventional domestic activities of the sort women commonly perform:

> i mean it's my house
> and i want to fry pork chops
> and bake sweet potatoes
> and call them yams
> cause i run the kitchen
> and i can stand the heat
>
> i spent all winter in
> carpet stores gathering
> patches so i could make

a quilt
does this really sound
like a silly poem
i mean i want to keep you warm (*MH*, 67–68).

Although the actions being described are apparently small and insignificant, the poem now begins to insist that it is not "a silly poem," but a serious poem making a serious statement. One of the most important parts of that statement is beginning to become clear, the fact that the speaker is taking control of all the activities precisely because of her ownership of this house. Although her actions are for the benefit of the lover, she is clearly the one deciding what the lover needs and how those needs might best be filled. Importantly, she also claims the right to use language as she wishes, to name things the way she wishes; in particular, she intends to call sweet potatoes "yams," an allusion to a frequent linguistic argument. Because she names the things in her house, she has control over them, a power she has earned through her ability to "take the heat."

Forcing us to notice that we are reading a poem combines with the speaker's appropriation of power over language to make explicit the fact that the poem is about the poet and her claims on the world. The poem's symbolic meanings become increasingly apparent in the remaining stanzas:

and my windows might be dirty
but it's my house
and if i can't see out sometimes
they can't see in either

english isn't a good language
to express emotion through
mostly i imagine because people
try to speak english instead
of trying to speak through it
i don't know maybe it is
a silly poem

i'm saying it's my house
and i'll make fudge and call
it love and touch my lips
to the chocolate warmth

and smile at old men and call
it revolution cause what's real
is really real
and i still like men in tight
pants cause everybody has some
thing to give and more
important need something to take

and this is my house and you make me
happy
so this is your poem (*MH*, 68–69).[12]

Although others might complain that her vision of the outside world is clouded (presumably by her own subjectivity), the speaker rightly observes that the vision the outside world has of *her* is equally clouded. The effectiveness of language itself—the poet's only medium—is called into question because people do not use language as a vehicle of emotional communication. In other words, the poet says, perhaps her own efforts to communicate through language will lead others to dismiss this as simply "a silly poem." In the penultimate stanza, the speaker restates the themes she has already developed. If her meaning was not clear in the first instance, she will try to reiterate it—"i'm saying."

On one level a love poem, "My House" is also a personal and artistic declaration or credo, which brings together many of the important themes and images we have seen throughout the volume: the difficulty of communication, the importance of old people, the idea that human connection and human love constitute the "real revolution," the poet's insistence on her right to see things from her own perspective, and, perhaps most important, her right to name and to define her world through language.

Giovanni's sense of humor, which is never absent for long from her poems, also surfaces toward the end of "My House." That humor, along with the domestic imagery used in the poem, allows Giovanni to make an extraordinarily powerful statement almost without the reader's (or listener's) realization.[13] In "Poem (For Nina)" we saw Giovanni insisting that race cannot be used as a tool of oppression once she decides to "let my world be defined by my skin and the skin of my people." In "My House," she similarly insists that gender cannot be used as a tool of oppression or trivialization once she decides to define the world as "my house." In her house, moreover, human connection is absolutely central; whether it takes the form of making a quilt to keep the other person warm, or of reaching out with a smile to another person, human connection *is* love, *is* the revolution.

In *My House*, then, Giovanni asserts her freedom and authority as rights to be claimed, not privileges to be granted. As a black woman in a white world and as a black woman poet in a male world, she transforms race and gender into her own sources of power; by embracing them, she converts them from tools of oppression in the hands of others into instruments of liberation in her own.

The Women and the Men

The accomplishment represented by *My House*, *Truth Is On Its Way*, and the *Dialogue* with James Baldwin gained Giovanni widespread recognition, making her life even more hectic and public than it had already become. She was also beginning to pour increasing amounts of time, money, and energy into *Encore*, to which she regularly contributed essays and reviews. In terms of her development as a poet, *My House* was a watershed publication that climaxed the first stage of her career. As she said in her 1974 conversation with Margaret Walker, "it wasn't really until I got into *Re: Creation* that I considered myself a poet. And it is only now [in 1973] . . . that I consider myself a writer" (*PE*, 57). In the years following the monumental achievement of *My House*, Giovanni brought together previously published poems in a volume titled *Ego-Tripping And Other Poems For Young Readers*, published her conversation with Margaret Walker, and released several more recordings of her poetry. Not until the appearance of *Cotton Candy on a Rainy Day* in 1978 was she to publish a new volume of poetry as significant as *My House.*

In 1975, however, Giovanni combined many of the poems originally published in *Re: Creation* with some 19 new poems and published them as *The Women and the Men*. Many readers know the poems of *Re: Creation*—which included "Ego Tripping"—only through *The Women and the Men*, which, like all of Giovanni's major volumes, has remained continuously in print. In fact, initial reviews and subsequent criticism often betray a lack of awareness of the dates of composition and original publication of more than half the poems in *The Women and the Men*, which has contributed to some of the mistaken conceptions about Giovanni's poetic and intellectual development.[14]

The new material in this volume is similar in theme and mood to the poems in *My House*, though much of it also anticipates *Cotton Candy on a*

Rainy Day. Of interest to the student of Giovanni's poetry is the arrangement of the poems in *The Women and the Men*, which is divided into three sections: "The Women," "The Men," and "And Some Places." New poems and old are more or less equally distributed across the three sections, but the new material in the first and last sections tends to be more intellectually engaging and aesthetically effective than that in the middle section ("The Men"). This fact is significant, I think, as an indication of the direction Giovanni's later work would take. The new poems in "The Men" are, with one or two possible exceptions, love poems—as are all of the old poems with the exception of "The Lion In Daniel's Den." The new material in "The Women," by contrast, like the old, covers a range of themes and moods. What this difference points to, I believe, is the fact that the world and the values that interest and engage the poet the most are the world and the values of women, and not women in relationship to men but rather in relationship to themselves or each other. This development, which was foreshadowed in Giovanni's first volumes, does not seem the result of the hostility toward men often evident in consciously feminist poets; it seems instead to grow out of an indifference toward or lack of interest in men. In later volumes, especially *Those Who Ride The Night Winds*, Giovanni's imagination is engaged by particular men who are public figures; but the everyday lives of men, or of men and women together, seem increasingly to hold little interest for her.

The first poem in "The Women," a new poem entitled "The Women Gather," concerns the ancient role of women as mourners of the dead. Although written for the journalist Joe Strickland, who was murdered in his Boston home by an intruder, the poem focuses on the mourning women who act as a catalyst in bringing a community together. To these women, "it is not unusual / that the old bury the young / though it is an abomination."[15] The poem implicitly compares this "abomination" to other abominations in our world:

> it is not strange
> that the unwise and the ungentle
> carry the banner of humaneness
>   though it is a castration of the spirit
>
> it no longer shatters the intellect
> that those who make war
> call themselves diplomats

we are no longer surprised
that the unfaithful pray loudest
every sunday in every church
and sometimes in rooms facing east
        though it is a sin and a shame (*WM*, 2).

The essential hypocrisy of the world can no longer shock or surprise the women who gather, although they recognize it for what it is.

The remainder of the poem explores the question of "how do we judge a man"; significantly, we who are women most often judge a man with a generosity born of the fact that we "know him through those who love him," that is, through women: "the women gather strangers / to each other because / they have loved a man" (*WM*, 3).

The poem's power comes in large part from the archetypal image it conjures of "the women gather." Giovanni seems to be trying to work toward a vision of female community that is not quite complete or even consistent in this poem. What seems clear, however, is that she locates a tremendous amount of significance and meaning in this image; there is a sense that the answers to the riddle of life are to be found in this image of women gathering to perform "ancient rituals" (*WM*, 2).

Several other of the new poems in this first section of *The Women and the Men* explore the related theme of the older woman as a symbol not simply of important values but also of unfulfilled dreams and isolation. What is significant in these poems, which include "Once A Lady Told Me," "Each Sunday," and "Mother's Habits," is the poet-speaker's identification with the older woman, even though she has enjoyed opportunities and freedoms never available to her older counterpart. As mother and wife, the older woman has led a life of caring for others, nurturing others, at the cost of forsaking whatever dreams she might have had for herself. Giovanni's remarkable ability to capture the consciousness of this figure is especially apparent in these lines from "Each Sunday":

i wonder did she dream
while baking cold-water cornbread
of being a great reporter churning
all the facts together and creating
the truth
did she think   while patching the torn pants
and mending the socks of her men   of standing

> arms outstretched before a great world
> body offering her solution for peace
> what did she feel wringing the neck
> of Sunday's chicken breaking the beans
> of her stifled life (*WM*, 7).

Although the older woman in this poem is "hopeful / that we never change / places" (*WM*, 7), we certainly sense that the speaker believes that she will one day be like the older woman. A continuity between generations of women is emphasized in both "Once A Lady Told Me" and "Mother's Habits"; in the latter, the speaker identifies herself as already possessing her mother's habits and indicates that her experience of the world and of life is and will continue to be similar to her mother's:

> i grow tired
> like my mother doing without
> even one small word
> that says i care
> and like my mother i shall fade
> into my dreams
> no longer caring
> either (*WM*, 23).

Complementing these poems about older women are two new poems about the poet-speaker's own aging process and final years, "The December of My Springs" and "The Life I Led." The latter poem, one of Giovanni's finest, presents a positive vision of age as well as an acceptance of the inevitable physical changes that age will bring:

> i know that the purple veins
> like dead fish in the Seine
> will dot my legs one day
> and my hands will wither while
> my hair turns grayish white   i know that
> one day my teeth will move when
> my lips smile
> and a flutter of hair will appear
> below my nose   i hope
> my skin doesn't change to those blotchy
> colors (*WM*, 10).

Physical comfort, connection to the new generation, and companionship comprise the speaker's desires for her old age, but her central concern is that she will be able to find comfort in the life she has led:

> i hope i die
> warmed
> by the life that i tried
> to live (*WM*, 10).

"The December of My Springs," by contrast, anticipates the mood of *Cotton Candy on a Rainy Day*;[16] it depicts maturity as a state which is void of joy and enthusiasm and in which direction is given by the intellect and the heart rather than the body. Although the speaker asserts that "it might be good / to decide rather than to need" where love is concerned, the poem's mood of disillusioned resignation calls into question how positive this "good" actually is. Love itself seems less an energy radiating from the self than a burden placed by others on the self:

> some say we are responsible
> for those we love
> others know we are responsible
> for those who love us (*WM*, 9).

A similar note is struck by one of the new pieces in the section "The Men." Unlike the other new poems in this section, "Something To Be Said For Silence" finds little of value in love or love relationships; indeed, the speaker finds herself unable to feel, even though she wants "to be in love":

> i guess it's all right
> to want to feel
> though it's better to really feel
> and sometimes i wonder
> did i ever love anyone (*WM*, 38).

As the poem continues, a mood approaching despair seems to settle over the speaker, who thinks that "somewhere something is missing" and "i feel we won't feel again" (*WM*, 38). Although these lines suggest a specific relationship that has somehow grown meaningless, the poem as a whole is less about a particular situation than it is about a mood that has engulfed the speaker.

Of the remaining new material in *The Women and the Men*, several poems continue the poet's reflections about and reactions to Africa, the result, no doubt, of a second extended visit in 1973. Especially noteworthy among these poems is "Africa," a poem in which Giovanni identifies herself as "a teller of tales / a dreamer of dreams," and a spinner of poems (*WM*, 42). Like a number of other contemporary women poets, Giovanni describes her creativity through the metaphor of a spider who, out of her self, generates something new, delicate, and beautiful. She also identifies herself with the traditional African *griot* (oral historian), a role appropriate to the possibility of kinship between Africans and black Americans articulated in the poem. This vision of a new kind of relationship with Africa is not radically different from the vision we saw in *My House*, for Giovanni once again recognizes that kinship with Africa could result only from acknowledgement of the truth:

> i dream of truth lubricating our words
> will that ease three hundred years
> and i dream of black men and women walking
> together side by side into a new world
> described by love and bounded by difference
> for nothing is the same except oppression and shame (*WM*, 43).

In another new African poem, "A Very Simple Wish," Giovanni protests the pan-Africanism that often leads black Americans to seek connections with Africans rather than with each other:

> i wonder why we don't love
> not some people way on
> the other side of the world with strange
> customs and habits
> not some folk from whom we were sold
> hundreds of years ago
> but people who look like us
> who think like us
> who want to love us   why
> don't we love them (*WM*, 46).

Finally, two other new poems in *The Women and the Men* deserve mention because they are rare instances of poems in which Giovanni takes her art as her subject. The first of these, "Poetry Is A Tressel,"[17] appears in the section of "The Men," and, like the other poems in this section, develops into a kind of love poem. Its opening lines, however, are important for the emphasis they place on poetry's primary function of communication:

> poetry is a tressel
> spanning the distance between
> what i feel
> and what i say (*WM*, 33).

A more serious consideration of poetry is presented in "Poetry," which appears in the last section of *The Women and the Men*. The idea of communication is again apparent, but several other ideas emerge as well. "We poets," Giovanni states, work out of our essential loneliness in order to create a poem that "no one understands." The reason the poem is misunderstood is that readers think they should love or accept poems, much as they might another person, when the poem actually exists to create "controversy." Because the poet creates in order to communicate, moreover, we see an implicit recognition of the reader. But the reader also has a responsibility, and in the final part of the poem Giovanni delineates that responsibility:

> a poem is pure energy
> horizontally contained
> between the mind
> of the poet and the ear of the reader
> if it does not sing discard the ear
> for poetry is song
> if it does not delight discard
> the heart for poetry is joy
> if it does not inform then close
> off the brain for it is dead
> if it cannot heed the insistent message
> that life is precious
>
> which is all we poets
> wrapped in our loneliness
> are trying to say (*WM*, 55).

In a reversal of the ordinary placement of responsibility, Giovanni in these lines suggests that if poetry is really poetry, then the failure to hear its music, delight in its joy, and understand its message is the reader's failure, not the poet's or the poetry's.

As I have tried to suggest, the new poetry Giovanni interwove with the old in *The Women and the Men* presents a voice in the process of transition. There are echoes here of the voice we found in *My House*, just as there are tones that will become fuller in *Cotton Candy on a Rainy Day*. If the new poems are not, as a group, as fine as those of either the prior or the subsequent volume, that is perhaps because of the magnitude of the different achievements represented by both those volumes.

Chapter Four
Cotton Candy on a Rainy Day

Three years after the publication of *The Women and the Men*, Giovanni brought out a new collection that took her readers by surprise, so little preparation had there seemed to be for the subdued, frequently dark voice that characterizes *Cotton Candy on a Rainy Day*.[1] Published on 25 October 1978, the new volume of poems sold well. Although some of the new poems in *The Women and the Men* can, in retrospect, be seen as anticipatory of *Cotton Candy on a Rainy Day*, no one, as Anna Robinson has said, "could have predicted the direction the poet" took in this volume.[2] Yet, reflecting as they do the poet's responses to events in her own personal life as well as to those in the social and political life of the 1970s, these poems record the voice of a maturing, developing writer; as Giovanni herself has observed frequently during her career, her work does show a logical kind of development. Perhaps because fame and recognition came to her earliest work, her poetry allows readers greater access to her own process of maturing than the work of writers often affords us. Even so, there is no question that the poems in *Cotton Candy on a Rainy Day* reflect the unusually dishonorable and disappointing history of America during the 1970s.

During the three-year interval between *The Women and the Men* and *Cotton Candy on a Rainy Day*, much of Giovanni's energy and money had been poured into *Encore American & Worldwide News*, a laudable enterprise that offered an alternative to the white perspective of most newspapers and magazines. As early as 1976, it was clear to everyone, except perhaps Ida Lewis, editor of the magazine and Giovanni's close friend, that *Encore* was in serious financial and managerial difficulty. Pushing herself at an almost unbelievable pace, Giovanni stayed on the lecture circuit to help keep the magazine afloat. In addition to the anxieties and disappointments attending this venture, Giovanni's personal life was also filled with turmoil and unhappiness during this period. In the larger life of the nation, the ideals and dreams of the 1960s were dead, and in their wake, the Vietnam War and the Watergate conspiracy had bred a cynicism and despair that President Jimmy Carter's hollow promises did nothing to dispel. As the decade advanced, the strength of the political right increased, and a growing backlash against black Americans became manifest.

Dedicated to her father, whose sudden illness had brought Giovanni home by the time the volume appeared, *Cotton Candy on a Rainy Day* leaves the reader with an impression of a speaker in crisis; it suggests a "dark night of the soul" without offering any assurance of deliverance or salvation. The volume's primary theme of mutability is examined from several angles and engenders a range of emotional responses in the speaker. Many of the poems focus on the process of aging as the most obvious manifestation of human mutability. Frequently, however, Giovanni superimposes the experience of disillusionment onto the process of aging, tacitly suggesting that unfulfilled dreams are a natural corollary to aging. Certainly what becomes evident as one reads through *Cotton Candy on a Rainy Day* is that the speaker's apparent recognition of human mortality seems actually the result of her having fallen from expectation to disillusion. Repeatedly, the poems show the speaker grappling with the emotional pain and often despair created by her realization that dreams and ideals are more likely to be shattered by reality than to reshape it. Her efforts to present this savaging of dreams as a universal experience, an inherent aspect of the human condition, are often at odds with her acknowledgement of the fact that it is an experience more common to some groups of people than to others. Thus, she sometimes attempts to rationalize the unnatural restrictions imposed by gender and race as merely constitutive of the human experience. These attempts account, I believe, for the fact that the mood of *Cotton Candy on a Rainy Day* is darker than her admittedly serious themes might otherwise lead us to expect.

"mankind alone among the mammals learns to cry"

The title poem with which *Cotton Candy on a Rainy Day* opens establishes the idea of life's ephemeral qualities, but the speaker's attitude toward her theme is perhaps more positive here than elsewhere in the volume and certainly more positive than critics have tended to acknowledge. In public readings of this poem, Giovanni typically provides information about its source that sheds considerable light on the speaker's tone. The cotton candy image had been with her for a long time before she wrote the poem, the result, she says, of her having taken her nephew to the zoo one day when he was still quite young—probably in 1963 or 1964. Because it was a rainy day, they had the zoo almost completely to themselves, but the concession stands were open so they decided to indulge themselves in their favorite treat, cotton candy. When the little boy and his aunt tried to make their purchase, however, the woman running the concession stand merely observed, "It's raining." "Yes," the poet acknowledged, wondering what the problem might be, but reiterating her order more firmly. Instead of serving up two cotton candies, the concession lady repeated, in a louder voice, "It's raining." Clearly, as the poet recounts the incident, she and her nephew were supposed to grasp some significant implication of this insistence on the weather conditions, but it eluded them. Finally, the concession clerk had to explain that, although she had cotton candy, she did not sell it on rainy days because the rain would melt it before the customer had a chance to eat it.

Giovanni found this logic both mystifying and infuriating. She was prepared to spend her money to buy something that was in fact available, and she could not believe that she was to be prohibited from enjoying as much of it as she could simply because it would not last, because it would melt before she was able to consume it. The whole episode stayed in her mind, she says, because it so vividly dramatized the belief held by many people that one should not invest in an experience that will be ephemeral or that one will not actually have time to complete. To her, cotton candy became an apt metaphor for life itself, which one invests in and strives to make better despite the inevitability of change and, ultimately, death.

In the opening lines of the poem, the speaker describes herself as elusive and insubstantial:

> Don't look now
> I'm fading away
> Into the gray of my mornings
> Or the blues of every night[3]

The vagueness and indistinctiveness that the speaker attributes to her identity impact primarily on other people,[4] as is indicated by the first line. But the second stanza suggests that this vagueness is both a function of change itself and a natural phenomenon:

> Is it that my nails
>   keep breaking

Or maybe the corn
   on my second little piggy
Things keep popping out
   on my face
   or
of my life (*CC*, 21).

Just as the speaker's body is unpredictable and subject to sudden change, so too is her life, which makes her a "difficult" woman for others:

It seems no matter how
I try I become more difficult
   to hold
I am not an easy woman
   to want (*CC*, 21).

For those who seek permanence or stability in a relationship, the speaker acknowledges, she may not be the best choice; she is "not an easy woman / to want" because she is "difficult / to hold." Although at this point in the poem, *hold* could conceivably suggest either "embrace" or "keep in one's control," the final parts of the poem make the latter meaning more compelling.

The next stanza of the poem states that "loneliness" will be what "this decade" of the 1970s "will be / known for," a line of thought that follows logically from the suggestions of human impermanence and resistance to change made in the poem's first three stanzas. Loneliness, though it is a function of isolation, is described in positive terms:

If loneliness were a grape
   the wine would be vintage
If it were a wood
   the furniture would be mahogany
But since it is life   it is
   Cotton Candy
      on a rainy day
The sweet soft essence
   of possibility
Never quite maturing (*CC*, 22).

Here the speaker asserts that loneliness is a fundamental condition of human life—in fact, "it is life." And what life presents us is "cotton candy on a rainy day," that is, something potentially wonderful that is never able to be realized. Unlike the best variety of grape, which yields vintage wine when it is allowed to mature, or the valuable mahogany, which reaches a kind of perfection when it is made into furniture, cotton candy on a rainy day will melt before the "possibility" it represents can be realized.

The tone of the poem seems to shift in the next stanzas as the speaker declares her own commitment to stay "in the great tradition / albeit circus / That the show must go on" despite, presumably, the fact that life's possibilities rarely come to fruition. Giovanni then smoothly segues into the next movement of the poem, using the food imagery that has been central all along as her unifying device:

> We all line up
>   at some midway point
> To thread our way through
>   the boredom and futility
> Looking for the blue ribbon and gold medal
>
> Mostly these are seen as food labels
>
> We are consumed by people who sing
>   the same old song   STAY:
>   *as sweet as you are*
>   *in my corner*
> Or perhaps   *just a little bit longer*
> But whatever you do   *don't change baby baby*
>   *don't change*
> Something needs to change
> Everything   some say   will change
> I need a change
>   of pace   face   attitude and life
> Though I long for my loneliness
> I know I need something
> Or someone
> Or . . . . . . (*CC*, 22–23).

Constructing her lines from the titles of popular romantic songs,[5] the speaker dramatizes the possessiveness typical of romantic relationships, a possessiveness that is "consuming." Not only do others want to possess us, but they want us to remain unchanged. This desire for permanence is, however, within the context of the poem, a desire for stasis, because mutability and impermanence have been established as defining features of life. Thus, though the speaker recognizes her need for "something / Or someone," isolation and loneliness seem to represent the only avenue away from the possessiveness of others.

In a final reconfiguration of her central metaphor, Giovanni concludes the poem with these lines:

> I am cotton candy on a rainy day
>   the unrealized dream of an idea unborn
>
> I share with the painters the desire
> To put a three-dimensional picture
> On a one-dimensional surface (*CC*, 23).

With the assertion that "I am cotton candy on a rainy day," the speaker makes clear the complete failure of others to understand her or life itself, a failure suggested earlier in the line "We are consumed by people." Their desire for her not to change is as impossible and preposterous as the rule followed by the concession woman at the zoo. Just as life, like cotton candy, represents "possibility / Never quite maturing," so the speaker herself is "the unrealized dream of an idea unborn." And, as the final lines of the poem make clear, just as the poet and her nephew wanted to buy the cotton candy despite the rain that would quickly melt it, so she, as a writer, emulates the painters. She, like the painters, desires "To put a three-dimensional picture / On a one-dimensional surface," a goal impossible of attainment but nonetheless worthy of pursuit. "Cotton Candy on a Rainy Day" thus refuses to view human mutability or human mortality as inhibitive of meaningful action; indeed, as Giovanni frequently states when she reads the poem, those conditions of human life—especially mortality—constitute a kind of imperative that we do as best we can with the short amount of time we have.

This theme of working toward goals one may never succeed in reaching recurs frequently in *Cotton Candy on a Rainy Day*. In "Age," for example, in which Giovanni develops the themes of aging and mortality, the speaker asserts that just as "lack of life / prevents death," so too "the unwillingness to try / is worse than any failure" (*CC*, 46). A bittersweet treatment of the theme may be seen in "The Beep Beep Poem," which delineates the frustrations and difficulties of being a writer. The problems the poet confronts include the absence of new subjects: "there's almost nothing / that hasn't been said / and said and said" (*CC*, 68). Pleasing one's audience, whether that audience be one's father or the editorial board of *Encore America & Worldwide News*, often seems impossible. Although these obstacles might seem to militate against writing at all, they are insufficient to prevent the poet from writing about subjects that please her. Suggesting an analogy between writing and driving, Giovanni concludes her poem by detailing the many pleasures she receives from driving her car through the countryside. The poem ends on an exuberant note rarely heard in this volume:

> the power within my toe delights me
> and i fling my spirit down the highway
> i love the way i feel
> when i pass the moon and i holler to the stars
> i'm coming through
>
> Beep Beep (*CC*, 69).

Even if she has only the moon and stars for an audience, the pleasure she takes from flinging her "spirit" down the highway—or the page—is sufficient unto itself.

In instances such as these, the speaker in the poems of *Cotton Candy on a Rainy Day* reveals herself to be a resolute idealist. More often in the volume, however, we see her grappling with the emotional costs inevitably and repeatedly exacted from the idealist. Her idealism is precisely what obliges her to traverse that downward arc from expectation to disillusion mentioned at the beginning of this chapter. Many of the poems in *Cotton Candy on a Rainy Day* describe that arc, including "Introspection," "Forced Retirement," "Crutches," "The Winter Storm," "Their Fathers," "Adulthood II," and several others. Frequent topical allusions tie the poet's disillusionment to the larger political and social ideals she shared with a generation; in "Being and Nothingness (to quote a philosopher)," for instance, the speaker points to the absence of meaningful action as evidence that the 1960s and the ideals associated with them are dead:

> i've always prided myself
> on being a child of the sixties
> and we are all finished
> so that makes being
> nothing (*CC*, 89).

Although poems such as this one connect the speaker's disillusionment to a larger historical and social context, her emotional experience remains extremely personal, and, in fact, connections to a larger context do not predominate in the volume. The repetition in the lines above of a phrase also used in "Cotton Candy on a Rainy Day" ("i've always prided myself") suggests the extent to which the speaker is dealing primarily with her own personal responses rather than with the responses of a generation.

In many of the poems in *Cotton Candy on a Rainy Day*, Giovanni presents the experience of disillusionment and loss as a function of aging and maturity. In "Turning (I need a better title)," for example, the speaker ties the radical shrinking of "her / life into one / tiny room with kitchen" to her thirtieth birthday (*CC*, 85). As we read through the volume, however, so dramatic is the change that maturity has brought her that her attempts to present her disillusionment as a function of aging begin to seem somewhat contrived; there is a sense in which she seems to be tying the two experiences together in order to make her disillusionment bearable. Somehow, if it can be seen as a common result of a natural process, it can be reduced to manageable proportions. That it may actually be the result of something bordering on cataclysmic—something greater than simply aging—is most evident in the very fine poem "The Rose Bush":

> i know i haven't grown but
> i don't fit beneath the rose
> bush by my grandmother's porch
>
> i couldn't have grown so much though
> i don't see why the back of the couch
> doesn't hide me from my sister
>
> the lightning that would flash
> on summer days brought shouts
> of you children be still   the lightning's
> gonna get you
>
> we laughed my cousins and sister and i
> at the foolish old people
> and their backward superstitions
> though lightning struck me
> in new york city

and i ran
to or from what   i'm not sure
but i was hit
and now i don't fit
beneath the rose bushes
anymore
anyway   they're gone (*CC*, 76–77).

Profoundly altered by the experience of being "struck" by the "lightning" in New York, the speaker finds she can no longer "fit beneath the rose / bush by my grandmother's porch," just as she can no longer hide behind the couch so her sister cannot see her. The first two stanzas of the poem cast her alteration in terms of physical size, even though the speaker is certain that she has not "grown so much." The second part of the poem suggests, however, that not physical growth but something explosive and diasastrous has altered her—something as perilous and uncontrollable as the lightning that "the foolish old people" had warned her would "get" her if she did not remain "still."

The alteration wrought in her by the lightning is measurable by the places and objects she remembers from her childhood; the innocence and hope and excitement associated with her grandmother's rose bush, and with the games of hide-and-seek she and her sister and cousins would play, seem to belong to a different person. But these remnants from the past that might allow the speaker somehow to integrate her younger self and the person she has become are also themselves "gone." The devastating final line of the poem suggests not that she has simply grown older but that the people and the very places from her childhood to which she might anchor her adult self have been eradicated. As we recall from *Gemini*, Giovanni's grandmother's home was obliterated by the "lightning" of urban renewal, which so disoriented her grandmother that she died. "The Rose Bush" evokes the poet's own comparable disorientation, though it does not identify the nature of the "lightning" she has experienced.

Although the experience inscribed in this poem and others like it can generate emptiness and despair in the speaker, it also enables her to empathize with others. The most poignant example of this newly acquired understanding of others is to be found in the poem "Gus (for my father)," which charts the ways in which the dreams of black men "tunnel under," never to be realized. Although "Langston says" such dreams "might explode," the speaker reflects that they "might also just die / Shriveling to the here and now" (*CC*, 63). Despite the "tunneling under" of his dreams, her father "always had pretty legs," gained not from playing tennis but from swimming "In a sink-or-swim mud hole somewhere / In Alabama" (*CC*, 62). Similarly, though he is a short man, "He hustled the ball on the high school court / Well enough to win a college scholarship" (*CC*, 62). We discover that her father has succeeded by dint of hard work—"he worked three jobs"—and even more, perhaps, by refusing to acknowledge obstacles and limitations: "The fact that he is short / Was an idea late reaching his consciousness" (*CC*, 62).

The speaker's admiration of her father is informed by an awareness of the cost paid by others as well as by himself for the oppression he experienced as a black man. She points out, for example, that "He was a stranger" to her because he was always working (*CC*, 63); and she suggests, as she has elsewhere, the painful effects on others of his culturally created idea of manhood, which made him believe that having something to give his loved ones was more important than

> understanding
> That even nothing is something
> As long as you are there
> To give the nothing   personally (*CC*, 65).

These lines echo the frustration with black men that Giovanni had expressed in her dialogue with James Baldwin. Baldwin, describing the process by which the black man is emasculated by a white racist society, explains that because the black man cannot provide his family what they need, he grows to hate them. Giovanni fails to grasp or credit this sort of logic: "I don't understand how a black man can be nothing in the streets and so fearful in his home, how he can be brutalized by some white person somewhere and then come home and treat me or Mother the same way that he was being treated" (*AD*, 43).

In the poem, despite such obviously ambivalent feelings of the speaker toward her father, she nonetheless achieves the insight that judging and condemning him was easy until she herself had to experience her "own possibility shrink / Back into the unclonable cell / From which dreams spring" (*CC*, 64). This idea is elaborated upon through concrete, specific details:

> Before our mettle is tested
> We easily consider ourselves strong

Before we see our children want
Not elaborate things
But a christmas bike or easter shoes
It's easy to say
what should have been done (*CC*, 64).

Whatever the "lightning" that radically changed her, one positive result is a new empathy with and tolerance toward others. The speaker attempts to present that "lightning" and its effects as a function of aging; her attempts are not, however, altogether convincing:

If the first sign of spring is the swallows
Then the first sign of maturity is the pride
We gulp when we realize
There are few choices in life
That are clear
Seldom is good pitted against evil
Or even better against best
Mostly it's bad versus worse (*CC*, 64).

In this poem and others in *Cotton Candy on a Rainy Day*, then, we find themes of disappointment, disillusionment, and diminishment tied to the process of aging and maturity. If we fail to be persuaded of the truth of this connection, it is surely because the painfulness described is out of proportion to the ordinary experience of aging. Moreover, Giovanni's refusal to relinquish the dreams and ideals themselves—despite their having been deferred and battered—suggests that they are something more substantive and reasonable than the naive visions of most people's youth. More like her father than her poem for him might acknowledge, the poet seems also to refuse to recognize obstacles because she knows they ought not be there—and, in fact, are not there for everyone. Like her father, that is, she refuses to be a victim of her gender or her race, even though she is a black woman in a sexist and racist culture. Although she may find "few choices in life / That are clear," she will claim whatever control over her life she possibly can. As she states in "Choices,"

if i can't do
what i want to do
then my job is to not
do what i don't want
to do (*CC*, 66).

This kind of choice is "not the same thing," she acknowledges, "but that's why mankind / alone among the mammals / learns to cry" (*CC*, 66). And, despite the frequency—even the predictability—of defeat, she continues to try:

> in youth our ignorance gives us courage
> with age our courage gives us hope
> with hope we learn that man is more
> than the sum of what he does
> we also are what we wish we did (*CC*, 46).

A New Awareness of Gender

As we have seen throughout this study, from the outset of her career, Giovanni often focussed her poetry on women and the limitations imposed by gender. And as early as *Gemini*, she thought about the differences created by the intersection of gender and race: "white women and Black men are both niggers and both respond as such. He runs to the white man to explain his 'rights' and she runs to us. . . . We Black women are the single group in the West intact. . . . We are . . . the only group that derives its identity from itself. I think it's been rather unconscious but we measure ourselves by ourselves, and I think that's a practice we can ill afford to lose" (*GE*, 144). As the second sentence in this passage suggests, Giovanni recognized distinct differences between black women and white women, differences that often seemed to overshadow the commonality of gender. Like many black women of her generation, moreover, she was alternately hostile toward, skeptical of, or indifferent about the women's movement. The women's liberation movement was, she said in a 1971 interview, for white women: "'Black women don't need to be liberated' (in the white woman's sense)."[6] In another interview given about the same time, she criticized women in the liberation movement: "All they do is complain that black women have not helped them. If they want to be equal to white men why do we have to help them. . . . If they were interested in women's lib why aren't they helping Angela Davis" (*Black Collegian*, 33).

Just as Giovanni's plain speaking early in her career angered many of the men in the Black Arts Movement, from the mid-1970s on it similarly has hurt her with white women in the liberation movement and, more recently, with some academic feminists. But, as Toni Cade asked in her 1970 anthology *The Black Woman*, "how relevant are the truths, the experiences, the findings of white women to Black women? Are women after all simply women? I don't know that our priorities are the same, that our concerns and methods are the same, or even similar enough so that we can afford to depend on this new field of experts (white, female)."[7] These questions are still being asked and explored by black feminists today, who continue to protest the double exclusion of black women writers from accounts of black literary traditions on the one hand, and from accounts of women's literary traditions on the other. In light of their justifiable anger at such exclusions, the systematic and almost universal exclusion of Nikki Giovanni from the spate of black feminist literary criticism published in the 1980s seems especially ironic, even reprehensible. Iconoclastic and plainspoken though Giovanni may be, her accomplishments as a black woman poet are far too significant to justify her virtual invisibility in literary criticism specifically aimed at recognizing and interpreting the artistic accomplishments of black women.[8] The dismissal of her work by feminist literary critics is all the more regrettable because of the decided feminist undercurrents in much of her poetry. Too often, however, these undercurrents have been missed by critics who, perhaps deceived by the simplicity of her language, have failed to bring to her poetry the kind of analysis they would to apparently more "difficult" verse.[9]

Although we have seen the prevalence of themes about women in earlier volumes of her poetry, she herself marks the poem "Woman" in *Cotton Candy on a Rainy Day* as the beginning of her *conscious* awareness of women and women's issues.[10] In this poem, the speaker describes a woman who had sought in numerous ways to define herself in relation to, or in terms of, a man; he, however, consistently has refused to play the parts she has projected for him. In each instance, the speaker has clearly *believed* herself unable to be what she wants to be without the man's cooperation: initially she wants

> to be a blade
> of grass amid the fields
> but he wouldn't agree
> to be the dandelion (*CC*, 71).

Similarly, he refuses to be a tree for her as a robin, a corner for her as a spider web, or a reader of her as a book. Quite obviously, the roles she projects for herself in these instances are not actually dependent on his playing the roles she projects for him. Equally clear, however, is that each of her roles is slightly more dependent than the previous one.

Consistent with this pattern of increasing dependence, the woman's final attempt to define herself in terms of the man places her in a wholly dependent role: "she turned herself into a bulb / but he wouldn't let her grow" (*CC*, 71). This series of roles culminates in the implicitly dependent status of woman; but the man's refusal to participate no longer prevents the woman from maintaining the identity she has chosen:

> she decided to become
> a woman
> and though he still refused
> to be a man
> she decided it was all
> right (*CC*, 71).

"Woman" thus makes a strong assertion of the necessity for women to define themselves without reference to a man, especially without dependent reference. Regardless of how "woman" and "man" are constructed, women must clearly go forward, construct their own identity, regardless of whether men choose to do the same. This theme had preoccupied Giovanni for a number of years; again, in her dialogue with Baldwin, she made an analogous statement: "black men say In order for me to be a man, you walk ten paces behind me. Which means nothing. I can walk ten paces behind a dog. It means nothing to me, but if that's what the black man needs, I'll never get far enough behind him for him to be a man" (*AD*, 47). Giovanni thus clearly had thought about these ideas long before she wrote "Woman," even though that poem, as she states, marked a new conscious awareness of them.

Several other poems in *Cotton Candy on a Rainy Day* also allude to or focus on gender or gender-related concerns. "Forced Retirement," for example, which explores the relation between internal responses and external conditions, concludes with lines that echo Giovanni's early "My Poem":

> i could say i am black female
> and bright
> in a white male mediocre world
> but that hardly explains why
> i sit on the beaches of st croix
> feeling so abandoned (*CC*, 28).

Although the external features of her situation may not adequately explain her feelings of abandonment, through the very act of identifying those external features the speaker of the poem implies a connection between them. These lines also illustrate the distance between the younger Giovanni of "My Poem," who recognized herself as a "black female poet," and the older poet who now delineates the context in which that poet must live.

"Their Fathers" makes further comment on that context. The speaker of this poem locates "the weakness / of our race" in the "sterility" of black men, who look to "past glories" rather than planning for the future (*CC*, 48). Toward the end of the poem, she again turns to the relationship between black men and black women. Just as the speaker in "Gus" tacitly criticized her father for withdrawing from his family because he could not give them what they wanted or needed, the speaker in "Their Fathers" similarly expresses the bitterness such behavior can create in the black woman:

> someone said the only emotion
> black men show
> is rage or anger
> which is only partly true
> the only rage and anger
> they show are to those
> who would want to love them
> and bear their children
> and with them walk into the future
> why do we
> who have offered expectation
> have to absorb pain (*CC*, 50).

The intersection of race and gender inevitably seems to result, these lines suggest, in black men's abuse of black women. In "Gus," the speaker observed that "Black men grow inverse / To the common experience" (*CC*, 65). In "Their Fathers" she shows—in much the same way Baldwin had—how the daily encounters with racism prevent black men from being able to conform to the socially constructed definition of manhood; as a consequence, black women become the target of their "rage and anger." Again, we see Giovanni working out in her poetry ideas that she had expressed earlier in other contexts.

Giovanni's new conscious awareness of gender as a source of oppression and limitation for women living in a sexist world constitutes another major contribution to the disillusioned, often despairing mood of *Cotton Candy on a Rainy Day*. The sense of limitation and restriction is even more apparent in a number of poems that consider gender in relation to writing. It seems probable, in fact, that Giovanni's heightened awareness of gender resulted, to no small extent, from her experiences in the literary world. Although we have seen that she asserted her intention to be the kind of writer she wished in *My House*, not until the poems of *Cotton Candy on a Rainy Day* do we see her confronting and responding to the price she had to pay for that independence. Again, like the image she gives of her father in "Gus," Giovanni herself seems to have been "late" in recognizing the obstacles, both tangible and intangible, thrown in the path of a woman who not only writes but writes poetry.

Poems in *Cotton Candy on a Rainy Day* that may almost be seen as companion pieces to earlier poems—such as "Forced Retirement" and "My Poem"—again illustrate Giovanni's new awareness of gender in relation to writing. In the earlier poem "Categories," for example, the speaker expressed her impatience and boredom with the categories people impose on her. A far more stultifying experience is evident in "Boxes"—indeed, even the contrast between the two titles highlights the qualitatively different emotions expressed in the two poems. "Boxes" opens on a note of tension and crisis:

> i am in a box
> on a tight string
> subject to pop
> without notice (*CC*, 34).

As the poem develops, the "box," in which "most of the time" the speaker "can't breathe," seems to be the result of her very success and strength—somewhat similar to the situation of black women described in "Their Fathers." As in the earlier "Categories," the speaker's strength is used against her:

> everybody says how strong
> i am
>
> only black women
> and white men
> are truly free
> they say

it's not difficult to see
how stupid they are

i would not reject
my strength
though its source
is not choice
but responsibility

i would not reject my light
though my wrinkles are also illuminated (*CC*, 34).

While the speaker resists rejecting her assets, even though they are misperceived and used against her by others, she does yearn to be free of the box in which they have placed her; she imagines her liberation would be akin to that experienced by Muhammad Ali when "leon spinks relieved him" (*CC*, 34). The poem's final stanzas reveal the speaker's awareness of the fact that she has allowed the way she has been "boxed" to tamper with her writing:

most of the time
i can't breathe
i smoke too much
to cover my fears
sometimes i pick
my nose to avoid
the breath i need

i do also do the same
injustice to my poems

i write because
i have to (*CC*, 35).

Just as she is destructive of the breath she most needs out of fear that it will not be available in her stifling box, so too, the speaker implies, she does "the same / injustice" to her poems because writing is so necessary to her—it is, in fact, as necessary as breathing.

More concrete treatment of the obstacles faced by the woman writer is given in "A Poem Off Center." The first section of this poem delineates the many domestic responsibilities that "decimate" the speaker's poems:

the women soon find themselves
talking either to babies or about them
no matter how careful we are
we end up giving tips
on the latest new improved cleaner
and the lotion that will take the smell away (*CC*, 39).

Not only do such domestic activities consume the daily lives of women writers, but the poems they do manage to write are always unacceptable to the "writing establishment":

if you write a political poem
you're anti-semitic
if you write a domestic poem
you're foolish
if you write a happy poem
you're unserious
if you write a love poem
you're maudlin (*CC*, 39).

Because the "writing establishment" is male, women's poems are dismissively judged by different standards than men's poems; virtually every subject or theme women's poems address is somehow used as a basis for attack. As a consequence, the speaker feels "sorry for the women" because "they have no place to go" (*CC*, 40). She recognizes, moreover, a parallel between male treatment of women and white treatment of blacks:

it's the same old story blacks
hear all the time
if it's serious a white man
would do it
when it's serious
he will (*CC*, 40).

The poem concludes with one of Giovanni's strongest statements about the impact of gender on her own life as well as on the lives of all women:

it's a little off center
this life we're leading

maybe i shouldn't feel sorry
for myself
but the more i understand women
the more i do (*CC*, 40).

The echo of the poem's title in the first line of this stanza reinforces the connections Giovanni is drawing between gender and writing; both women's lives and women's poems are "off center," that is, have been marginalized by men.

Conclusion

Of the 36 poems comprising *Cotton Candy on a Rainy Day*, only a handful strike a lighter or more hopeful note than the ones I have discussed. Of these, "That Day," which is the final poem in the volume, is especially deserving of attention. Written in the fast, upbeat rhythm reminiscent of the early "Beautiful Black Men,"[11] "That Day" is a raunchy, humorous poem that celebrates sex. Unlike the other poems about love in this volume, which consistently chart love's failures, disillusionments, and disappointments, "That Day" ignores the complications of love to express joy in the simplicity of sex. In some ways almost a nonsense poem, it makes an appropriate conclusion to *Cotton Candy on a Rainy Day*. The reader is forcibly caught up in the speaker's pleasure and excitement:

now time is money
and money is sweet
if you're busy baby
we can do it on our feet

we can do it on the floor
we can do it on the stair
we can do it on the couch
we can do it in the air (*CC*, 92–93).

Like the fleeting but delightful pleasure of eating cotton candy—which is made all the more ephemeral on a rainy day—sex provides an opportunity rare in this volume for two people to delight in and with each other. "That Day" provides an effective ending to the volume as a whole, in some ways bringing us full circle back to the title poem.

Just as "That Day" celebrates sex despite the fact that it is one of the most ephemeral of life's experiences, so, as we have seen, "Cotton Candy on a Rainy Day" insists that the inherent mutability and mortality of human life do not mean we ought not invest our best in it. Giovanni's idealism remains intact despite her recognition of life's fragility and despite her awareness and experience of the restrictiveness and oppressiveness imposed on certain human lives because of race and gender. What is responsible for the predominant mood of *Cotton Candy on a Rainy Day* as a whole, which even "That Day" cannot dispel, is her concern in most of the poems with measuring the downward arc from expectation to disillusionment, the distance between the ideal and the actual. As we will see, in her final volume of poetry, *Those Who Ride The Night Winds*, Giovanni began to center her poetry on human efforts to reach the ideal rather than on the gap between the ideal and the real. Through this shift in focus, as well as through her development of a new poetic form, Giovanni was able to move beyond the crisis inscribed in *Cotton Candy on a Rainy Day*.

Chapter Five
Those Who Ride The Night Winds

New Explorations

Published in 1983, *Those Who Ride The Night Winds* presents yet another facet of a poetic voice that, as we have seen, has remarkable range and spans several registers. After the disillusionment and despair sounded in *Cotton Candy on a Rainy Day*, readers are apt to take unusual comfort from the mature, serious, yet consistently hopeful voice of *Those Who Ride The Night Winds.* Although the poems in this volume continue to measure the gap between the ideal and the actual, the poet subverts the centrality of that measure in several ways. Many of the poems focus, for example, on the courage of those individuals who have striven to attain the ideal, rather than on their failure to reach it; occasionally, in fact, they are even successful. Regardless of failure or success, however, their effort, not the outcome, is what Giovanni applauds in *Those Who Ride The Night Winds*, as the volume's dedication makes clear:

> This book is dedicated to the courage and fortitude of those who ride the night winds—who are the day trippers and midnight cowboys—who in sonic solitude or the hazy hell of habit know—that for all the devils and gods—for all the illnesses and drugs to cure them—Life is a marvelous, transitory adventure—and are determined to push us into the next century, galaxy—possibility.

The distance between the ideal and the actual that leads to the somber quality of *Cotton Candy on a Rainy Day* not only receives less emphasis in *Those Who Ride The Night Winds* but is also presented by a reflective rather than an introspective speaker. Most often, the speaker looks outward at other individuals whom she in some way sees as heroic; and although their lives may illustrate the kind of unrealized potential or thwarted idealism examined in *Cotton Candy on a Rainy Day*, the speaker is better able to celebrate the intention because it is not her own failure she confronts. Her perspective as an observer, in other words, removes the emotional distortion often evident in *Cotton Candy on a Rainy Day*. Thus, the poems in *Those Who Ride The Night Winds* celebrate courage and idealism without denying other truths.

In part because these poems often focus on public figures, and in part because they tend toward the reflective rather than the introspective, the oppressive sense of constriction and even entrapment that we experience in *Cotton Candy on a Rainy Day* has been replaced by a sense of expansion and possibility. The speaker in these poems is not, to be sure, the young, swaggering, confident speaker of "Ego Tripping" or "My House"—nor would we expect such a speaker from a poet who was turning 40 when *Those Who Ride The Night Winds* was published. Instead, we hear in these poems a voice that is serious but not without a sense of humor; hopeful but not naive; mature but not cynical. Nowhere is this new persona given clearer or fuller expression than in "A Journey," where she invites others to travel on a journey in which she "will be your fellow passenger" rather than "the guide" or "technical assistant."[1] Although others have "ridden" the "rail" of this journey before, clear signs no longer point the way, meaning that "we must provide our own guideposts" (*NW*, 47). Sometimes, the road itself "washes out," forcing the travellers "to continue groping . . . or turn back" (*NW*, 47). The "rough spots" and "lonely times" apt to be encountered do not daunt the speaker, nor is she afraid of "the success of this endeavor," for she is, she states, the Egyptian sun god, Ra, and the journey is to "a space . . . not to be discovered . . . but invented" (*NW*, 47). None of us who take this journey together can promise each other anything, because "we are simply riding . . . a wave . . . that may carry . . . or crash" (*NW*, 47). The outcome of the journey is not, however, important; as the speaker states in the final line, "It's a journey . . . and I want . . . to go . . ." (*NW*, 47).

"A Journey" provides good illustration of the new voice Giovanni creates in *Those Who Ride The Night Winds*, a voice, incidentally, that is now expressed through a capitalized first-person pronoun. Especially significant is the poem's insistence on the equality of footing shared by the speaker and her readers; she claims no special vision or ability to "guide" others, nor will she serve as "technical assistant." The poem's theme of exploration is a unifying thread throughout the volume, as is the idea of "inventing" rather than "discovering" the space toward which we journey.

The title of the volume itself reflects the poet's rediscovered resolution and courage. In both history and folklore, the night has always belonged to forces of evil and destruction, be they vampires or men in white sheets.

For black Americans, the image of "night riders" has been especially powerful, for some of the most shameful chapters in American history have recorded the terrorizing, often murderous, midnight attacks by Ku Klux Klansmen on innocent black people. The night has also been, of course, a particularly dangerous time for women, and its threat of violence has been used as a mechanism for controlling them. Like the "Women Take Back the Night" demonstrations generated by the women's movement, Giovanni's title aims to reclaim the night for the forces of good. Giovanni explains that the title first came into her mind when she found herself one night stranded in an airport, waiting for a connecting flight; she suddenly realized that *she* is a "night rider."[2] More important, she began to realize that, collectively, we have given over the night to the frightening, dangerous, and evil things. Yet, as she states in "Love: Is a Human Condition," both the day and the night are necessary: "we live in a world requiring light and Darkness" (*NW*, 45).

Those Who Ride The Night Winds is thus divided into two sections, a structure Giovanni seems to favor,[3] "Night Winds" and "Day Trippers." Although each of these sections consists of 14 poems, the poems in "Night Winds" tend, overall, to be longer and more serious than those in "Day Trippers." All of the poems about or for well-known or public individuals are also in "Night Winds," while the love poems and humorous pieces are all placed in "Day Trippers."

A New Poetic Form

Those Who Ride The Night Winds marks one further development in Giovanni's poetry, which is the important change in poetic form that is to be found in the majority of poems in the volume. In these poems, she employs a new lineless form, consisting of groups of words or phrases separated by ellipses; these groups are combined into units having the appearance of prose paragraphs. This new lineless form allows Giovanni to retain the rhythmic effects on which she, as an oral poet, has always relied. At the same time, she is able to write more expansive pieces without moving into prose.

McDowell argues that this new lineless form results in a less oral poem and speculates that perhaps Giovanni is in fact "moving away from the emphasis on the oral" (McDowell, 158); in public readings, however, Giovanni routinely includes poems from *Those Who Ride The Night Winds*, and they seem no less "oral" than poems from earlier volumes. Mitchell finds the new form "reminiscent of telegraphic communication," giving the impression of being "hot off the mind of the author" (Mitchell, 150), an assessment that strikes me as being oddly inaccurate: such an impression seems a more likely goal for a journalist or a serial novelist (a Charles Dickens, for example) than for a poet.

Giovanni herself has stated that the new lineless form enabled her to accomplish several purposes. She was looking, she says, for a way to create a fuller and visually more accessible page, which she believes the lineless form allows. Beyond this consideration, she was seeking a formal mechanism for responding to what she saw as a trend toward absolutism in public discourse. Especially since the late 1970s, she maintains, the rhetoric of our public figures and publications has been a rhetoric of absolutes and certainty. Giovanni wanted to call into question the truthfulness of such rhetoric, to suggest that everything is not quite as clear or clear-cut as the rhetoric of our public discourse implies. The ellipses separating groups of words in her new lineless poems are intended to indicate that something is missing or has been omitted.[4] These absences or omissions thus become an important thematic part of the text itself; they represent a structural device for suggesting our limited access to knowledge and truth, for acknowledging the incompleteness of even a poet's perceptions.

The new lineless form that Giovanni uses in the majority of poems in *Those Who Ride The Night Winds* is, in addition, a much more flexible vehicle than the free verse characteristic of her previous work. McDowell suggests that Giovanni "may also be seeking a bridge between the freedom of prose and the more exact structuring of poetry" (McDowell, 158). While I do not entirely disagree with this speculation, I do believe that Giovanni's use of a lineless form reflects, paradoxically, her own concerns about the breakdown and inadequacies of language more than it does her desire for a less "exact" poetic structure; that is, the lineless form allows almost endless qualification, equivocation, and restatement. These rhetorical strategies become necessary only when the writer begins to find the single image or dazzling metaphor a deceptive and misleading simplification.

Because *Those Who Ride The Night Winds* contains poems in free verse as well as poems employing the new lineless form, we can test the validity of this speculation by considering possible correlations between subject and form. Of the 28 poems comprising this volume, only nine are written in free verse, and seven of those nine appear in "Day Trippers." As earlier stated, the poems in "Day Trippers" tend, overall, to be shorter and somewhat less serious or "weighty" than those in "Night Winds." Of the nine poems written in free verse, five are love poems ("Sky Diving," "Resignation," "I Wrote A Good Omelet," "Love Thoughts," "You Were Gone"); one captures the rhythm of music and dance ("Three / Quarters Time"); one is a light and clever playing with words ["Cancers (not necessarily a love poem)"]; one is a playful celebration of a particular parent-child relationship ("Eagles"); and one pays tribute to the artist Charles White ("Charles White").

By contrast, of the 19 poems written in lineless form, only one is a love poem ("A Word for Me . . . Also"), which appears, predictably, in "Day Trippers." In addition to this one love poem, one lineless poem addresses a relatively "light," though not humorous, subject ("Wild Flowers"), and it is likewise in "Day Trippers." The remaining 17 lineless poems concern serious subjects, including the writer and writing, the Atlanta child murders, the vilification of tennis star Billie Jean King, the murder of John Lennon, and the significance of a Phillis Wheatley or a Lorraine Hansberry.

This brief description of Giovanni's use of free verse and of the lineless form in *Those Who Ride The Night Winds* suggests that her increasing preference for the latter (which she has also used in more recent, individually published poems) is directly connected to the kinds of subjects she began to address in her poetry. Just as the poems in *Those Who Ride The Night Winds* depart from the introspective mode of *Cotton Candy on a Rainy Day*, so, too, they have become more expressive of thought than of emotion, and more analytical than lyrical. At the same time, the lineless form that clusters groups of words separated by ellipses does not seem to presage Giovanni's eventual turning away from poetry to the essay. The poems in *Those Who Ride The Night Winds* written in lineless form continue to capture the rhythms and to employ the diction of speech; they also rely on the hesitancies, the asides, the qualifications, and the interjections common to spoken as opposed to written language. Finally, although these poems are more analytical and less lyrical than many of Giovanni's earlier poems, they do not offer the kind of straightforward, linear analysis typical of the essay form. Instead, they approach their subjects indirectly and from many angles, and rarely, if ever, do they provide the stitching together into a seamless whole that we usually expect of the essay form.

In "Hands: For Mother's Day," the second poem in *Those Who Ride The Night Winds*, Giovanni uses quilts as the appropriate symbol of women's lives and women's art:[5]

Some people think a quilt is a blanket stretched across a Lincoln bed . . . or from frames on a wall . . . a quaint museum piece to be purchased on Bloomingdale's 30-day same-as-cash plan . . . Quilts are our mosaics . . . **Michelle-Angelo's** contribution to beauty . . . We weave a quilt with dry, rough hands . . . Quilts are the way our lives are lived . . . We survive on patches . . . scraps . . . the leftovers from a materially richer culture . . . the throwaways from those with emotional options . . . We do the far more difficult job of taking that which nobody wants and not only loving it . . . not only seeing its worth . . . but making it lovable . . . and intrinsically worthwhile . . . (*NW*, 17).

Both visually and, often, thematically, Giovanni's new lineless form is itself quiltlike, though it is probably not consciously designed to resemble this powerful symbol of female art and creativity.

The improvisational quality of this lineless form might also usefully be seen as analogous to jazz. Whereas Giovanni's earlier poetry frequently employs the structural devices of the blues, these more recent poems draw on the formal techniques of jazz. Like some jazz musicians, Giovanni sometimes states a theme and then improvises on it—such is the case, for example, of "Hands." In other poems, such as "A Poem on the Assassination of Robert F. Kennedy," she offers improvisation around the theme but never directly states it, in much the same manner as a musician such as Thelonius Monk. When we consider the overwhelming influence of black musical forms on Giovanni's poetry, the new lineless form of *Those Who Ride The Night Winds* represents a logical evolution from her use of free verse, comparable to the evolution of jazz from the blues. It is not simply a more flexible form, but it both allows and reflects a more complex perception of, response to, and commentary on reality.

Some Night Riders

The central image of *Those Who Ride The Night Winds* is found in "This Is Not for John Lennon (and this is not a poem)." As the title of the poem suggests, Giovanni's purpose here is less to commemorate the slain musician than it is to question and to criticize the kind of society in and by which the John Lennons of the world are routinely destroyed. Because we are a society that values, even showcases, violence, the poem argues, we cannot be surprised by, and must in fact take responsibility for, the Mark David Chapmans we have spawned. After all, we reward such individuals with "book contracts and possible made-for-TV movies" as well as "the 15 minutes of fame Andy Warhol so solemnly promised" (*NW*, 19). Similarly, we give attention and significance to those who "try to die by drugs or pills or slicing" their wrists, while ignoring those who "try to live by getting a job or creating one" (*NW*, 20).

The murder of John Lennon, then, is not an aberration, the poem suggests; rather, it is typical and symptomatic, because "Those who have nothing to offer take something away" (*NW*, 20). Those night riders who use the cloak of darkness to conceal their destructive actions do not "love the stars," will, in fact, bring them down as Mark Chapman brought down John Lennon. Those of us who want to reclaim the night, to become night riders of a different sort, "must learn to love the stars," and "do learn to love the stars . . . even while crying in the darkness" (*NW*, 20–21). John Lennon was such a night rider:

> He was an astronaut of inner space . . . He celebrated happiness . . . soothed the lonely . . . braced the weary . . . gave word to the deaf . . . vision to the insensitive . . . sang a long low note when he reached the edge of this universe and saw the Blackness (*NW*, 20).

These very gifts, however, are essentially what made John Lennon vulnerable to someone "who having nothing to offer" took "something away." Thus, the poem concludes,

> No this is not about John Lennon . . . It's about us . . . And the night winds . . . Anybody want a ticket to ride? (*NW*, 21).

The poem's concluding question (taken from a Beatles's song title) underscores the dangers awaiting those who would attempt to wrest control of the night away from the destructive forces that have traditionally held it. As the poem's earlier lines about John Lennon's gifts to human beings indicate, "night rider" becomes for Giovanni a metaphor for those who are explorers, whether of inner or outer space. Quite clearly, such individuals explore not simply for the adventure but, more important, in order to enhance the quality of human life. Yet their efforts to bring joy or comfort to others are likely to be rewarded with their destruction by these others, not with gratitude. And that destruction does not hurt them, for they are dead; rather, it hurts us, for we, collectively, are diminished by that loss: "the whole may be greater than the sum of its parts . . . we'll never know now . . . one part is missing" (*NW*, 21).

This theme recurs in a number of poems in "Night Winds," including "A Poem on the Assassination of Robert F. Kennedy," where it is implied rather than directly stated. One of the shortest of the new lineless poems in *Those Who Ride The Night Winds*, this piece conveys the senselessness and wantonness underlying the destruction of our best by our worst:

Trees are never felled . . . in summer . . . Not when the fruit . . . is yet to be borne . . . Never before the promise . . . is fulfilled . . . Not when their cooling shade . . . has yet to comfort . . .

Yet there are those . . . unheeding of nature . . . indifferent to ecology . . . ignorant of need . . . who . . . with ax and sharpened saw . . . would . . . in boots . . . step forth damaging . . .

Not the tree . . . for it falls . . . But those who would . . . in summer's heat . . . or winter's cold . . . contemplate . . . the beauty . . . (*NW*, 31).

By drawing an analogy between Robert Kennedy and the tree, Giovanni emphasizes the *unnaturalness* of his assassination. This kind of destruction is perpetrated by individuals who disregard the interdependence of all human beings and fail to recognize that the damage they inflict is ultimately of themselves and us. The parallel syntax of "Yet there are those" and "But those who" distinguishes the destroyers from the rest of humanity. But the pun on "would" in each instance suggests their kinship with each other and separates them from the "tree"—which was considerably more than simply wood—that has been destroyed.

A variation on this theme may be seen in "Mirrors (for Billie Jean King)," which concerns a different kind of destruction to which our heroes and "stars" are frequently subjected. Although the occasion for the poem is the painful public exposure of Ms. King's private life by a woman with whom she had shared a relationship, Giovanni presents this exposure as symbolic of our failure, as a society, to distinguish private lives from public ones. Using mirrors and windows as metaphors for the private life and the public life, the poem argues that "The face in the window . . . is not the face in the mirror," nor should it be (*NW*, 22). The only aspect of a tennis star's life that should be available for public view is her performance and behavior as a tennis player. Her private life, including

love . . . and promises made after midnight . . . the rituals and responsibilities of courtship . . . have no place . . . in the court yard (*NW*, 23).

Ms. King's dignified handling of the combined efforts of the media and her former friend to destroy her makes her "One of my heroes" because she "has the courage of her game . . . and her life" (*NW*, 23).

While the poems we have discussed thus far address the destructive hatred that extraordinary individuals seem to inspire in others, "Linkage (for Phillis Wheatley)" and "Harvest (for Rosa Parks)" examine some of the ways in which we attempt to diminish the accomplishments of extraordinary human beings. The impetus for the first poem is the dismissive, pejorative criticism that Phillis Wheatley's poetry has often received. Again, as in the poems about John Lennon, Robert Kennedy, and Billie Jean King, the attackers operate from a position of safety and fail to recognize the risks incurred by the night rider:

> The critics . . . from a safe seat in the balcony . . . disdain her performance . . . reject her reality . . . ignore her truths . . . How could she . . . they ask . . . thank God she was brought . . . and bought . . . in this Land . . . How dare she . . . they decried . . . cheer George Washington his victory . . . Why couldn't she . . . they want to know . . . be more like . . . more like . . . more like . . . (*NW*, 26).

Especially sensitive to such disparaging criticism of Wheatley—a sister poet—Giovanni offers an effective two-pronged counterattack. Implicitly locating the source of their criticism in their sexism and their abusive treatment of children, Giovanni first indicts such critics for their failure to understand what it might have meant to be brought as a slave to America, especially as a young female slave. The poem opens, in fact, with an invitation to the reader to try to imagine that experience:

> What would a little girl think . . . boarding a big . . . at least to her . . . ship . . . setting sail on a big . . . to everybody . . . ocean (*NW*, 25).

Later in the poem, Giovanni reminds us of the kind of life Wheatley, as a female, would have left behind her in Africa: "clitorectomies . . . infibulations . . . women beaten" (*NW*, 26). Given such conditions of life, Wheatley might have "willingly shed" the perhaps frightening world of "MAGIC" for the more benign possibilities of Christianity and "the Enlightenment" (*NW*, 26).[6]

But the even more devastating attack Giovanni launches on detractors of Wheatley is executed through a comparison of Wheatley's options with those of today's young children who are trapped in such urban hells as the Minnesota Strip:

The block . . . that little Black girls . . . stood upon . . . is the same block . . . they now walk . . . with little white boys and girls . . . selling themselves . . . to the adequate . . . bidder (*NW*, 25).

This kind of abuse of our children is not new with us, any more than it was with America's white slaveholders:

Hagar was a little Black girl . . . chosen by Sarah and Abraham . . . looked like a breeder . . . they said . . . Phillis . . . a little Black girl . . . chosen by Wheatley . . . looked intelligent . . . make a cute pet . . . for the children . . . Old men . . . sweat curling round their collars . . . choose a body and act . . . on the wait . . . through the tunnel to Jersey . . . Looked like fun . . . they say . . . Family members . . . and family friends . . . inhale to intoxication . . . the allure of the youths . . . destroying in conception . . . that which has never been . . . born . . . (*NW*, 25).

Like Hagar before her and the young children of today—who are not safe from abuse and exploitation even with family or friends—Phillis Wheatley, as she stood on the auction block, looked out on a world ready to sell her and buy her; what, if anything, the poems asks, would distinguish the people she saw:

Do you see those who purchase . . . or those who sold . . . Do you see those who grab at you . . . or those who refused to shield you . . . Are you grateful to be bought . . . or sold (*NW*, 26).

With betrayal behind her and before her, then, "We cannot be surprised that young Phillis chose poetry . . . as others choose prostitution . . . to express her dismay . . ." (*NW*, 26). And yet, her critics have been disdainful of the poetry she wrote, wishing she could have been like Harriet Tubman or Sojourner Truth, failing to recognize that "Phillis was her own precedent . . . her own image . . . her only ancestor" (*NW*, 27).

Although Giovanni asserts "linkages" between Wheatley and both male and female children who are exploited by adults today and in the past, she also makes the additional "linkage" between Wheatley and women in general who live in a patriarchal society, between "house slaves who read and write" and "housewives who have time for neither" (*NW*,

27). Those whose imaginations are incapable of recreating the historical circumstances in which Wheatley was caught need only examine the present in order to understand the past. For, the poem argues, our own children and women are as enslaved as young Phillis Wheatley was, and we "deride their condition . . . yet purchase their service" (*NW*, 27). Giovanni's indictment of those who have created such horrifying conditions of life is brought to a powerful conclusion in the following series of questions:

> What must life be . . . to any young captive . . . of its time . . . Do we send them back . . . home to the remembered horrors . . . Do we allow them their elsewheres . . . to parade their talents . . . Do we pretend that all is well . . . that Ends . . . (*NW*, 27).

"Linkage" is one of the finest poems in *Those Who Ride The Night Winds* and one of the most strongly feminist poems in Giovanni's oeuvre. I have discussed it in considerable detail because many of the lineless poems in "Night Winds" are similarly constructed. It provides a representative example of the jazz-like improvisations this new form allows Giovanni to execute. Thematically, it also illustrates the kind of social criticism we find throughout the first section of *Those Who Ride The Night Winds*. As the discussion of "Linkage" should make clear, Giovanni is making very specific and detailed criticisms of American society in this volume; narrowing the general theme of society's responses to exceptional individuals, she attempts to identify and distinguish the relative significance of race, gender, and even age within the context of the particular individual or situation addressed in any given poem.

If we turn briefly to "Harvest (for Rosa Parks)," which, like "Linkage," offers a kind of revision of history or reputation, we find a somewhat different kind of structure than Giovanni has normally used, either in earlier volumes or in this one. The poem consists of a framing preface and epilogue spoken by the poet-narrator, who relates "an old story" that she

> learned in church . . . one evening . . . about a preacher . . . and his deacon . . . fishing (*NW*, 39).

The deacon of the story seems to have consistently bad luck at fishing: every time he gets a nibble, the fish somehow gets away. In response to his loss, the deacon curses. The preacher takes him to task for this cursing, and the deacon vows to desist; naturally, the deacon is severely tested, losing one fish after another. Each time, he restrains himself, bites his tongue, says nothing. When, however, he loses a "big big" fish, the deacon "turned to the preacher . . . and remarked Reverend . . . Something Needs To Be Said" (*NW*, 39).

This parable, printed in boldface type, frames the body of the poem, a monologue spoken by Rosa Parks. Outlining the important details of her life, she finds them unremarkable; but we recognize something remarkable in her attitude:

> You always felt . . . you should do something . . . It just wasn't right . . . what they did to Negroes . . . and why Negroes . . . let it happen (*NW*, 39).

After telling us of her and her husband's long involvement in the NAACP, she comments that

> Many people just think History . . . just fell on my shoulders . . . or at my feet . . . 1 december 1955 . . . but that's not true (*NW*, 40).

She then recreates the scene of the key event of that December day in 1955, pointing out the fact that she received no support or encouragement from the other black people on the bus, who moved to the back of the bus at the driver's command. Though she places no blame on these others, she herself "just didn't . . . couldn't . . . get up":

> I just thought . . . we should let them know . . . *I* should let them know . . . it wasn't right . . . You have to realize . . . I was forty years old . . . all my life . . . all I'd seen . . . were signs . . . that everything was getting worse . . . (*NW*, 40).

Subsequent to the success of the Montgomery boycott, Mrs. Parks was frequently asked to reenact the scene on the bus, and yet somehow no one ever wanted to know about *her*—about her life, or why she moved to Detroit, or what she and others like her were trying to accomplish. Despite her acknowledgment that "Our people . . . can break . . . your heart . . . so can other . . . people," the one thing she knows for certain is that "what one person does . . . makes a difference" (*NW*, 41).

In the epilogue to the poem, Giovanni's purpose in this poem becomes clear. Like the deacon who felt that "something needs to be said" about his loss of the fish, Giovanni feels that

> Something needs to be said . . . about Rosa Parks . . . other than her feet . . . were tired . . . Lots of people . . . on that bus . . . and many times before . . . and since . . . had tired feet . . . lots of people . . . still do . . . they just don't know . . . where to plant them . . . (*NW*, 41).

Although understated, Giovanni's point in the poem's conclusion is unmistakable. By explaining Rosa Parks's refusal to move to the back of the bus as simply a function of her "tired feet," we not only unfairly diminish her contribution to history; we also diminish our conception of human potential and strength. And once we thereby deny the human capacity for heroism, how will we ourselves rise to heroic behavior that social change and growth inevitably require? The poet's function, the frame of "Harvest" suggests, is to protest such reductive and inaccurate accounts of human action. Like the deacon, the poet recognizes that "Something Needs To Be Said" about the loss to our own humanity these accounts create. Without question one of Giovanni's night riders, Mrs. Parks, in her refusal to move to the back of the bus, was motivated not by physical exhaustion but by spiritual and moral determination and commitment. She recognized, as Giovanni states in "Love: Is a Human Condition," that "there must be more to all our lives than ourselves . . . and our ability to do more of the same" (*NW*, 45).[7] And, as with the other heroes celebrated in "Night Winds," Mrs. Parks knows that "what one person does . . . makes a difference." A more constant theme in Giovanni's work would be difficult to identify.

No discussion of the heroic night riders celebrated in *Those Who Ride The Night Winds* would be complete without the inclusion of "Hands: For Mother's Day." In some senses, this poem brings together many of the images and emotions found in poems for or about women throughout Giovanni's career. Centered on the central image of women's hands, the poem works associatively, building to a conclusion that asserts the primacy of women and women's nurturance of life in the evolution of the species. The lineless form works especially well for Giovanni in this poem, allowing her to move from a quick, staccato series of very concrete images, to brief vignettes, to more analytical, abstract passages—and, in fact, this is the sequence of the first three paragraphs of the poem.

At least part of the accomplishment represented by this poem is

Giovanni's success in avoiding sentimentality in addressing an almost inherently sentimental subject. As Giovanni explains when she reads the poem, it was written at the request of the *Los Angeles Times* for a Mother's Day poem—as dangerous a subject as a poet is likely to confront. Remarkably, Giovanni avoids sentimentality and yet writes a strongly emotional poem. One reason for this success is that she focuses not on one mother but on a multiplicity of mothers and grandmothers, from her own grandmother to the mother of Emmett Till to Betty Shabazz to Ethel Kennedy. She also avoids sentimentality by allowing her meanings to accumulate around actions rather than essences. Finally, she expands the ordinary meaning of *mother* to include virtually all women, to whom she attributes nurturance, comfort, discipline, toil, support, and strength.

The poem implicitly contrasts these actions to the unnamed actions of men, just as it implicitly contrasts women with men: "The wives and mothers are not so radically different"; "It is our hands which . . . soothe the longing of the brothers"; "We of the unacceptably strong"; "Quilts are our mosaics . . . **Michelle-Angelo's** contribution to beauty." These implied contrasts become explicit in the poem's concluding paragraph, which attributes the evolutionary development of human beings from four-legged creatures to upright, two-legged ones to women and their life-sustaining actions; woman the nurturer, not man the hunter, is the logical explanation of human evolution:

> Some of us . . . on special occasions . . . watch the ladies in the purple velvet house slippers with the long black dresses come in from Sunday worship and we realize **man** never stood up to catch and kill prey . . . **man** never reared up on his hind legs to free his front parts to hold weapons . . . WOMAN stood to free her hands . . . to hold her young . . . to embrace her sons and lovers . . . WOMAN stood to applaud and cheer a delicate mate who needs her approval . . . WOMAN stood to wipe the tears and sweat . . . to touch the eyes and lips . . . that woman stood to free the arms which hold the hands . . . which hold (*NW*, 18).

A poem such as "Hands" makes the neglect of Giovanni by many feminist scholars confounding. Of all the poems in *Those Who Ride The Night Winds* that pay tribute to heroic night riders, none surpasses this celebration of women. Though the poem does not make the brash, swaggering assertions of "Ego Tripping," its claims for the superiority of women are no less extraordinary. They may even, in fact, be more credible because they are rooted in everyday, apparently unimportant, actions—no hyperbole of the sort found in "Ego Tripping" is necessary here.

On Writers and Writing

Of the many souls who "ride the night winds" in this volume of poems, the writer or artist is, perhaps not unexpectedly, of special concern. As we have already seen, "This Is Not for John Lennon" and "Linkage" are written for or about artists, as are "Lorraine Hansberry: An Emotional View," "Charles White," "I Am She," and the poem that constitutes the preface to the volume. In addition, the final poem in *Those Who Ride The Night Winds*, "A Song for New-Ark," is at least partly concerned with the writer. Perhaps a volume of poems marking a new development in the poet's form might logically be expected to reflect in its content a special interest in the artist and in art; such is, at any rate, the case of *Those Who Ride The Night Winds.* Taken together, several of these poems constitute an important statement by Giovanni about her conceptions of art and of herself as a writer.

In the prefatory poem, Giovanni considers the origins of language and poetry and their current stage of development. Because the origins of poetry remain concealed and unknown, they may reside in either the ridiculous or the sublime. But however the first poem came to be written, what is certain is that human beings, alone of the animals, "can give vent to our understanding . . . of the tenuousness of Life . . ." (*NW*, 7). As she had in *Cotton Candy on a Rainy Day*, Giovanni emphasizes here the fragility and the mutability of human life:

> change . . . both gradual . . . and violent . . . is a necessary ingredient . . . with Life (*NW*, 7).

This "necessary ingredient" of change is, she argues, what gives rise to art and artists. One of art's functions, in fact, is to give expression to—and to help us understand—changing perceptions and conceptions of reality, changing needs, changing social relations.

In the final section of the poem, Giovanni charts some of the many ways in which, in our lifetime,

> language has opened . . . becoming more accessible . . . more responsive . . . to what people really think . . . and say (*NW*, 8).

Not only have the "written arts" become "more accessible," but political, religious, and social ideas that were once unthinkable are now realities. The combined efforts of movements in which Giovanni herself participated in the 1960s and early 1970s have, she states, in 1982, resulted in profound—and positive—changes.

The "tenuousness" and impermanence of life that in *Cotton Candy on a Rainy Day* frequently gave rise to despair are in this poem converted into sources of hope. Change, Giovanni recognizes, was in fact the purpose and goal of the 1960s. The journey from expectation to disillusion that structures many of the poems of *Cotton Candy on a Rainy Day* has been replaced here by an acknowledgement that not *all* ideals were shattered, not *all* hopes destroyed. Social and political realities in America did change for the better, and "While there is surely much . . . to be done . . . some change has rent . . . its ways" (*NW*, 8).

Finally, Giovanni does not exempt herself from the phenomenon of change, but indicates that she, too, is now moving in new directions; as an artist, she continues to be a night rider:

> I changed . . . I chart the night winds . . . glide with me . . . I am the walrus . . . the time has come . . . to speak of many things (*NW*, 8).

Although she does not specify the change she has herself undergone, the poems that follow, as we have seen, do in fact reflect changes in poetic form, in mood, and even in subject.

Giovanni's conception of the writer is expanded in the first poem of the volume proper, "Lorraine Hansberry: An Emotional View." Interestingly, this poem was first published as an essay in 1979;[8] the only change Giovanni has made in it is to shape it into the new lineless form, thereby revealing and highlighting its underlying patterns of rhythm. Less about Lorraine Hansberry than the kind of writer she symbolizes in Giovanni's imagination, the poem develops from the central metaphor of the artist as "bookmaker," a term whose negative connotations mystify the speaker:

> It's intriguing to me that "bookmaker" is a gambling . . . an underworld . . . term somehow associated with that which is both illegal . . . and dirty . . . Bookmakers . . . and those who play with them . . . are dreamers . . . are betting on a break . . . a lucky streak . . . that something will come . . . their way—something good . . . something clean . . . something wonderful . . . We who make books . . . we who write our

dreams . . . confess our fears . . . and witness our times are not so far . . . from the underworld . . . are not so far . . . from illegality . . . are not so far from the root . . . the dirt . . . the heart of the matter. (*NW*, 13)[9]

The aptness—even brilliance—of the bookmaking metaphor becomes apparent as we read through the rest of the poem. The writer, like the bookmaker, is a dreamer and a gambler, despite the fact that the odds are against her; the writer has "no reason . . . to be hopeful," no reason to write of love or courage or hope. Writers themselves walk a "fine line between insanity and genius," and, having seen "all sides of the coin," "cannot justify . . . our faith . . . Yet faith we do have . . . and continue to share" (*NW*, 13). The writer or artist, by definition almost, is a gambler about humankind and human possibility.

Unlike the bookmaker, who simply shoots "craps . . . with the white boys . . . downtown on the stock exchange" (*NW*, 13), the writer

is shooting craps . . . with God . . . is wandering into a casino where you don't even know the language . . . let alone the rules of the game (*NW*, 14).

The risks involved in being a writer are, in other words, enormous; but, the speaker goes on to say, "that's proper . . . that's as it should be," for there are many other safe paths one could have taken if one had not wanted to be a writer—one could have worked for the post office, for example, "or taken a graduate degree in Educational Administration" (*NW*, 14).[10]

Using as a transition the idea that the success of the writer's bookmaking will be determined by history—"time . . . is the only judge"—Giovanni segues into the next section of the poem, which improvises on the meaning of time for black Americans. Weaving in allusions to such historical events as the African slave trade, the *Brown vs. Board of Education* decision, the Montgomery bus boycott, and the murder of Emmett Till, Giovanni shapes a commentary on black Americans' experience of time as "a burden." Controlled by white Americans and Europeans, time has never been "right" for those things black Americans want or need. As "a colored poet," Giovanni states, "my wishes . . . no matter which star I choose . . . do not come true" (*NW*, 14–15). But, she adds,

I'm also a writer . . . and I know . . . that the Europeans aren't the only ones . . . who keep time . . . some of the time is going . . . to be my time . . . too . . . (*NW*, 15).

At this point in the poem, we begin to become aware of the yet unstated relevance of these ideas to Lorraine Hansberry. As we begin to recall the conflicts and realities informing the lives of the characters in *A Raisin in the Sun*, we can appreciate even more fully the appropriateness of Giovanni's bookmaking metaphor, the necessity for black Americans to be dreamers and gamblers, and the special imperative placed on the black writer to take the risks inherent in writing and be willing to offer hope for a different future. In the final section of the poem, Giovanni brings Hansberry explicitly into the poem for the first time, celebrating her as a writer who

seeing both sides of the dilemma . . . and all sides of the coin . . . still called "Heads" . . . when she tossed . . . And in her gamble . . . never came up snake eyes (*NW*, 15).

The poem offers a remarkable tribute to the playwright; it also, however, gives eloquent expression to the exigencies affronting the black writer.

Toward the end of *Those Who Ride The Night Winds*, Giovanni comments more lyrically on her conception of herself as a writer. In "I Am She (for Nancy)," which she identifies as one of only two "personal" poems she has ever written, "Nikki–Rosa" being the other, she states: "I am she . . . making rainbows . . . in coffee cups" (*NW*, 56). Suggesting once more that the writer gambles against the odds on hope and beauty, Giovanni links herself at the end of the poem to the other night riders in the volume:

Floating to shore . . . riding a low moon . . . on a slow cloud . . . I am she . . . who writes . . . the poems . . . (*NW*, 56).

The final section of "A Song for New-Ark," which is the last poem in *Those Who Ride The Night Winds*, reveals Giovanni's sense of affinity with musicians and her desire to create poems that are songs. The passage provides fitting closure to the changes in form and mood that we have seen throughout this volume of poems:

When I write I want to write . . . in rhythm . . . regularizing the moontides . . . to the heart/beats . . . of the twinkling stars . . . sending an S.O.S. . . . to day trippers . . . urging them to turn back . . . toward the Darkness . . . to ride the night winds . . . to tomorrow . . . I wish I understood . . . bird . . . Birds in the city talk . . . a city language . . . They always seem . . . unlike humans . . . to have something . . . useful . . . to say . . . Other birds . . . like Black americans . . . a century or so ago . . . answer back . . . with song . . . I wish I could be a melody . . . like a damp . . . gray . . . feline fog . . . staccatoing . . . stealthily . . . over the city . . . (*NW*, 62).

A number of associations should be triggered in the reader's or listener's mind by some of the images in this passage. Giovanni's obvious sense of affinity with music and musicians is of course apparent, as is her reiteration of the theme of exploration, of creating a new space by becoming a night rider rather than remaining a day tripper. Her invocation of birds seems likely to suggest, given her personal and poetic interest in jazz forms, the late Charlie Parker. The bird also, of course, has more immediate associations in her own work, especially in the final line of "Ego Tripping": "I . . . can fly / like a bird in the sky." Here, however, she wishes she "could be a melody"—which is, as we have seen, what her new poetic form has allowed her to create in her poems.

Chapter Six
The Connecting Voice of Poetry

Since at least the early 1970s, Nikki Giovanni has insisted that her poetry reflects the "logical evolution, at least of my own mind" (Seifullah, 9). When critics have attacked her, especially in the early stages of her career, for changing, their attacks have been meaningless to her because she sees change as both inevitable and desirable: "If my next book isn't at least an emotional improvement over my last book, I would never submit it to a publisher. I like to think there's growth. If there's no growth, there's no reason to publish" (Tate, 75). As we have seen, to Giovanni's critics, changes in her poetry have often been equated not with growth but with some sort of "selling out," or loss of integrity, even when they have been described in apparently neutral language. How does Giovanni herself describe the "evolution" of her poetry? What have been and are her goals as a poet? What was and is her conception of poetry itself?

Answers to these and related questions have been provided throughout Giovanni's career by her poetry. In the course of this study, we have charted the changes in subject, mood, and form in her poetry, from the earliest to the most recent. During the last decade, however, Giovanni's poetry and her goals as a poet have received additional illumination from several different publications, including major interviews with her by Arlene Elder and Claudia Tate and two essays by the poet herself, which she recently reprinted in *Sacred Cows . . . And Other Edibles.* Taken together, these provide us with a more comprehensive context within which to understand her poetry.

"the self is a part of the body politic"

Claudia Tate's 1983 interview with Giovanni begins with Tate's observation that "The black revolutionary fervor of the sixties seems to be gone" (Tate, 61), a comment that indicates how generally prevalent has been the identification of Giovanni as a revolutionary poet. Tate follows this comment with the question, "Does this suggest that the revolution is over?" (Tate, 61), and both the question and Giovanni's response to it underscore the fact that Giovanni is unquestionably a political poet—in the broadest possible sense of the word—regardless of whether she is a "revolutionary" poet. As she herself has stated even more recently, she is "a poet of information, of content, rather than a strict adherent to structure. I like the story and I care more about *what* is being said than *how* it is said, which is quite different from poets to whom structure means everything."[1]

Precisely because Giovanni is a "poet of information," critics have felt especially free to focus on the *kind* of information her poetry expresses. Having been identified as a "revolutionary" poet at the beginning of her career, she has had to confront both the desires of others that she remain unchanged and the rigid definition of "revolution" that these others are likely to maintain. As her response to Tate's question reveals, Giovanni herself objects to what she sees as the ahistorical nature of the position such individuals take. First, she explains to Tate, "We're looking at a phenomenon as if it were finished. . . . From where I am, I see a continuous black revolution going on for the last four hundred years in America" (Tate, 61). As for the particular revolutionary struggle of the 1960s, she says, "black Americans won their objectives. We didn't like the segregated buses. We didn't like the segregated schools. We didn't like the way we were treated in stores. We didn't like the housing patterns. We didn't like the number of doctors or lawyers we had. We didn't like our lack of professionals. We won" (Tate, 61).

These victories were neither, Giovanni hastens to add, sufficient nor final, because "We're talking about a struggle for freedom that keeps going on and on" (Tate, 62). But the strategies of the 1960s cannot be the strategies of the 1980s or 1990s, or, as she explains in another interview, "you can't use yesterday's methods to solve today's problems and you must never give up just because everything didn't work out like you thought it would" (Rosenthal, 30).

The underlying biases and assumptions of Tate's next interview question suggest that Giovanni's critics often fail to understand that a "poet of information" will not "use yesterday's methods to solve today's problems": "Your earlier works, *Black Feeling*, *Black Talk/Black Judgement* and *Re: Creation*, seem very extroverted, militant, arrogant. The later work, *The Women and the Men* and *Cotton Candy on a Rainy Day*, seem very introverted, private, lonely, withdrawn. Does this shift in perspective, tone, and thematic focus reflect a conscious transition?" (Tate, 62).[2] Giovanni's response to this question is of considerable significance: "I'll tell you what's wrong with that question. The assumption inherent in that question is that the self is not a part of the body politic. There's no separation" (Tate, 62). The identity of the individual self, in other words, is constituted by and through larger social and political realities; there can be no private self that exists outside or apart from the larger world. As Giovanni herself states it elsewhere, "in life all things are political. What we do every day and how we do it."[3]

As a poet who emerged during the 1960s, moreover, Giovanni has consistently believed in a connection between art and action, a central impetus of the Black Arts Movement; in Larry Neal's words, "It is a profound ethical sense that makes a Black artist question a society in which art is one thing and the actions of men another. The Black Arts Movement believes that your ethics and your aesthetics are one" (Neal, 1971, 275). Although we have seen that Giovanni objected to the prescriptiveness that eventually would destroy the Black Arts Movement, her poetry, both early and late, reflects the kind of ethical concerns described by Neal. As she goes on to explain to Tate, the "militant stance" prescribed by adherents of a black aesthetic was as repugnant to her as any prescriptiveness; but beyond this, it also lost its usefulness: "What are we going to do with a stance? Literature is only as useful as it reflects reality" (Tate, 63). Ironically, prescriptive assumptions of just this sort are evident in Tate's question. Had Giovanni's poetry continued to be "extroverted, militant, arrogant" (if one accepts Tate's terms) in the 1970s and 1980s, it would have ceased to "reflect reality." The "shift" to which Tate refers is not, Giovanni's answers make clear, the result of a decision to write a different kind of poetry. Instead, as the social and political realities of her world changed, both she—who is "a part of the body politic"—and her poetry—which deliberately attempts to "reflect" the world—also changed.

Elsewhere Giovanni identifies some of the changing realities that her poetry reflects. "I started as a writer concerned about the black situation in America and have grown to be a writer concerned about the black situation in the world. I have come to realize that gender bias is a real problem. It's difficult to be a woman, but being black and female produces a double bind."[4] In addition to this kind of expansion in her awareness and focus, she points to the implications that space exploration has for human beings: "A lot has happened. I don't want anybody to think it's just me. It's all of us. It has to do with the way we conceptualize the world. We are earthlings. When Viking II took off we became earthlings. Nobody knows what an earthling is, and how an earthling relates to other earthlings" (Tate, 71). Our world, in other words, looks very different now than it did in 1968 when Giovanni began her career as a poet. And her poetry will inevitably reflect those differences because they give shape to who she is.

In "About A Poem," included in *Sacred Cows . . . And Other Edibles*, Giovanni writes of some of the significant changes that have occurred in the black community since the 1960s. One is the realization that "violence doesn't work" (*SC*, 70). Comparing violence to a savings account, which is "only helpful if you don't have to use it," Giovanni asserts that "Once you use it you have nothing to fall back on and you have to start resaving and rebuilding. Our community had nothing to rebuild with" (*SC*, 70). Moreover, once the trump of violence had been played, once the savings account was empty, the black community made the mistake of turning "our backs upon who we are and who we could become," and consequently, "We began to sour" (*SC*, 71). "Somewhere during the sixties," Giovanni argues, "Magic came into our movement," and "Freedom, which is clearly a list of responsibilities, became a list of wishes" (*SC*, 71). In particular, she takes to task those people in the movement who "turned our backs on those who had freed us—the old men and women who had worked the fields; the young couples who built homes; the folk who insisted on going into places where Blacks were not wanted"—and her list of ordinary, insignificant, but crucially important individuals goes on at length (*SC*, 72). "We soured," she says, "because we failed to honor our forefathers. We wanted freedom to be so much more than paying our bills at the end of the month; seeing our children grow up and go to college; retiring after twenty years on the same job. We wanted Freedom to be some kind of emotional lottery where when our number came up we would be rich and famous. We wanted Magic, and we soured because Freedom is reality" (*SC*, 72).

Although Giovanni does not herself explicitly tie the changes in her poetry to these changes she watched in the black community, the connections are not difficult for us to recognize. We have followed the emotional curves of her work, from the angry poems of *Black Judgement* to the despair of *Cotton Candy on a Rainy Day*, emotions that parallel her analysis of the black community during the 1960s and 1970s. Her emphases in the passages above on the responsibilities of freedom and the resources within the black community also place *Those Who Ride The*

Night Winds in yet another light. As she stated in the Tate interview, "the self is . . . a part of the body politic."

Because "there's no separation" between the self and the body politic, and because Giovanni consistently accepts the idea that art must be connected to human actions, the poet has a responsibility not simply to focus on current issues and events but to comment on, analyze, and interpret them. As she states in "In Sympathy With Another Motherless Child," also included in *Sacred Cows . . . And Other Edibles*, "I have even gone so far as to think one of the duties of this profession is to be topical, to try to say something about the times in which we are living and how we both view and evaluate them" (*SC*, 33). Partly because she sees herself in the tradition of the griot, traveling "the length and breadth of the planet trying to bring people closer to the truth," she also believes that "rage" is the impetus behind writing: "I have been considered a writer who writes from rage and it confuses me. What else do writers write from?" (*SC*, 33, 31).

Significantly, however, although Giovanni's conception of herself as a poet is as a kind of truthteller, prompted by the wrongs she sees around her, she insists that poetry cannot persuade its readers or listeners to change their attitudes and behavior: "I don't think that writers ever changed the mind of anybody. I think we always preach to the saved. Someone from the *Post* asked me, how would I describe myself, and I said, 'I'm a preacher to the saved.' And I don't think that anybody's mind has ever been changed. It has been enhanced by an already-meeting-of-the-minds."[5] This position can partly be seen as Giovanni's reaction against the idea popular among the writers of the Black Arts Movement that somehow the "revolution" could be effected through poetry. Giovanni viewed this idea as dangerously connected to the sort of prescriptiveness she found anathema, but it also just did not make sense to her: "There will never be the poem that will free mankind. . . . anybody that thinks that is a fool" (Elder, 69–70). Partly, however, Giovanni seems to take the position that she is "preaching to the saved" out of a desire to disclaim credit for significant events. At most, she argues, "There are people who charismatically embody an age"—people such as Martin Luther King, Jr., or John F. Kennedy (Elder, 70). Such people "personify the best within us," but they are not the force that made, for example, the 1960s happen. Instead, she argues, "It was the little old ladies that said, 'I'll walk,' that made Martin Luther King" (Elder, 70). While Giovanni seems to believe that she, too, may at times "charismatically embody" an idea or a set of values, she does not believe that what she writes is itself the cause or source of change.

The vital writer, she says, functions as both historian and prophet: "We're a little bit of a prophet, and we are a little bit of the historian. And we're saying, 'this is the meaning that we find. You have to take what you can'" (Elder, 71). To function as a historian and a prophet requires arrogance, but "writers are arrogant" (Tate, 75). They are not, however, superior to other human beings: "The writer is not god. It's what we do for a living. It's not who we are . . . writing is not who I am. It is what I do. And I think that anybody who fails to separate what they do from who they are . . . is in serious, mental trouble" (Elder, 75).

As these statements from a variety of sources indicate, Giovanni conceives of the poet as being, at different times, a voice of, a voice for, and a voice about her people. The poet's responsibility is to speak the truth, as she sees it; and it *is* a responsibility: "I think that I have a view of the world, that I have an obligation, not just your basic right, to share" (Elder, 75). To speak, to "share" her view of the world through her poetry, does not make the poet a leader of the people but an empowerer of the people—of whom the poet is also a part. Such empowerment is critical to the survival of the people, in much the same way as the spirituals enabled the slaves to survive by empowering them. These functions of the poet and poetry define the nature of the poet's subject matter to the extent that that subject matter must have relevance to the lives of the people to whom it is addressed—hence, frequently, its topicality.

One of the reasons that many writers seek to avoid topicality, of course, is that they do not wish to see their work dated; those writers hope to "transcend" the particulars of their lives so as to make their work "timeless" and "universal." Such goals are far removed from Giovanni and many other Afro-American writers; when art is connected to survival, concern about its "timelessness" or "universality" tends to lose importance.[6] It is not surprising, then, that Giovanni defines poetry as "a way of capturing a moment," "a single stroke" (Tate, 73). For this reason, she says, "I date all my work because I think poetry, or any writing, is but a reflection of the moment. The universal comes from the particular" (*SC*, 57). Especially because she believes that "A poem's got to be a single stroke," she does not do a lot of revising. When she does revise, she revises the poem in its entirety, rather than focussing on its individual parts: "If that means I start at the top a dozen times, that's what I do"

(Tate, 73). Her goal is to create "an accurate picture of what I saw. It's that simple. And I keep working until I have the best reflection I can get. Universality has dimension in that moment" (Tate, 74).

Dancing Naked on Your Own Floor

Giovanni's conception of how universality is achieved in a poem parallels her insistence that, although she may function as historian and prophet for her people, "Nobody's going to tell me what to write about because it's about me dancing naked on that floor. And if I'm going to be cold, it's going to be because I decided to dance there" (Tate, 73). The poet's freedom to write what she or he wants to write is, in fact, one of the freedoms gained from the 1950s and 1960s. Giovanni argues that the liberating insight for black Americans was the realization "that no matter what we did, no matter how much we abided by the rules and regulations, no matter how straight our hair, correct our speech, circumscribed our behavior, no matter *what*—we were, in the words of Moms Mabley, 'still a Negro' " (*SC*, 53). This recognition carried a tremendous advantage for all black Americans because it allowed them to be individuals: "The advantage to a people who have clearly defined an issue is this: the individual is relieved of the burden of carrying his people forward. He can dance upon his own floor in his own style. Though white Americans would try to this very day to make Black Americans responsible for each other, Black people recognize that just as individual accomplishments open no doors, individual failures close off no avenues" (*SC*, 53).

There could hardly be a freedom more necessary to an individual like Giovanni than this freedom to dance on her own floor without feeling that her people would be affected by her success or her failure. The freedom to fail is especially important to her concepts of the writer and of poetry; writing is a risky activity because it amounts to "dancing naked on the floor." And clearly, if the cost of failure is prohibitive, most people will not place themselves in so vulnerable a position:

A lot of people refuse to do things because they don't want to go naked, don't want to go without guarantee. But that's what's got to happen. You go naked until you die. That's the way it goes down. If you don't want to play, you're not forced to. You can always quit. But if you're not going to quit, play. You've got to do one or the other. And it's got to be your choice. . . . You're going to sweat, and you're going to get hit, and you're going to fall down. And you're going to be *wrong*. Probably nine times out of ten you're going to be wrong, but it's the tenth time that counts. Because when you come up right, you come up right beautifully. But after that you have to start again. (Tate, 69)

Because failure is an unavoidable cost of success, the writer must accept it and be willing to risk it. For successful writing cannot occur if the writer is unwilling to "dance naked on the floor." This seems to constitute the only requirement Giovanni imposes on the writer: he or she must be honest: "once you have given up your basic integrity, then you really have nothing else to offer" (Elder, 71).

The writer's honesty or integrity is essential, Giovanni argues, because writing "is only half the process; someone must read" (*SC*, 66). And the relationship of the writer to the reader must be a relationship of trust, a trust that the writer's dishonesty will violate:

Because the only thing you bring, the only thing any of us, any professional brings, is your honesty. You don't mind that the patient died on the table, as long as the surgeon wasn't drunk. It's sad if he did. It's sad to you; it's sad to the patient. It's probably sad to the surgeon. But you feel like, "well, he tried." And in my profession, if you're not going to be honest. . . . I mean, I'm a reader. You'd feel raped to think that you involved your heart and your mind and your time, that there were things you could have been doing, and you were sitting there reading a book to find out that it's essentially dishonest. . . . I mean, it's not acceptable. Absolutely unacceptable. (*SC*, 72)

If the writer is honest, even if she or he fails, the reader and the reader's trust are not violated.

Correspondingly, because by being honest "the writer is totally vulnerable to people we shall never see" (Elder, 74), the critic also has a responsibility to respect the writer's intention. Giovanni's impatience with critics is based on her sense that they often do not accord writers that kind of respect; thus, early in her career she felt that writers should ignore critics, because the critics "can wipe you out just as quickly with praise as with condemnation" (Terrell, 7). More recently, she has objected to the tendency of critics to dislike, rather than value, change in writers: "One reason that America has, I believe, always preferred its writers dead is that not only can it then be determined what we wrote and why we wrote that way, but we are not there to change our minds or correct any misgivings" (*SC*, 59). As Giovanni sees it, however, the critic has a responsibility to read all of a writer's work and to write criticism that is informed by a knowledge of changes in that work: "You can't quote the last book as if it were the first. You can't make a critical judgment based on one book. It doesn't work" (Tate, 75).

As a black woman writer, Giovanni also takes exception to the racist and sexist biases often to be found in criticism: "If Black writers write about slavery we are told it's parochial, no one is interested in this stuff; but when Jewish writers write about their history it's called the Old Testament. When women write about the reality of our lives, it's called too dull; when white men write their lives, it's called heroic" (*SC*, 33). Critics have a responsibility to try to meet a work on its own terms and understand it. And if a black woman is capable of reading and understanding the work of a white male writer, then the white male critic can surely read and understand the work of the black female writer—"That's the critic's job" (Tate, 64).

In the course of this study, we have seen that Giovanni's quarrel with the critics has considerable justification. Rarely have her critics based their judgments on a reading of all of her books. Slotted early in her career as a "revolutionary writer," Giovanni's subsequent work has often been measured against that description as if it were a norm. Very rarely have her critics wished to grant her, as Henry James would put it, her *donnée*.

Fortunately for Giovanni, however, she has consistently found a large audience for her work, even though that audience has included few literary critics. Her enormous popularity suggests that her own conception of poetry as "a connection," "a link," between lonely and isolated human beings has considerable accuracy and validity. For ultimately, I believe she sees her poetry as serving similar purposes and functioning in ways parallel to the spirituals and the musical forms that grew out of the spirituals. At the conclusion of Claudia Tate's interview with her, Giovanni makes explicit this conception of her work:

> If you look through *Cotton Candy* you'll hear a lot of music. 'Cause if you're in trouble, you don't whistle a happy tune and hold your head erect. You hummm (*sic*). You hum a basic gospel tune. Can you imagine what a slave ship must have sounded like? Imagine what a slave ship must have sounded like to the women. All the slave-ship stories we've heard so far have been from men. All the men heard was the agony of the men. That's valid. But just imagine what a slave ship must have sounded like to a woman. The humming must have been deafening. It had to be there. The hum, the gospel, the call-and-response came over because it's here. The men didn't bring it over. I'm not knocking the men. They brought

the drum for sure. But they didn't bring the hum; they didn't bring the leader-call; they didn't bring the field hollers, because they didn't know them. They were not field men. They were hunters. Hunters don't make noise. So what we're hearing in the music is the women. . . . We women were the ones in the fields in Africa. The music is not something we learned on these shores. We were communal even then, and as we got into bigger fields, we would call to one another. If you didn't answer back, we went to see about you. The hum, the holler, the leader-call are women things. . . . So what you're hearing in our music is nothing but the sound of a woman calling another woman. (Tate, 78)

Although some might disagree with Giovanni's interpretation of the roots of black spiritual music, her statement is of value for what it reveals to us of her own conception of poetry and of herself as a poet. As we have seen throughout this study, not only is Giovanni's poetry oral, but it has close connections to music. Her remarks in this passage make clear that she intends her poetry, like the spirituals, to be "the sound of a woman calling another woman," that is, an expression uttered to bridge the distance between herself and others. In this view, poetry becomes as serious and vital as anything can be. And, like the spirituals, Giovanni's poetry functions for her countless readers and listeners as a life-sustaining force: "We affirmed in those dark days of chattel through the White Knights of Emancipation that all we had was a human voice to guide us and a human voice to answer the call" (*SC*, 52). More than anything else, the poetry of Nikki Giovanni offers a human voice that says, "I am here."

Appendix

A Conversation with Nikki Giovanni

The following interview took place between Virginia Fowler and Nikki Giovanni in Nikki Giovanni's study on 12 October 1991. During this weekend, the Clarence Thomas/Anita Hill confrontation was being televised from the U. S. Senate.

VF: I notice from the stack of magazines and newspapers about the Clarence Thomas nomination that you must be as consumed as everyone else by the current hearings. What do you think about the fact that the whole nomination process seems to have come down to a confrontation between a black man and a black woman?

NG: Quite frankly, until you mentioned it, I hadn't thought of Anita Hill as a black woman. Perhaps I should have. But I thought of Anita Hill as an abused woman—I'm saying in terms of sexual harassment, in terms of her relative position. Despite that abuse, having come through almost exactly the same process, in fact, as Clarence Thomas did, she reached a very different conclusion: that at some point something has to be of value here besides *my* survival. I don't understand Clarence Thomas. I don't understand affirmative action babies. And if he says that affirmative action is not good, he now, in this hearing, with this that we're going through, has proven his point. If you had asked me this last year about Clarence Thomas, you know, "What do you think about his stand against affirmative action?" I would have said "Well, Clarence Thomas is exactly what you hope affirmative action will do. It empowers people. It puts them in a position to realize their lives, their dreams, their possibilities." But if what we're seeing is the result of affirmative action, then I'm not sure it's worth it. An entire generation has paid for their education. And the end result is that they're saying, "Well, this isn't working." I don't know what happened to the character of black people. I really don't.

VF: If I could shift our conversation just a little, I wonder if you'd comment on the extent to which gender was an issue in the Black Arts and black power movements, at least as you saw it?

NG: One of the issues in SNCC, going back to the mid-1960s, was a gender issue. And it was raised by, among other people, Casey Hayden and Mary King.

And, of course, we had the horrible statement from Stokely Carmichael, when the press said to Stokely, "What is the position of women in the movement?" and he said, "Prone." And that constitutes harassment. And he ultimately said it was a joke. I don't know anyone who thought, in fact, that it was funny. But as an artist I just couldn't see that I would ever benefit myself by thinking in terms of gender. And I suppose benefit is going to be a bad word and somebody will beat me over the head with it, but I didn't see how I could ever grow if I thought of myself as anything other than Nikki.

VF: And yet, would you say in looking back at it that had you been a man, had you been male, would your career have taken a different track?

NG: We're not talking politics, we're talking art. The first thing you have to be as an artist is you. And I think it's very important to own yourself. So you're asking me would my career have flourished better, or would I have what? produced better books or gotten more awards? or made friends?

VF: No. Not better, but one of the things that strikes anyone who looks at your career is that the critical reception from the literary establishment and the black intellectual establishment is way disproportionate to the success that you have had. Even today it is not given the kind of attention that the work of writers like LeRoi Jones or Don Lee has received. I can't help but wonder the extent to which gender enters into that. You knew both LeRoi Jones and Don Lee. At what point did they become critical of what you were doing?

NG: I never had any reason, and I don't know any other way to say this, to think that LeRoi Jones would ever hold me in any affection or uphold my work, or in any other way appreciate what I'm trying to do.

VF: Why?

NG: I just never did.

VF: Can you say why?

NG: Because I can read his work.

VF: I don't understand.

NG: In my opinion, LeRoi has always been an opportunistic man. I liked his essays a lot. I think he's quite a musicologist; I think that his essays are quite outstanding, in fact. I was a good friend of LeRoi's sister, Kamako. She's dead now. I always liked her. I liked his mother very, very much, and I thought that LeRoi picked on his father. I didn't get to know his father nearly as well. I didn't know any of his previous wives. I know his current wife. But to me, LeRoi's always been all over the page. I met LeRoi Jones when he came to visit Fisk University, and I suppose that was 1964, might have been 1963. I don't remember the date exactly. It's a look-upable because it was a Black Arts

Conference at Fisk University, and he was the primary speaker. But LeRoi came, I think on that Saturday afternoon and just riveted everybody. He was reading that poem "Up Against The Wall Motherfucker, This Is A Stickup." That was great because you never heard somebody read a poem that said "Up Against The Wall Motherfucker." And he's quite a charismatic fellow. People were asking about publishing. That's when the "Should we publish with white publishers?" and all of that stuff came up. And LeRoi categorically said, he was still LeRoi then, categorically said, "No, we shouldn't publish with white publishers. We should start our own publishing houses." And you know how you listen. Maybe you don't. I listen. It was interesting because all of LeRoi's books were with William Morrow. And as it turned out, of course *Black Fire* came out that following September. And it was of course with Random House, right? And then other books came out. So, several years later when I saw him, I said, "Gee, LeRoi, I remember when you were at Fisk you were saying we shouldn't publish with white publishers." "Well," he said, "we have contracts." So I said, "Oh, if we have contracts we should publish with white publishers, but if we don't we shouldn't." I mean, come on.

The guys and I were not going to get along because the guys were into power. They like to tell you what you should do. I remember reading Don [Lee]'s book, *Dynamite Voices*. And if he weren't such a poor writer I would have puked. The nerve of this son of a bitch, if I may, to say what my writing should be. I think that he should deal with what his writing is. Don was too young and not nearly well-read enough to be a critic. Don just didn't know what he was talking about. But of course the joke to me was Don's position on me at one point was that what I really needed was a good man, you know. Ishmael Reed used to say that to me all the time, too. Finally, I said one day to Ish, "This issue is settled. If I need a good man and you're a good man, take me, I'm yours. Let's go." He was quite shocked, but I didn't hear about that any more from him. Eventually, Ish and I became friends. But I got tired of hearing what was wrong with me. I don't think there's anything wrong with me. And I really don't countenance too many people who do. I never did really ever want to be around people that think that what's wrong with me is that I was born. That's insurmountable. I can't handle that in white people, and I wasn't going to handle it in black people. But mostly, it's my life, and I wanted the mistakes to be mine.

I do think that men when they are unsure seek to control, and the natural victim of that control would be women. They would seek to show their power to women. As I looked at men and women, it just was not a situation I wanted to place myself in. If I would fail, it had to be because, and I'm speaking now as a poet, it just had to be because there was nobody out there that wanted to hear my poetry. It couldn't be because I failed to please LeRoi Jones or Ron Karenga or

Don Lee, people like that. Any failure that I would experience had to be because there was nobody out there.

VF: Sure, I see.

NG: And I thought that I owed it to myself to find out is there somebody out there. In other words, if you put me in a rocket and you sent me into space, I probably wouldn't come back because I simply wouldn't believe that nobody's there and I would keep looking. And I just felt that my obligation was to keep finding my audience. Because I didn't want anybody else's audience. I just wanted my own.

VF: Well, to back up just a minute. You said that anybody who has read LeRoi Jones would know that there's no way that he would like what you did. Would you pursue what you see as the basis of his dislike? Is it based on values? On personality? On aesthetics? I know that in the case of the anthology he did several years ago of black women poets, from which he excluded you, his reasons for doing so were clearly ideological; he indicates that in a note. Were they always ideological?

NG: Well, you know, LeRoi's a liar; that goes back to the South African controversy.

VF: Yes. Were you always at odds with each other?

NG: Not really, because I used to go to his house and smoke. He didn't smoke, either. He used to drink teas all the time when he lived in Newark. But, his statement in the anthology was a lie and LeRoi knew it. I wrote to Jim Finkenstadt at Morrow and said, you know, LeRoi's got a note in his book saying that he excluded me because I went to South Africa. One, I didn't go to South Africa, but, two, that is not why he excluded me. He wrote me and asked me for poetry. I wrote him back because LeRoi has never been kind to women and he's never been kind to me. And I knew that there was no way that I was going to put myself in a position of LeRoi Jones rejecting my work. I wrote him back and said, "Dear LeRoi, since you and I share the same publisher why not simply get your permissions from William Morrow? Sincerely, Nikki Giovanni." And of course that didn't please him, I'm sure. The end result was that the book that sold about three copies had that note in it as if that was supposed to hurt me. Well maybe it did. You know, you were asking me earlier about the critics and things like that. I can't deal with that. I don't know what I've missed. I know I haven't won things like book awards and, you know, I understand that I'm not the Poet Laureate of Virginia or Tennessee or Ohio, or something of that nature. To be excluded I didn't mind. I still don't because I think that what I do is what I do and what they do is what they do. What I don't like is the intrusion. I don't like the lies, you know, because I really don't have anything to say about LeRoi other than I'm saying something now because I'm responding to your questions. I'm not going to spend my life responding to LeRoi Jones or Don or any of the rest of those people. That's not what I do. I don't care. I just know that I can't spend my life responding to either what I'm excluded from, whether I feel excluded or not, or what they've said. I try to correct whatever records I can and the rest of the time I just try to go on, and that's the truth.

VF: Some critics have pointed out that perhaps one of the reasons that you fell into disfavor with people like LeRoi Jones was for ideological differences. Could you talk a little bit about what you see as being the relationship between art and ideology?

NG: All of that's bullshit. And I said that as clearly as I know how. I don't have any ideology, and I think that that's probably the most confusing thing about me in terms of my writing. I don't have any ideology. I don't have a lifestyle, either. I have my ideas and I have a life. And I think that people really confuse it. They think that your life is in service of either an ideology or some cause. I didn't have a cause. I was offended. It wasn't like "Oh, my goodness. These poor negroes can't drink from a water fountain in Rich's [department store in Knoxville]. I should go picket for them." No. I don't think that at all. I thought, you know, what the hell does Rich's think it's doing putting a sign up like that? And I think that I should do something about it. Or, in this case, my grandmother thought I should do something about it. It was personal. My concerns have always been quite personal. So I only take up a few things. I don't have a lot of big issues that I'm trying to deal with. I'm not trying to convince anybody, you know; I didn't ask for a vote. I don't even recall asking people to buy my book. I've had book parties, but I don't think I've ever walked up to anybody and said, "Please buy my book." I don't need validation like that. I do think that it's fair to ask people to listen. I'm not seeking agreement. I don't know; I just don't believe in ideology. All of those *isms* all to me come down to one thing. Some white boy is in control. I don't see the point of going from one white boy to another; I don't want to change white men. And I suppose George Wallace is more unattractive than, for example, Patterson, speaking of governors of Alabama. But the reality is I don't want any of them. If I can't have a free world, then I'm not going to engage in the minutiae of the enslavement.

VF: So you don't want to have to choose between evils.

NG: Not don't want—I'm not going to pretend that somehow it can be better. I was born in this country and my mother was born in this country and my grandmother, if I follow matrilineally, and my great-grandmother and her great-grandmother were born in this country. So this is where I am. There may be a search for truth. But I think ultimately the search is for freedom. How do we achieve freedom in a world of multiple responsibilities? One of the things you have to do is own yourself. You just have to. And that's always going to cost you something. It is, and I just happen to think it's worth it. Hurston is dead and we can't even find the grave, but there are people like Zora Neale Hurston who just said, "I think I still want to own myself whatever else is wrong with me." And I am not a big Zora Neale Hurston fan. But what I admire about Hurston is that, whatever she was, she was herself. I do like that. But I do think she paid a disproportionate price to be herself. They owed Zora what Chicago in my opinion owed Carolyn Rodgers. Carolyn was quite an excellent poet, quite a good writer and I think that her desire to realize herself went against the grain. I'm not Nikki Corleone and so I don't get to make wonderful statements like Don Lee has to pay for Carolyn Rodgers. But, to some degree, Don should have to answer for Carolyn.

VF: Do you think you've had to pay a price for insisting on owning yourself?
NG: That comes back to the question you asked me, you're asking me to contemplate something that is uncontemplatable to me. I'm sure I have but I don't know what; I do look at my career and at my life and I am compelled to say it's good.

VF: What about the whole South Africa episode?
NG: Well, truly that was ugly and unfortunate. I mean, there's no question. I think again what happened with that was that it was so foreign. If somebody had said, "Name a million things that will happen in your life," the one million and twenty-fifth would have been black people will turn against you. So it really caught me quite off guard. I think as much as anything I didn't like the way my mom was treated and people don't. But Mom has to pay a price for being my mother, and I'm really sorry about that. Thomas has to pay a price for being my son. If somebody had said, "You can avoid that," we would also have avoided all the things that made me the target when I spoke out against it. But something happening to me is the price you pay for being a public figure. I don't like those aspects. I don't want to be that kind of a public figure. I never did. I just want to be me. And again, I think, Jesus, I just want to do what I do. I want to go and do my reading. I like to talk to people. I do. I like interacting. I like the kids and I like the old people. I haven't had a whole lot of regard for contemporaries because, well, it's cutthroat. And anybody that says anything different is either not an artist or not quite aware. Their minds got pickled someplace. It's a cutthroat world.

VF: Are you suggesting that there's not enough room in the world for more than one writer at a time?
NG: No. I think that there's plenty of room, and I personally like artists. That's

the truth. I'm certainly not going to be harmed by other writers. But you still have to have the right to be yourself. I couldn't be a part of the school. I can only be myself. I think you should write what you believe, you know. I wrote that poem, you know, that at the end says something to the effect that maybe this isn't a poetic time at all. But I never took that to mean I shouldn't write poetry. And so you write something and somebody says "What does this mean?" I've never been an artist who wouldn't try to explain herself. And I didn't want anybody to think that it means that this is what *you* should do. Clearly I wrote poetry. Anything else that I was doing, and I did say that several times until people quit asking me, is none of your business. Somebody would say, you know, what are you doing for black people? What do you mean, what am I doing for black people? Who are you to ask me? Yeah, it's like the people who run up to you and ask, "What are you doing for Jesus?" That's between me and Jesus. It's none of your business.

VF: Well, that goes back to the question of the relationship between art and ideology. But the people who would be asking you that question clearly were thinking that somehow, as a writer, you should be writing in the service of black people.

NG: But I am black, and I've never not tried to be. And I am a woman, and I've never not tried to be. I'm from Ohio, and I'm connected to Tennessee and Georgia. I am what I am. And it's there. You can take it or leave it. I'm a good cook, too. And I'm compulsive and I keep a clean house. I mean, pick what you want. You can't pick my words and try to pillory me on them because they're my words. And I've always stood by my poetry and I don't think in this life I would write a poem that I don't. But standing by your poetry and somebody saying, you know, that I should follow this, I'm not a guru. What I do believe is that you should think for yourself. If you're not capable of doing that, I suppose then you should find the best person you can to ask. But I'm not trying to lead the people. I'm not an ideologue. I think I can think for myself. I do believe that honorable people will resolve differences honorably, and that from that resolution will come something better because we all compromise. I never had a problem with the word *compromise*. People argue that we won't compromise. Sure we will. It's a human thing. You have to find what's important. What you don't want somebody to do, and what I would advise against doing with me and what I would try not to do with somebody, is you don't want to cross the line that's important. Because once that line is crossed then essentially it's war. Psych 101 teaches us, don't corner a rat. A simple little thing like a rat. Now rats we do know are vicious, but they're quite small. If you want the rat out of your house, open the door. It can't corner you. One of you has to die.

VF: What should the relationship between you as an individual and the larger group be? Whatever the larger group may be—the larger group that is your family or the larger group that is your immediate community. To what extent do you take your identity from the larger group?

NG: I take a lot of my, if not identity, certainly comfort from the larger group. I like to feel that I am a responsible relative. I certainly like to feel that I am a responsible citizen. I don't think that people have a right to intrude but I feel that I am a worthwhile member of my immediate community. I'm also a citizen of Earth. And I think that's overriding. I think that I am quite rural. I am a poet who lived in urban areas. But I don't think I have an urban sensibility. As individualistic as I am I don't think anybody, even on my worst day, I don't think my worst enemy would accuse me of looking out for myself. I don't think that anybody would ever say that I'm not generous with my talent, with my money, with whatever I have. I grew up, and of course that's my Tennessee and Georgia roots showing, thinking that you're supposed to give something back. You just can't go through life looking out for yourself.

I believe that you do strive to give something back, because none of us are products of ourselves. And as individualistic as I am, to be an individual is to simply recognize the entity that is you. But so much goes into making that happen. I mean, what a different person I would be (forgetting the family and the genes and things like that) without an Alfredda Delaney or an Emma Stokes or a Sister Althea. How very different I would be without a Flora Alexander or a Teresa Elliot. But goodness, all of these people did so many wonderful things. Mostly it's not that they did something. They didn't buy you shoes and crap like that, but they believed in you and they encouraged you and, you know, there's an obligation. Well, I can't pay Teresa's bill. Miss Delaney's dead; Miss Stokes is dead. Flora's alive, but you can't pay these people back. How do you pay back somebody for believing in you when you were 12 years old, for Christ's sake? So what you do is find someone that you can give something back to. To me the human experiment requires that you continue to go forth. It's so basic. And it's emotionally quite rewarding, you know.

VF: How does this sort of giving back differ from writing poetry in service of a movement or a cause or an ideology?

NG: It's my determination. What I want to contribute is my right. I would add, and I don't have any problem with that, my obligation or responsibility. But it's *my* right. And nobody can determine what *I* need to do for my people. No one. I deal in words. And to a great degree words are the most nebulous of all weapons and, to another degree, the strongest. It's the only thing you cannot ever really take back, you know. So on the one hand you have an intangible that no one can see, and on the other hand you have a very strong, very powerful thing. I think that my words should be as true as I can make them.

VF: Do you have an aesthetic out of which you see yourself working? What are the components of good poetry?

NG: I judged a contest in Indiana, Illinois, some small college there. Maybe upstate New York. And I chose a poem that I thought, for a high-school competition, was really quite wonderful. Something to do with an orange burst. I don't remember. It was like a metaphor for her menses beginning. I thought it was wonderful. I got this really vicious letter from the mother of one of the boys who was in the competition but whose poem didn't win. I wrote her back and said, actually when you're in a poetry contest it's a crap shoot. And on any given day, any given piece of poetry at a certain level of competition could go the other way. It could have been exactly the other way. It was a subjective judgment and when I judged the contest I subjectively chose that one. I said, in other words, that it was a game, and people hate to hear things like that. But it was a game. I was charged to pick a winner. That makes it a game. It cannot be life because in life there are no winners. It's a little bit better or little bit worse, but there's no finalization. I thought I was really wonderful with this mother, you know, but she didn't appreciate it. And I always give detailed comments in a contest because I want to say to the other people that in reality this is, one, a game, and, two, most of us, the majority of us, will not be number one. So you can't worry about it. Most of us are not going to be. I mean, it's like watching the World Series. Four teams win their division; two teams win the pennant. One team wins the World Series. But the reality is, if the last team didn't play then the first team couldn't win. And you have to keep that in mind.

VF: Well, I think that I understand what you're saying. But what if you remove the element of competition? What makes a poem good?

NG: My problem is always that I'm accused of grading easy and I think it brings up the dilemma of what you're asking me, because I don't grade my kids against each other. Which means that a lot of my grades are high because I look at it as "How did this poem achieve it?" "What did it set out to do?" The number one thing I'm looking for when I'm teaching is "What are the premises? How well did the writer fulfill his or her task?" If I'm judging the contest I'm also asking "Did it delight me?" When I teach I'm interested in "Will it help my writer to grow?" When I do a contest I'm not teaching these people. They have presented to me what they see as their best shot and then I think I have a right to say "Is it delightful?" "Is it insightful?" "Does it touch me?" "Are the words anchored in something?" Because a lot of people think you can just throw some images out: "a sky—light blue against the green crown hills." You know, some crap like that. What the hell is this all about? I'd rather have a good poem about Mother Stirred the Soup on Saturday, you know. Something that makes them grounded in something. Make some concrete images out of it. Build a house, you know, shelter. Make something you can crawl into and wrap yourself around. So that's what I'm looking for, if that's what you're asking.

VF: So for a poem to be good, in your opinion, it has to delight you, or provide some insight and be anchored in some kind of world that you know and recognize?

NG: My language gets poor sometimes and I would say delight but I don't mean that lightly.

VF: Okay.

NG: I don't mean it like, "ho, ho, ho." You have to sort of see what the writer's doing. There has to be a reason for it, you know.

VF: Of the writers who have come up most often in your lectures as writers that you admire, I would say that the three names that occur most frequently of living writers are Toni Morrison, Gloria Naylor, and Alex Haley. All three of them are writers that I've heard you refer to any number of times as writers whose works are wonderful, that you loved. There's something in common in those three writers.

NG: Yes, they delight me.

VF: But beyond the fact that they delight you, or maybe, not beyond it, but *how* do they delight you? or why are you delighted by what they write when you might not be delighted by what somebody else writes?

NG: We could add Ernie Gaines because we've been talking about him lately. I mean, Ernie writes like an angel. Ernie is like a great wine. He just gets better and better. But Toni and Gloria and Alex are very different writers.

VF: Yes.

NG: And so I don't have to compare them and I hope that they don't compare themselves because that's just foolish. They all set about to do different things. I think Toni and Gloria, because they're women, get compared, and I think it's to the detriment of the reader, not to the detriment of either writer. Both novelists should just thank God every morning that they exist because they should push each other. They should make each other continue to dig. Toni was so far out through the stratosphere, she was just so far out alone that I'm really happy for her. I don't know that she's happy. I'm not speaking for Morrison. But I'm really happy that Gloria Naylor came along because it gives Toni something to push against.

VF: When you say that she was out in the stratosphere alone, what do you mean?

NG: Well, Toni is a black writer, and I think what has totally delighted me is that she's never apologized for being black. And that's really an unusual sort of situation. She decided to write *The Bluest Eye*, and she doesn't take on the white characters and the black characters are not responding directly to them. What Pecola's mother was doing was fantasizing at the movies, you know. What she wanted was what they had. And then she abuses Pecola because of the little white child. It's the contradiction of her own life. It's not, you know, what Margaret Walker called omniscient beings who tower over us and laugh. Toni didn't credit the white people with being that important. They just kind of float through. And I think that it's been critically conceded, how she has made place a character. And the way that none of those other people, I mean, *Winesburg, Ohio* is not a character. And that other thing they do on stage all the time, a stupid play that they do with props, everybody sits around and reads. Really dumb. Not *Winesburg, Ohio*, but something like that.

VF: *Our Town?*

NG: *Our Town*. You know what I'm saying? I don't think that the place exists. But Toni has made a place living. Place has taken on a life, not of the characters but of its own. And, you know, how could you not love that? I mean, it's a certain genius at work. I think it's fantastic what she has achieved, you know, in that area. And of course Gloria is always looking into the human heart. I introduced Gloria Naylor when she came to [Virginia] Tech, and I said she is an archaeologist because she mines the human soul. And she really does. She just keeps looking at the person, at the person, at the person. So Gloria's into magic with Mama Day and really it wasn't so much Mama Day's magic as it was the boy's magic.

VF: George?

NG: George. George was willing to do whatever. Talk about a knight in shining armor and all of that. But the magic was that George loved her. And it takes a Naylor to bring that kind of scene where the trees are talking and the bridge is falling and, you know, all that is going on and yet the *true* magic was George's love. It's wonderful.

VF: How do you place Morrison and Naylor and yourself within the larger context of Afro-American literary history?

NG: Well, I think what my generation did was to change our focus of address; if I had to say what is outstanding in my own career—and I don't say this for any meanness or bitterness or anything like that—I address my people. And I think coming from that basis I clearly belong in the tradition of Langston Hughes. But Langston had a situation that I didn't have, in that Langston was a part of the Harlem Renaissance and was carrying the burden of a voiceless people. The

Black Arts Movement carried the voice of a voiceless people and then the people were given a voice. We were also fortunate that advances in technology meant we didn't have to go through white publishers, so there was the confluence of technology with the political group, and I think that that made a big, big, big difference in what the novelist could do. The novelists never want to give the poets the credit. But the poets created, or rather, we solidified an audience, because black people have always read. I mean, that's been the white rap, that black people won't read. Why should anybody in their right mind spend time with Tom Pynchon, or people like that? Who the hell is going to read, "Rabbit is rich, Rabbit is dead, Rabbit is poor, Rabbit has an erection, Rabbit doesn't have an erection"? This is not literature, so why should people read it? So, the black community gets a rap that we don't read. But the poet showed that indeed black people read. Now the question is, is the literature going to be interesting? People like Morrison, who is chronologically older, but artistically, or at least in terms of publishing, younger, can as a novelist capture the audience that the poet created. And of course Gloria Naylor would be, in essence, her child. It was a question of who was going to come along and capture part of that audience created by the poets. I guess we'd have to give some credit here to Alice Walker because of *The Color Purple*. But I'm not so sure about *The Color Purple* because I don't think that Alice has done what Toni and Gloria have done, neither in theme nor in address. I think that Alice gave up. I think that she almost had it. She had it with *Grange Copeland*. *Grange* was a very important, is a very important, novel. And I think of Alice as being one of the better short story writers of the 1960s and 1970s. She wrote beautiful short stories. I'm really sorry that Alice didn't continue. That she didn't pick up the story of Grange's granddaughter. I'm just saying for me I've lost Alice, and I guess there are people who say, well, gee, I've lost Nikki. So I don't know. That's fair enough.

VF: In what ways do you see yourself connected to Langston Hughes?

NG: Well, it's a continuum. I mean, one of the things Langston taught us, and taught us very well, is that you can write what you believe. And Langston was of course quite estranged from the black literary establishment.

VF: Yes, he was.

NG: I always appreciated that because it always seemed to me that the people I really loved never got along with the people I never did love. And so it gave me great comfort to know that if you're doing what you believe, you probably won't be liked by other people who want you to do what they want you to do. It's my low-level quarrel with DuBois. I'm tired of the control freaks. And I said it earlier, but the only thing I believe in is the people, and the people will break your heart. I say that all the time, and it's quite true. But you do separate. Even when we were doing the South African thing I did very much have it in my mind that these were not the people. These were in fact the fanatics and the ideologues, because the people won't act like that. And I think I was justified and I think I've been vindicated in that the ordinary black person to me is a wonderment. If somebody just had to drop me someplace and say "You can't move. You just have to sit there, you know, for the next five years," then I would say "Please, drop me in the middle of some small town no higher up than Virginia." Georgia, Alabama, Mississippi, Tennessee. I can handle it because it's a constant fascination how southern black people negotiate with their dignity intact. And so I have a lot of faith in those people. You were talking about voices; once we released those voices no one needed to speak for them. They're an elegant people. They're capable of speaking for themselves.

VF: Did that therefore change what you saw as being your job as a poet? what your role as a poet is?

NG: I think that clearly I have deemphasized the "we." And I think if we look at my earlier work, you'll see there's a lot of "we" because I listen and I talk a lot. But I listen very well. But then the people were able to speak for themselves. I think the key book there is *My House*. And the turn around is that if we believe in what we say, and I do, that the people should be free, then we have to allow the people to be free as they see themselves to be free. Not as I would see them to be. And I don't see that I am any different than the people. I'm certainly one voice. I might have been one of a few at one point. But clearly by the time we hit the 1970s I was one of many. And I think that that's a great burden off your shoulders because your level of accuracy can change because you're not trapping anybody with your words, you know. You're not putting a spin on somebody else's life. You can just put it on yours and somebody can use it or not. That depends. But the people are free. No matter what the other problems we're having in America. We're having quite a few, between Bush and Reagan. There are quite a few. I'm serious. They're financial. And any time you have severe financial problems you're going to have emotional problems that are concurrent with it. But we are free. And what we're now having to decide is "What is our responsibility as a free people and a free nation?"

VF: One of the ways in which it could be said that you follow Langston Hughes is that he also performed his poetry with music, didn't he?

NG: He did a lot with jazz. He loved jazz. And I clearly regret not having met Langston. He and Lorraine Hansberry are the only two people I know that, if I could have dinner with anybody, living or dead, I would love to have dinner with either of those. You know, if somebody could bring them, I would love to have that, because Langston loved jazz as I love gospel, and we would just probably sit all night and argue about music. So I'm sure that Langston and I could have had a big, big argument, because I've got—he has the age but I have the music. My music is older than his. And I'm sure it would just be fun to watch what each of us is doing. Because I really went back beyond Langston just because of my love for gospel music. For that matter, to tell you the truth, LeRoi Jones did it first. That was really funny because LeRoi, you know, bitched about *Truth Is On Its Way*, and I said to somebody, *New York Times*, *Washington Post*, somebody, I don't know what he's upset about. I'm only doing what he did. My career has followed LeRoi Jones's career in very interesting kinds of ways. We're both with William Morrow, you know. He recorded an album, and it's not my fault nobody bought it. He's of course made movies and things like that and he writes plays. I don't do that.

VF: In fact, your performance with gospel music and the release of *Truth* certainly made your name known to an even larger audience.

NG: It was a width thing. It wasn't a depth thing. I don't know how else to say it, but I was a star way before any of that. I just did very well. And stardom or name recognition or the ability to walk down the street or not, can in fact be quite a hassle. When *Truth* came out I had already been doing television, I'd already been doing readings. I think *Truth* is good because it gave people who normally did not think of poetry an opportunity to reconsider. And the two groups that I was delighted to see pick up the album were the older people and the kids.

When *Truth* came out, I was in Africa. I'd gone to West Africa. I'd gone to Nigeria and to Ghana, Togo. In fact, I was in Ivory Coast, in the airport in Abidjan, and I was walking from the plane into the airport, and there were some black Americans coming out. And they said, "I [*sic*] love your album." I said, "What are you talking about?", because the album was released and I went on to Africa without thinking about it. I'd been gone for awhile. They said, "You know, that record album with James Cleveland"—everybody always said James Cleveland [instead of Benny Diggs]; it used to drive Benny Diggs nuts. And I said, "Where did you hear my record?" "They're playing it all over the states." I said, "Are you kidding?" They said, "No, we're not kidding." So I did put a call in. I called home and said I just ran into some people in Abidjan who said my record is being played. They said, "Oh, you're number 12 on the charts." I said, "You're kidding." Who would have thought a recording of poetry and gospel would have such success?

VF: Why do you think it was such a phenomenal success?

NG: It was true. It was good. And we did it with a lot of love. But when you do something like that you don't expect it to become popular. I did it with a little record company. I didn't expect it to get a proper hearing at all. But WWRL in New York started to play it on FM and then we made AM gospel. And in retrospect I can see, of course, that radio was absolutely key. I won a NATRA award for it, and that's radio. And so all of a sudden you had a lot of air play, you know. And there were so many ways to approach the album. "Ego Tripping" was played for the kids. And "Peace Be Still" really did flip out the gospel people, who were not sure about me. I mean, the sanctified, right? But they knew Benny and they knew him to be one of theirs. And so the question that Benny had to answer was, "Who is she?" "Well," he'd say, "Nikki's all right." The first thing they had to find out was actually I do know what I'm talking about. I do know my gospel music. And so your gospel people wanted to say—James Cleveland for that matter—well, you know, how did you come to this? What do you mean, how did I come to this? I know my history; I know my spirituals and I know my gospel. I grew up in church. And to be a backslider, which I've always said I am, doesn't mean that I don't know and appreciate the music. I've never disliked the church or church people. I had already had a Father's Day concert at Bryant Walker's church in New York. I had it with LaBelle [a female rock group]. We did a free Father's Day concert. But I'd always been looking for ways to extend the voice. And that's all you try to do is see that it's out there. It's one reason I was so proud of Ntozake Shange. She took another way to extend the voice; the choreopoem was a wonderful thing. I was really glad to see that Ntozake was extending it, because you keep extending the form. You keep making something happen.

VF: What do you see as being the qualities in your poetry that make it go with gospel so well?

NG: Well, the main thing that I think my work offers is a singular voice. I don't, I really don't think that there's a whole lot of confusion. If you hear my poem you'll know it's me. And I think I have as much a signature voice for what I do as Aretha Franklin has a signature voice as a singer.

VF: Your voice is the main source of consistency from your earliest work to your most recent.

NG: It's me. And I keep working on making that remain, you know, more me. I'm 48 and so there are lots of different ways of looking at it. But I think that that's important. But I am one who values the oral connection. I think that writers who deliberately try to make words stand alone are crazy because words have to connect. And the first way that words connect is that you can wrap yourself around them, both your eye and your tongue. And if you do that then your heart can follow, you know. I guess that's a play on that phrase, what is it—you got 'em by the balls, their heart and mind will follow. I think if you've got 'em by the eye and the tongue, the heart and mind can follow. So whatever else my poetry is, I wanted it to be clear that a human being wrote it.

VF: A lot of your time and your energy have gone into performances of your poetry or readings of your poetry. To what extent do you think an understanding and appreciation of your poetry is dependent upon its oral presentation?

NG: Well, oral presentations tap something primal. There's something about the reading voice that's very different. I'm sure if we had a voiceogram, whatever they're doing now, that the voice prints of something read and something spoken would be different. It's one reason I hate to be read to by politicians.

VF: Or by anyone else.

NG: No, I like to be read to. I mean, but I don't want anybody to read me something I should read myself.

VF: So you're saying that poetry is not something people should necessarily read themselves?

NG: I'm saying that poetry functions like any other lullaby, I guess. You can sing it to yourself and we all have, I'm sure. You know, we all sing ourselves to sleep. But it's also very nice when someone comes and sings it to you. And so I don't—what do I want to say—I don't want to be misunderstood. The thing that is wonderful about television is that it gives us a common visual. In addition to the visual, though, it gives us a common voice. Television is preeminent in a way that even radio is not because people would gather at the radio in a group. But television you can do alone. And I think if you talk to TV stars, let alone people like me, you'll find that more people still recognize their voices than their faces.

VF: Really?

NG: Yes. And it's an amazing thing. I can get in cabs, certainly even yet, I can get in a cab and the cabbie will know my voice without recognizing my face. I know it happened to Bette Davis as distinct as that face was. The voice will get you every time. I know that there's something comforting about the human voice. I enjoy poetry readings, first of all. I like to hear someone speak to me who's speaking *to* me. If you've been to my poetry readings, and I know that you have, you notice that at least half of what I'm doing is talking with the audience.

VF: Right.

NG: Because I'm not there to insult them by saying "I'm here to read a poem because you are too dumb to read it." I know that they can read the poem. What I'm trying to say is, we are having an experience; it's why I said I don't like politicians to read a speech. I would rather they came and said to me whatever it is that was on their mind. And I think about the great political speeches that I've heard. There have been speeches that, I'm not going to say extemporaneous because politicians are not extemporaneous people, but they've already put it in their head that they're going to do. They're not flipping pages. They are in fact looking you in the eye and saying, "This is an experience." I hate the press for having ruined that, because more and more people are afraid to talk to people. But there's something wonderful about that commonality of experience. Now singers do it. But when you do a singer you've got the song. And the song generally does stand between the singer and the audience. And so the first thing you respond to is the song. Whether you respond to the beat, you know, whatever. But there's the song and the singer can hide behind it. The writer cannot hide behind her words, and so when we're on stage we're essentially naked. And it's kind of wonderful because people need to know it's all right to be vulnerable. I think all of us who read do that.

VF: So you think one of the things that you accomplish with an audience is by allowing yourself to be vulnerable on the stage, you make it seem less frightening?

NG: Yes. Because it's not going to kill you. The worst that's going to happen, and believe me your feelings can get hurt, is that they're not going to like you. And yet, even if you would be in front of a hostile audience, or in front of an audience that for some reason is totally just not going to like you, you've shown, if to no one else but yourself, that you can survive it. You can handle it.

VF: There have been so many powerful black preachers and orators—Frederick Douglass, Frances Harper, or, more recently I guess one thinks of Martin Luther King, Jr. Do you see yourself as having anything in common with the tradition of the preacher?

NG: Yes, the preacher's important. No one in their right minds would compare themselves to King.

VF: Well, what is the difference between what you do with an audience and, I'm not trying to be sacrilegious at all, but it seems to me that there are lots of similarities between what you do with an audience and what a preacher does with a congregation. What are the differences?

NG: The main difference, you mentioned King so let me center on Martin as opposed to *the* preacher.

VF: Okay.

NG: I think the main difference between a Martin Luther King, Jr., and a Nikki Giovanni is that Martin had a charge to get people to do something. I don't.

VF: Although you often urge your audiences to go out and, I'm trying to recall some of the things . . .

NG: Certainly I do. Think for yourself. Read something. Do something different.

VF: Not a specific action.

NG: No.

VF: Yes. Okay.

NG: And you don't have to call me to let me know you did it. What I'm doing is trying to simply hand back the power that they have. I mean, I just want to hold the mirror up and say, "See, you're wonderful," because I believe that. And when I don't I won't. That's why I have to limit my speaking engagements. There're places where I can't speak because I don't think that those people are wonderful. I don't want to say it, you know. Martin was charged with talking to the saved and the sinners. I mostly talk to the saved.

VF: That's quite a difference.

NG: Yes, it is. A very big difference. And again he had a, oh Jesus, he really had such a charge. So did Frederick Douglass. But these men had a payoff. There was an action. They wanted something to happen. I wouldn't mind to see something happen. I don't know how much of that is a result of being a woman because I've always been a woman. It's not something that I—it's not a dress I put on. And so I don't know how much of my conditioning, my socialization, whatever—I don't know how much of that has put me in a position. I'm not passive. But I don't, I truly don't expect people to do what I would like to see done.

VF: So, unlike the preacher, you preach to the saved. What, if anything, do you have in common with the preacher?

NG: I do think the slave preacher is an important person and I do think that he's maligned. What he did and what we all do is work with what we have. What he did by embracing the Christian religion, first of all, was to be able to get the day off. You have to remember that slaves used to work seven days a week, which could not be right. If God rested on one day, they had to as well. So he did something. His primary audience would, of course, have been the slaves. But his secondary audience was the slave master. So he's serving two different communities and trying to satisfy the needs of both. He did not start slavery, and he wasn't going to stop it. And that's a fact. I mean, no matter what the dream, he didn't start it, and he wasn't going to stop it. But if you can remind people that, "Didn't my lord deliver Daniel, and why not every man," you are preparing them for when slavery does end. I'm sure that the slave preacher did not anticipate it would be 200 years. He was hoping it would not. He was hoping that if he didn't see it, his children would. And that's been the charge of each generation up until mine, that what I have not done I hope that you can. And nobody would have anticipated there would be 10, 15 generations before any modicum of freedom came. And so I look at it that it's preparatory. I look at his job as preparatory.

The black church of course is the greatest repository of black history. There's just no getting around it. I respect what the church did, and so I guess if you want to look at it, at least the way I'm looking at it, what they did was plant, and I would like to think of myself as a planter. I don't know who is going to reap. James Cleveland said the harvest is plentiful but the laborers are few. He may be right. All I know is that the ground is there. I'm going to try to furrow it. That's all I can do. My generation is just not going to be available to harvest. And so what you're hoping is that you planted well. I think that's all you *can* do. And so I think you have to give up any idea of monuments to—there'll be no monuments to people like me. And I'm not the first person like me. You're happy because you know what you've done, but there'll be no monument.

VF: That's an interesting comment. In your dialogue with Baldwin, and in other places as well, you made a statement that you thought Baldwin had always been more interested in morality, while you were more interested in power. You weren't that interested in being the most moral person in the world, but you could handle being the most powerful.

NG: I think I was 26 or 27 when I did that interview with Jimmy in London. It was good. I took Tommy with me. We all stayed in the same hotel and so we had a week to talk to each other, to get to know each other. And of course I would have loved Baldwin anyway because I'd read him. I mean, everybody had read Baldwin. But he was very, very kind to Thomas. And Jimmy's a night owl, and that's probably an understatement. We would be having breakfast when he would just be coming in. And Thomas called him Jimmy Baldwin. "Jimmy Baldwin! Jimmy Baldwin! Take me for a walk." And you know, Jimmy's hung over, but he would take Tommy for his morning walk before he would go to bed. It was really, I mean, he would have won my heart anyway. Plus, he's great to talk to.

But I was a young woman talking to a man old enough to be my father, and so we were doing generational differences. This was not a private conversation between Baldwin and me that some camera sort of overheard. We were having one of the generationals. I did the same thing with Margaret Walker. We talked generationally. And I was trying to explain the world as I think my generation saw it, and I do think my generation is very much interested in power. I have not reread my dialogue with Jimmy and I have not reread my conversation with Margaret Walker. But I'm fairly sure that I'm accurate at least in tone if not in exact words that what I said was I would always rather have power than have power be held over me—even at 48, and that would be to some degree giving up my soul. If I had a chance to have real power, I'm not talking about, you know, I'm a policeman I can write a ticket. No bullshit like that. I'm not going to sell it short. But if I had a chance to have some real power, if I had been Clarence Thomas at EEOC [Equal Employment Opportunity Commission], if I had had the EEOC suit, they would probably have bombed the building. Because that's a chance to make a difference. There's enough power in just something that simple to make people's lives better. You can do something with it. You teach school or something like that you can make changes in the individual. But if you could be provost or president, and the advantage of being president is that you get to hire the provost, then that would be worth doing because then you have a chance to make an institution bend to your will. I would always accept that. Jimmy would have shied away from it. He never liked that kind of responsibility. That kind of responsibility doesn't frighten me because I know what I want done.

VF: Another thing that you say in the dialogue with Baldwin and elsewhere is that everybody should take care of their own little block, something to that effect. Does that mean you don't really believe in the possibility of large, organized social movements for change?

NG: It's very limited. If I, Nikki, had been primary advisor of Martin Luther King, Jr., or of Huey Newton, or of Rap Brown, I would have recognized, "This is finished. We have done the best that we could do." King would never have been in Memphis. In all fairness, I don't say it was a mistake. I really don't. But a social movement is stolen time, as it were; it's a glitch, and you maximize it. You do exactly what you can do and then you have to trust that what you've done will work out. As I said, I'm a planter; you have to put the seeds in there and water them and you do everything you can but then you have to recognize they have to grow on their own. It's not a permanent position. No matter what it is, it can't be. And I'm very leery of large groups. I belong to the Deltas, I belong to the National Council of Negro Women, and things like that. I'm very proud of things like that. But it's very limited what we try to do and what we can do. Mass social movements of necessity have to come to an end, because either the people understood it and did it or not. As a leader, you're only representing the legitimate desires of someone else. No leader created the movement. And that's what everybody seems to miss. Movements create leaders. But once you're a leader the existentials of it change, and then you have to be the one that's saying, "I've done the best that I can." And no matter how much the people clamor for you to come back, if you're wise you've given back the power to the people. Because the power, if I may quote Huey Newton, resides with the people. And when the changes occur you have to be able to do that. I mean, you did what you did. Then someone else must take it up. I mean, it's just that basic. I think that movements are dangerous. The people is always dangerous because the . . .

VF: I thought you believed in the people.

NG: I believe in the people, but I don't fool myself. The people will put palms down on one Sunday and scream for Barabbas the next Friday. And I'm not against the people. I'm just saying any people of any color in large numbers are dangerous. And so when you draw them together there should be a reason. And when that reason is as well fulfilled as possible they should be dispersed. Otherwise you've got what is called a standing army. And we could certainly assess the 1960s in that regard. A standing army is always dangerous because it's always looking for a war.

VF: Is that what went wrong with the [civil rights] movement?

NG: Nothing went wrong. I'm the only person who's ever going to answer this question this way that I know of. Nothing went wrong with the movement. We did what we set out to do. There were some people that were late in getting the word. Hey! We won. Nobody wanted to admit that. It's finished. It finished honorably. It finished well. We did not finish in 1968. I think the murder of Robert Kennedy is quite sad. I think you know that. It's a great loss. Truly a great loss. But in terms of the 1960s we had already, way before that, way before the murder of King, we had done what we were to do. The people were not going to stop, and the movement has not stopped. Anita Hill is an extension of that. The women's movement is an extension of that. The anti-war movement is an extension of that. For that matter, the sexual revolution, and I don't care what they say about AIDS or anything else, the sexual revolution belongs to us; and though we aren't proud of AIDS, we're proud of freeing women to relate to their bodies. The gay movement belongs to us. We freed people. We did it. So why should the leadership that led, the people that led the marches, why should they now be compelled to do yet more? At some point somebody needs to say, "Enough. I've done enough." You do it or you don't. But I . . .

VF: . . . it's a difficult position if you're a revolutionary and the revolution is over. You write yourself out of a job as it were.

NG: But you try to look down the pike because you figure, okay, one day we'll all be 50, or we'll all be 60. And look at what we will have accomplished. And should we survive, all of us won't, you know, I mean, I didn't have that kind of a problem. But you don't, you just don't want to lose somebody for no damn reason. And it just seemed to me that as young people we had put so much of our lives into a cause; we were public figures. And so the hardest thing to do is to come back and say, "No, I'm going to create a space and make a life that makes some sense. And then I can reflect. Then I'll have an opportunity to assess what we did and to help in a smaller way for sure." But I think in a truer way, too, to a great degree, to help make it really solidify. To make it—you know, it's not the personal flake. The flake lets you know; you see a few snowflakes. But it's the other cloud that joins it that makes the snowstorm. And that's what, you know, in terms of a wish, I mean, that's what I really want for my generation. That we be capable, that we be around to assess what we've done.

VF: One last question that you may or may not want to answer. I know you're fond of the spiritual "It Is Well With My Soul" . . .

NG: I like it 'cause the song leaves me in charge. Even though . . .

VF: Even though I'm dead I can speak for my soul.

NG: It is well. It's a beautiful song.

VF: Yes.

NG: It was my grandmother's favorite song.

VF: Yes, I know. I just wondered, what does that mean to you? The easiest question saved for last of course.

NG: I thought the question you were going to ask is, "How am I going to justify, 'and I really hope no white person ever has cause to write about me because they never understand Black love is Black wealth.'"

VF: You can certainly respond to the question that I didn't ask.

NG: I like that poem. Margaret Walker called me and I had only briefly met Miss Walker. She was Miss Walker. She's Margaret now. At that point I was living in New York and she talks, you know, and her bottom lip quivers. "This is Margaret Walker," and I was just thrilled out of my mind. "Yes, Miss Walker." "That poem, my dear, is your signature poem." And I'd really have to search my memory to think of something that made me happier than Margaret Walker saying that to me because I admire her as a writer and as a human being. She's quite bright. I was driving home and I was trying to think, if I could pick three people from whom to pick the Supreme Court justices, you know, if George [Bush] called and said, "Well, give me three choices," I thought, well, the first one I'd trust would be Leon Higginbotham of course. But I think Leon is too old if he's not actually dead at this point. But let's deal with some realities—Barbara Jordan of course. Or if you couldn't do Barbara, my next real choice would be John Hope Franklin, for obvious reasons. He's a great historian, and it would be nice to get some of those lawyers off the court and get some real people on it. But then, I was laughing to myself and thought, if I could make a pick, though I doubt that she would accept, my third choice would be a very strong Margaret Walker because she's far better educated, I think, than probably any black American since DuBois.

VF: Really.

NG: Yes indeed. I mean, she's a brilliant woman. She just chose to practice poetry and of course she chose to live in Mississippi. But her mind is a catholic mind. She really pulls it all together. She would be wonderful on the Supreme Court. I was laughing to myself. I could see George Bush calling her now and saying, you know, "Margaret, Nikki Giovanni recommended you for the Supreme Court, and I'm going to make this appointment."

VF: You wish.

NG: But, to get back to the poem, "Nikki–Rosa" is doing two things, and I don't analyze my poetry and I know you're not asking me to. It's doing two things. It says, it is indeed well with my soul, and for those who would tamper with it, that's a no-no. I will not allow myself to be tampered with by those who don't care about me. And so I made a blanket statement about people who don't care about me. It's a fair statement to make, and any exception to that would be an exception. Margaret and I in our dialogue talked about white people. And I used to perplex her. What she called me was a brazen hussy.

VF: Oho.

NG: I love it. I used to perplex her because she said I lumped people and she looked at them as individuals, and I said, "That's not true." It's not. What I do is I look at exceptional white people as exceptional, and she wants to look at exceptional white people as the rule. And so I've never, if I would have changed anything in the philosophy of nonviolence I would not have ever loved in general. I would have said, "Let us hate in particular." There are a lot of hateful things that happen. How could you not hate the men who killed Emmett Till? And to say, "We're going to hate the act and love you" is ridiculous. I'm not going to love you. I hate you for doing that. And I recognize you as being exactly what you are—a representative of your people. The people who mourned Emmett Till with us were the exceptions. But white Americans, if I may, have always gotten away with their exceptional people doing the general, and the general people being taken as the exceptional. And so I didn't think it was fair. So I don't have to justify that.

VF: I never dreamed of asking you to justify it.

NG: I answered a question you didn't ask, and I answered it in a way . . .

VF: Well, it is a question that we talked about very early on because of the fact that I am white.

NG: James Baldwin says that's your decision. I love Baldwin for that. But for me at 48, menopausal, with a kid in college, that dog, a mother and my sister who are all significant to me—I think that I discharge my responsibilities to my family and to my community and to planet Earth as responsibly, and I might add, as joyfully as I can. I am not given toward deep depression. If things bother me I do the best I can. I connected with Anita Hill when somebody asked her, "Well, what do you expect us to do?" and she said, "I just brought you the information. That's your job." I thought, she's right. I mean, I don't know this woman, what world she lives in. But I would imagine that she lives in that world that says, "All I want to do is my best and the rest of you have to do whatever it is you have to do." If you do what I would say is the right thing, I'm glad. If you don't, people being people, *c'est la vie.*

VF: Yes.

NG: And I think that that's the only way to be, you know, sane. But I think that I would disappoint myself if I had to be less. I would be sad if I had to write things that I didn't believe or didn't like to write. On the other hand, I'm sure I would if it was a question of my kid going to law school, and people have said that "What you need to do, Nikki, is write a novel." I'm sure that I could write a really shitty novel and do pretty well with it. I just think if I was going to write a novel—this is where all of this kicks in and maybe ties up for you—I'm no novelist, and I know good novelists. And if I'm going to write I have to write at least on the level of *The Bluest Eye.* I'm not going to charge myself with writing on the level of *Song of Solomon* because it took her four novels to get there. But at least on the level of *The Bluest Eye.* At least on the level of *Brewster Place.* At least on the level of "A Cold Gray Day in November," because that's where Gaines started. And if I can't start where they started I don't want to do it. I really don't. And I don't mind falling short. I don't. I can handle that I wasn't able to do it, but I can't handle that I know that I can't as I start it.

VF: I see what you mean.

NG: I have to feel like I have enough knowledge and enough skill to at least think that I can achieve on that level. And if it would fall short I would like to think I wouldn't publish it. Once you know where the bottom line is, then you just don't want to fall below that. I'm living in a golden age of black literature. I think that I've been a part of it and I think that my sanity—you didn't ask me "What did I think is the basis of my sanity?"—I think a part of my sanity is that I know when I was a part of it, when I started it and where I fit on this end of it. It keeps me happy on both ends. I know what I achieved as a young writer. Not only in the writing but in the visibility of the writing. But having achieved that, it's nice to watch other people take center stage on it and I'm really proud of that. And I really think that I continue to be innovative. You know, that I have something to say. I do today's job today.

Notes and References

Chapter One

1. Nikki Giovanni, *Black Feeling, Black Talk/Black Judgement* (New York: William Morrow, 1970), 58; all references to poems in Giovanni's first two volumes, *Black Feeling, Black Talk* and *Black Judgement*, will be to this combined volume and will hereafter be cited in text as *BF*.

2. Giovanni frequently introduces this poem to audiences by discussing the outrage she felt when Moynihan published his report.

3. Margaret Walker was the first to call "Nikki–Rosa" a "signature poem." See *A Poetic Equation: Conversations Between Nikki Giovanni and Margaret Walker* (Washington, D.C.: Howard University Press, 1974), 53; hereafter cited in text as *PE*.

4. Ida Lewis, "Foreword" to *My House* (New York: William Morrow, 1972), xi.

5. Nikki Giovanni, *Gemini: An Extended Autobiographical Statement on My First Twenty-Five Years of Being a Black Poet* (1971; rpt. New York: Penguin, 1985), 33; hereafter cited in text as *GE*.

6. Nikki Giovanni, Unpublished Juvenalia. Nikki Giovanni Collection. Mugar Memorial Library, Boston.

7. Margaret B. McDowell, "Groundwork for a More Comprehensive Criticism of Nikki Giovanni," in *Belief vs. Theory in Black American Literary Criticism*, ed. Joe Weixlmann and Chester J. Fontenot, Studies in Black American Literature, vol. 2 (Greenwood, Fl.: Penkevill Publishing Co., 1986), 136; hereafter cited in text.

8. Eugene Perkins, "The Black Arts Movement: Its Challenge and Responsibility," in *The Black Seventies*, ed. Floyd B. Barbour (Boston: Porter Sargent Publisher, 1970), 86.

9. Quoted in Diana Ketcham, "Giovanni Changes and Stays On Course," *The Tribune*, 20 May 1984.

10. Kalamu Ya Salaam [Val Ferdinand], Review of *My House* and *Like A Ripple On A Pond, Black World*, July 1974, 65. McDowell offers a detailed discussion of Salaam's "political background," which suggests that his disapproval of Giovanni's politics was expressed as disapproval of her poetry. See McDowell, 149–51.

11. Quoted in "Princess of Black Poetry: Nikki Giovanni," *Soul Sounds & Stars*, 15 August 1971, 14; hereafter cited in text as "Princess."

12. Larry Neal, "And Shine Swam On," in *Black Fire: An Anthology of*

Afro-American Writing, ed. LeRoi Jones and Larry Neal (New York: William Morrow, 1968), 655; hereafter cited in text.

13. Carol Clemmons, Review of *Truth Is On Its Way, Cold Truth Magazine*, July 1971, 36.

14. Peter Bailey, "Nikki Giovanni: 'I Am Black, Female, Polite . . . ,'" *Ebony*, February 1972, 52; hereafter cited in text.

15. "Women of the Year, 1973: Winners and Women," *The Washington Post*, 15 May 1973.

16. Jeanne Noble, *Beautiful Also Are The Souls of My Black Sisters* (Englewood Cliffs, N.J.: Prentice-Hall, 1978), 197.

17. Interview with Nikki Giovanni, *Today's Health*, May 1974, 28; hereafter cited in text.

18. "Black Perspective," *Time* , 30 October 1972, 85; hereafter cited in text.

19. Barbara Reynolds, Interview with Nikki Giovanni, *USA Today*, 19 September 1985, 11A; hereafter cited in text.

20. Michael A. Tucker, "Nikki Giovanni: The Poet From Lincoln Heights Is No Stranger to Controversy," *Tristate: The Cincinnati Enquirer Magazine*, 20 April 1986, 4.

21. Giovanni in fact protested the blacklisting of a number of people, both the famous and the relative unknown. She was especially irate over the treatment of Dannabella Hall, a gospel singer who went to "witness" for God in South Africa. The Hollywood chapter of the NAACP had wanted to give her an Image Award, but after her trip to South Africa, Randall Robinson—a key figure in these activities—put pressure on the chapter to rescind the award. Giovanni protested. Eventually, Giovanni's protests against the blacklisting tactics, and the reprisals she in turn received, led Charles Kuralt to interview her for his television program; she also appeared on Phil Donahue's television talk show.

22. In 1973, in order to visit Swaziland, Lesotho, and Botswana, the tourist was obliged to make a "courtesy stop" in South Africa, where changing planes was necessary. This "courtesy stop" could be made in one of two ways: through a visa or through a house arrest upon the tourist's arrival in Johannesburg's Jan Smuts Airport. Giovanni applied for and received a four-day visa that allowed her to travel through Johannesburg to Swaziland, back through Johannesburg to Lesotho, and back through Johannesburg to Botswana. From Botswana she was then able to travel directly on to Uganda. The visa application seems to have been the only "evidence" of the false accusations made against her. The absurdity of the accusations was underscored by the fact that her books were at that time banned in South Africa.

23. Quoted with the permission of Nikki Giovanni, who made some of her correspondence files available to me, and Betty J. Blackman, author of the letter.

24. Nikki Giovanni, "A Poet's Reflections," *Encore*, 7 (18 September 1978), 39.

Chapter Two

1. Barbara Reynolds, *And Still We Rise: Interviews With 50 Black Role Models* (Washington: Gannett New Media Services, 1988), 94; hereafter cited in text.

2. For a discussion of these similarities, see, for example, Bernard W. Bell, "New Black Poetry: A Double-Edged Sword," *CLA Journal* 15 (1971), 37–43; and Stephen Henderson, *Understanding the New Black Poetry: Black Speech and Black Music as Poetic References* (New York: Morrow, 1973); hereafter cited in text. Bell finds parallels in four areas: "a nostalgic interest in Africa . . . ; a rediscovery and reevaluation of black folk values . . . ; the elevation of members of the black masses, especially the working class, as heroes, and . . . the introduction and validation of the blues, jazz, ballads, sermons and black idiom as poetic material" (40). Henderson locates the primary difference between the two movements in the attempt of the Black Arts Movement "to speak directly *to* Black people *about themselves* in order to move them toward self-knowledge and collective freedom. It is therefore not 'protest' art but essentially an art of liberating vision" (16).

3. For a discussion of this defensive position, see Lance Jeffers, "The Death of the Defensive Posture: Toward Grandeur in Afro-American Letters," in *The Black Seventies*, ed. Floyd B. Barbour (Boston: Porter Sargent Publisher, 1970), 253–63.

4. Quoted in Hoyt W. Fuller, "Toward A Black Aesthetic," in *The Black Aesthetic*, ed. Addison Gayle, Jr. (New York: Doubleday, 1971), 5.

5. W. E. B. Du Bois, *The Souls of Black Folk*, 1903; rpt. W. E. B. Du Bois, *Writings*, ed. Nathan Huggins (New York: Library of America, 1986), 364; hereafter cited in text.

6. *Negro Digest*, the first publication of Johnson Publications, was modeled after *Reader's Digest.* Eventually, however, *Ebony*, another Johnson publication that became enormously successful, overshadowed *Negro Digest.* Thus, when Hoyt Fuller became the editor of *Negro Digest*, Johnson allowed him to take it in new directions, which he did by seeking original articles by black writers. Fuller hired David Llorens, who traveled to black colleges and generally made known the *Digest*'s interest in publishing material from young writers. Eventually, because of these young writers, the nature of *Negro Digest* changed. For a discussion of the history and role of the little magazines in the Black Arts Movement, see Abby Arthur Johnson and Ronald Maberry Johnson, *Propaganda and Aesthetics: The Literary Politics of Afro-American Magazines in the Twentieth Century* (Amherst: University of Massachusetts Press, 1979).

7. Lerone Bennett, Jr., *Before the Mayflower: A History of Black America*, 5th ed. (New York: Penguin, 1982), 423; hereafter cited in text.

8. Larry Neal, "The Black Arts Movement," in *The Black Aesthetic*, ed. Addison Gayle, Jr. (New York: Doubleday, 1971), 272.

9. James Turner, "Black Nationalism: The Inevitable Response," *Black World*, January 1971, 8; hereafter cited in text.

10. Amiri Baraka, "Foreword: The Wailer," in *Visions of A Liberated Future: Black Arts Movement Writings By Larry Neal*, ed. Michael Schwartz (New York: Thunder's Mouth Press, 1989), x–xi.

11. Don L. Lee, "Toward A Definition: Black Poetry of the Sixties (After LeRoi Jones)," in *The Black Aesthetic*, ed. Addison Gayle, Jr. (New York: Doubleday, 1971), 235.

12. Henry Louis Gates, Jr., "Canon-Formation, Literary History, and the Afro-American Tradition: From the Seen to the Told," in *Afro-American Literary Study in the 1990s*, ed. Houston A. Baker, Jr., and Patricia Redmond (Chicago: University of Chicago Press, 1989), 17.

13. Ron Karenga, "Black Cultural Nationalism," in *The Black Aesthetic*, ed. Addison Gayle, Jr. (New York: Doubleday, 1971), 32.

14. Lorraine Dusky, "Fascinating Woman," *Ingenue*, February 1973, 81; hereafter cited in text.

15. See McDowell for a detailed discussion of this issue.

16. William J. Harris, "Sweet Soft Essence of Possibility: The Poetry of Nikki Giovanni," in *Black Women Writers (1950–1980): A Critical Evaluation*, ed. Mari Evans (New York: Anchor/Doubleday, 1984), 222; hereafter cited in text. Harris cites this poem as an example of "the sort of frivolousness that Giovanni's critics, such as Madhubuti and Wallace, rightfully attack."

17. Suzanne Juhasz makes a similar argument in *Naked and Fiery Forms: Modern American Poetry by Women, A New Tradition* (New York: Octagon/Farrar, Straus and Giroux, 1976), 155–76; hereafter cited in text.

18. Sarah Webster Fabio, "Who Speaks Negro? What Is Black?" *Negro Digest*, September/October 1968, 33.

19. From a conversation with the author, August 1991.

20. Abdul A. Seifullah, Interview with Nikki Giovanni, *Bilalian News*, 4 March 1977, 9; hereafter cited in text.

21. For a detailed analysis of this poem, see Margaret A. Reid, "A Rhetorical Analysis of Black Protest Poetry of the Revolutionary Sixties," *Middle Atlantic Writers Association Review*, 1 (1982), 52.

22. See Henderson, 47 ff.

23. C. W. E. Bigsby, *The Second Black Renaissance: Essays In Black Literature*, Contributions in Afro-American and African Studies, no. 50 (Westport, Conn.: Greenwood Press, 1980), 295. I would, as should be clear, disagree with Bigsby's conclusion that "it is not a collapse which produces compelling poetry" (295).

24. Sherley A. Williams, "The Blues Roots of Contemporary Afro-American Poetry," *Massachusetts Review*, 18 (1977), 549.

25. Ralph Ellison, *Shadow and Act* (New York: New American Library, 1966), 90.

26. Nikki Giovanni, "First Steps Toward A True Revolution," *Negro Digest*, December 1966, 86.

27. Nikki Giovanni, "Black Poems, Poseurs and Power," *Negro Digest*, June 1969, 34; subsequently reprinted in *Gemini.*

28. This number includes the poem of dedication.

29. Ruth McClain, Review of *Re: Creation, Black World*, 62–63. As McDowell shows, however, most of Giovanni's readers did not notice a shift of emphases in her poetry until the publication of *My House.*

30. Giovanni explained her decision not to marry in several different ways. In one statement, she indicated that she did not have the financial pressures that often lead women to marry: "I had a baby at 25 because I *wanted* to have a baby and I could *afford* to have a baby. I did not get married because I didn't *want* to get married and I could *afford* not to get married" (Bailey, 56). In another interview, she stated: "Yes, I consider myself a loner. . . . I have never thought about getting married. It's a drag. To men who say, 'How come a pretty girl like you is not married?', I say, 'How come a handsome dude like you *is* married?'" See Patricia Coffin, "Nikki Giovanni: Princess of Black Poetry," *Single*, 1 (December 1973), 64.

31. Nikki Giovanni, *Re: Creation* (Detroit: Broadside Press, 1970), 34; hereafter cited in text as *RC.*

32. Mary Burgher points out that the valorization of motherhood is common in autobiographies by black women: "Black women autobiographers consistently expand motherhood into a creative and personally fulfilling role." See her "Images of Self and Race in the Autobiographies of Black Women," in *Sturdy Black Bridges: Visions of Black Women in Literature*, ed. Roseann P. Bell, Bettye J. Parker, and Beverly Guy-Sheftall (New York: Anchor/Doubleday, 1979), 115.

33. Juhasz similarly points out that, "Somehow the black woman must be true to herself as she *is* to be both a poet and a revolutionary, for the nature of the revolution itself is in question" (168).

34. A political activist throughout his career, Robeson consistently fought on behalf of black Americans, which led to his victimization by the McCarthyites. For a number of years during the 1950s, he was denied a passport and barred from concert halls.

35. Michele Wallace, one of Giovanni's more venomous detractors, misreads the poem by quoting the first two lines of the second stanza completely out of context: "Although she rarely chose to reflect it in her work, Giovanni did realize the black woman's dilemma to some extent. A line from one of her later poems is unfortunately more typical: 'what i need to do / is sit and wait / cause i'm a woman.'" See Michele Wallace, *Black Macho and the Myth of the Superwoman* (1978; rpt. London: Verso, 1990), 169.

36. Juhasz argues that the concluding stanza suggests that "the less she does do, the more possible becomes the awaited reward; the workings of society are totally out of her hands" (164).

Chapter Three

1. From a conversation with the author, August 1991.
2. For an excellent discussion of the challenge to literary critics that a popular writer poses, see Harris, pp. 218–19. Harris also draws useful distinctions between the good popular writer and the bad popular writer, arguing that Giovanni falls into the first category.
3. Bailey draws attention to this issue in his otherwise favorable article: "There are black artists—those in what is called 'the black power literary establishment'—who are convinced that Nikki's emergence as a 'star' will hinder her development as a *black* poet. Says one member of that group: 'In the beginning I thought that Nikki was going to be one of the stabilizers in the black cultural scene; one who could be counted on to maintain her integrity. Unfortunately, she is off on an ego trip. That might be alright in and of itself; but her talent doesn't match her reputation. She needs to retire for a while and develop her talent rather than continue the quest to be a personality. What is happening to her happens to many committed black people when they get status, money and recognition. They start ego-tripping.' The critic makes it clear that the success and acceptance of her album is important. 'It is important because it reaches many new people. Black people respond to oral works and that makes it extremely important. That's why she must not get into the wrong bag'" (Bailey, 52). The most vicious attack came from Salaam, who argued that "The philosophy of *My House* is strictly European literature regurgitated. We are not Europeans, however. Not even those of us trying with all our might to be that" (Salaam, 67).
4. *A Dialogue: James Baldwin and Nikki Giovanni* (Philadelphia: J. B. Lippincott, 1973), 60; hereafter cited in text as *AD*.
5. Grounds for Giovanni's complaints may be found in a review of *A Dialogue* by Hilda-Njoki McElroy. McElroy complains that "there is nothing profound in the dialogue," but that "it could provide a source for character studies of Baldwin and Giovanni. In fact, it could be staged as a one-act drama. I would title it, 'Who's Afraid of James Baldwin and Nikki Giovanni; A comedy for white audience.'" See her review in *Black World*, December 1973, 48.
6. Thomas Lask, "Soul Festival: A Cool Nikki Giovanni Reads Poetry," *New York Times*, 26 July 1972.
7. Nikki Giovanni, *My House* (New York: William Morrow, 1972), 5; hereafter cited in text as *MH*.
8. From a conversation with the author, August 1991.
9. From a conversation with the author, August 1991.
10. Giovanni seems to be quoting Toni Morrison's *The Bluest Eye*, which

was published in 1970. The statement comes near the very end of that novel and is made in reference to Cholly Breedlove: "Love is never any better than the lover." See *The Bluest Eye* (New York: Holt, Rinehart, Winston, 1970), 163.

11. Giovanni also explains her preference as being based on the fact that *Afro-American* suggests an immigrant status; black Americans were not, however, immigrants. They are Americans whose skin color is black. Giovanni's American centrism is also expressed in an interview from about the same time period. See "Nikki Giovanni On Race, Sex, & Age," *The Black Collegian*, December–January, 1970–71, 30–34; hereafter cited in text as *Black Collegian.*

12. In the final line of the poem's penultimate stanza, *need* is a typographical error and should read *needs*. When Giovanni reads this poem, she reads "and call / it revolution" as "and call / that revolution."

13. Such is the case of Harris's reading of the poem. He reductively claims that in the poem "Giovanni has exchanged the role of revolutionary Mother Courage, sending her Black troops into battle, for the role of domestic Black woman, making fudge for her Black man. While the poem may make the reader uncomfortable—has it set the feminist movement back fifty years?—one can sympathize with Giovanni's desire to retreat into domestic comforts in the face of a disappointing world" (223).

14. Mozella G. Mitchell, for example, states that *The Women and the Men* "marks another milestone in the life and career of Nikki Giovanni. In this collection of poems, we find that she has permitted to flower fully portions of herself and her perception which had been evident only in subdued form or in incompletely worked-through fragments. . . . Furthermore, the delicate, charming, poetic expression they are given in these verses show [*sic*] superior skill and mature creative development." See her essay, "Nikki Giovanni," in *Afro-American Poets Since 1955*, ed. Trudier Harris and Thadious M. Davis, *Dictionary of Literary Biography*, vol. 41 (Detroit: Gale Research, 1985), 148.

15. Nikki Giovanni, *The Women and the Men* (New York: William Morrow, 1975), 2; hereafter cited in text as *WM.*

16. Paula Giddings argues that both "The December of My Springs" and "Something To Be Said For Silence" anticipate the "direction" Giovanni would take in *Cotton Candy*. See her "Nikki Giovanni: Taking A Chance on Feeling," in *Black Women Writers (1950–1980): A Critical Evaluation*, ed. Mari Evans (New York: Anchor/Doubleday, 1984), 214; hereafter cited in text.

17. The misspelling of this crucial word perhaps exemplifies the indifferent editing black writers so often seem to receive from their publishers. Giovanni is herself a notoriously poor speller.

Chapter Four

1. Harris calls *Cotton Candy on a Rainy Day* "Giovanni's bleakest book" (226) and Mitchell finds it "her most sobering book of verse yet" (149).

2. Anna T. Robinson, *Nikki Giovanni: From Revolution to Revelation* (Columbus: State Library of Ohio, 1979), 20; hereafter cited in text.

3. Nikki Giovanni, *Cotton Candy on a Rainy Day* (New York: William Morrow, 1978), 21; hereafter cited in text as *CC*.

4. Robinson maintains that these lines reflect the speaker's feeling that she is "vaguely defined, capable of fading away, of being fogged-in by the drabness of her existence" (20). It is important to note, however, that the speaker is addressing another person, to whom she is, as she acknowledges, elusive.

5. "Stay As Sweet As You Are" is an old song. "Stay In My Corner" was a hit song by The Dells. "Stay (Just A Little Bit Longer)" was sung by Maurice Williams and The Zodiacs, and later covered by the white group The Four Seasons. "Don't Change" was a song by The Five Stairsteps. "Everything Will Change" was a 1970s Quincey Jones song.

6. Janelle Anderson, "The Sister Speaks," *Soul Illustrated*, 3 (Winter 1971), 42.

7. Toni Cade, Preface to *The Black Woman: An Anthology* (New York: New American Library, 1970), 9.

8. Audre Lorde has addressed the hostility that seems endemic in black women's responses to each other. She asks, "Why do Black women reserve a particular voice of fury and disappointment for each other? Who is it we must destroy when we attack each other with that tone of predetermined and correct annihilation? We reduce one another to our own lowest common denominator, and then we proceed to try and obliterate what we most desire to love and touch, the problematic self, unclaimed but fiercely guarded from the other." See her "Eye to Eye: Black Women, Hatred, and Anger" in *Sister Outsider: Essays and Speeches*, by Audre Lorde (Trumansburg, N.Y.: Crossing Press, 1984), 159.

9. See, for example, Harris's comments on *My House*, quoted above in note 12 to Chapter 3.

10. From a conversation with the author, August 1991.

11. The poem was written to the rhythm of a song by Johnny Taylor, "Your Love Is Rated X (That Means You're Extra Special)." From a conversation with the author, August 1991.

Chapter Five

1. Nikki Giovanni, *Those Who Ride The Night Winds* (New York: William Morrow, 1983), 47; hereafter cited in text as *NW*. "A Journey" is included in the volume's second section, "Day Trippers."

2. From a conversation with the author, August 1991.

3. Erlene Stetson has argued that "Polarity is characteristic of Giovanni's poetic message." See *Black Sister*, edited by Erlene Stetson (Bloomington: Indiana University Press, 1981), 51.

4. From a conversation with the author, August 1991.

5. The quilt has, in the last decade, begun to receive acknowledgment as a legitimate art form, mostly because of the efforts of feminist scholars. In light of my subsequent discussion of analogies between Giovanni's new lineless form

and jazz, it is interesting to note that at least one art historian has commented on the analogous neglect suffered by jazz and quilts: "Quilts have been underrated precisely for the same reasons that jazz, the great American music, was also for so long underrated—because the 'wrong' people, for sexist and racist reasons, have not been allowed to represent or define American culture." See Patricia Mainardi, "Quilts: The Great American Art," in *Feminism and Art History: Questioning the Litany*, edited by Norma Broude and Mary D. Garrard (New York: Harper & Row, 1982), 344.

6. In an interview with Claudia Tate, published the same year as *Those Who Ride The Night Winds*, Giovanni expresses similar sentiments about Phillis Wheatley: "There is nothing wrong with the poems she wrote. And I dare say, from what I see of history, there was no particular reason why Phillis Wheatley didn't mean exactly what she said. There is no reason for me to reject what Phillis Wheatley had to say about her experience. And I don't. People get upset because she talks about Africa in terms of how delighted she was to discover Christianity. Well, from what little I know, she might have been damned delighted. Life for an African woman can be very difficult even today, and she was writing in the eighteenth century." See *Black Women Writers At Work*, ed. Claudia Tate (New York: Continuum, 1983), 63.

7. "Love: Is A Human Condition" is among the poems in *Those Who Ride The Night Winds* viciously attacked by Paula Giddings, who finds this poem "typical of the quality of thought in this book—which often borders on the incoherent" (Giddings, 215). Since Giddings wrote the introduction to *Cotton Candy on a Rainy Day*, one might have expected more sympathetic, if not more astute, criticism from her. Her remarks on *Those Who Ride The Night Winds* seem, as McDowell argues about other criticism of Giovanni's work, generated by some personal animosity.

8. Nikki Giovanni, "An Emotional View of Lorraine Hansberry," *Freedomways* 19, no. 4 (1979), 281–82.

9. It is interesting to note that Giovanni's regular column for *Encore* was entitled "The Root of the Matter."

10. Even in serious poems, Giovanni's sense of humor reasserts itself in *Those Who Ride The Night Winds*. Several of the poems in "Day Trippers" are entirely playful and humorous.

Chapter Six

1. Lois Rosenthal, "Writing As Breathing: Nikki Giovanni." *Writer's Digest*, February 1989, 34; hereafter cited in text.

2. Tate's grouping of poems is itself illogical because, as discussed in chapter 3, most of the poems in *The Women and the Men* were first published in *Re: Creation*. Tate's omission of *My House* from either group is also striking.

3. Nikki Giovanni, "An Answer To Some Questions On How I Write: In Three Parts," in *Black Women Writers (1950–1980): A Critical Evaluation,* ed.

Mari Evans; rpt. in *Sacred Cows . . . And Other Edibles* (New York: William Morrow, 1980), 62; hereafter cited in text as *SC*.

4. Nikki Giovanni, "Writing and Being," *Career Insights* (1984), 99.

5. Arlene Elder, "A *MELUS* Interview: Nikki Giovanni," *MELUS* 9, no. 3 (Winter 1982), 69; hereafter cited in text.

6. This is far from saying, however, that works by Afro-American writers in general or Nikki Giovanni in particular are not in fact timeless and universal in their themes, which they clearly are.

Selected Bibliography

PRIMARY SOURCES

Chief Printed Works (exclusive of foreign and anthology editions)

A Dialogue: James Baldwin and Nikki Giovanni. Philadelphia: J. B. Lippincott, 1973.

——— (paperback edition). Philadelphia: J. B. Lippincott, 1973.

A Poetic Equation: Conversations Between Nikki Giovanni and Margaret Walker. Washington, D.C.: Howard University Press, 1974.

——— (paperback edition, with new postscript). Washington, D. C.: Howard University Press, 1983.

Black Feeling, Black Talk. Privately printed, 1968.

Black Judgement. Privately printed, 1968.

Black Feeling, Black Talk/Black Judgement. New York: William Morrow, 1970.

——— (paperback edition). New York: William Morrow, 1971.

Cotton Candy on a Rainy Day. New York: William Morrow, 1978.

——— (paperback edition). New York: Morrow Quill, 1980.

Ego-Tripping And Other Poems For Young People. Illustrated by George Ford. New York: Lawrence Hill, 1973.

——— (paperback edition). Illustrated by George Ford. New York: Lawrence Hill, 1973.

Gemini: An Extended Autobiographical Statement on My First Twenty-Five Years of Being a Black Poet. New York: Bobbs-Merrill, 1971.

——— (paperback edition). New York: Viking, 1973.

——— (paperback edition). New York: Penguin, 1976.

My House. New York: William Morrow, 1972.

——— (paperback edition). New York: William Morrow, 1973.

Night Comes Softly: Anthology of Black Female Voices. Privately printed, 1970.

Re: Creation. Detroit: Broadside Press, 1970.

——— (paperback edition). Detroit: Broadside Press, 1970.

Sacred Cows . . . And Other Edibles. New York: William Morrow, 1988.

——— (paperback edition). New York: William Morrow, 1989.

Spin A Soft Black Song. Illustrated by Charles Bible. New York: Hill and Wang, 1971.

——— (revised edition). Illustrated by George Martins. New York: Hill and Wang, 1985.

——— (paperback edition). Illustrated by George Martins. New York: Sunburst/Hill and Wang, 1987.

Those Who Ride The Night Winds. New York: William Morrow, 1983.

——— (paperback edition). New York: William Morrow, 1984.

Vacation Time: Poems for Children. Illustrated by Marisabina Russo. New York: William Morrow, 1980.

——— (paperback edition). Illustrated by Marisabina Russo. New York: William Morrow, 1981.

The Women and the Men. New York: William Morrow, 1975.

——— (paperback edition). New York: William Morrow, 1975.

Recordings

Cotton Candy on a Rainy Day. Folkways Records FL 9756, 1978.

Legacies. Folkways Records FL 9798, 1976.

Like A Ripple On A Pond. With The New York Community Choir, Benny Diggs, director. Niktom Records. Distributed by Atlantic Recording Corporation, 1973.

The Reason I Like Chocolate. Folkways Records FC 7775, 1976.

Spirit To Spirit. Directed by Mirra Banks. Produced by Perrin Ireland. PBS Television, 1987. Videocassette.

Truth Is On Its Way. With The New York Community Choir, Benny Diggs, director. Right On Records, 1971.

The Way I Feel. With Music Composed by Arif Mardin. Niktom Records. Distributed by Atlantic Recording Corporation, 1975.

Essays, Short Stories, Speeches, Individual Poems, and Letters (a chronological listing)

"First Steps Toward A True Revolution." *Negro Digest* 16 (December 1966): 86–88. Gender issues in the movement.

"Revolution: A Definition." *Conversation* 4 (June 1967): 7–8. Excerpt from a speech on black history.

"A Revolutionary Tale." *Negro Digest* 17 (June 1968): 70–83. Short story later incorporated into *Gemini.*

"The True Import of Present Dialogue, Black vs. Negro (For Peppe, Who Will Ultimately Judge Our Efforts)." *Black Graphics International* 3 (1969): 27–28. Poem, later included in *Black Feeling, Black Talk.*

"A Short Essay of Affirmation Explaining Why (With Apologies To The Federal Bureau of Investigation)." *Black Graphics International* 3 (1969): 24–25. Poem, later included in *Black Feeling, Black Talk.*

"Kitty Litter (A New Definition of Genius)." *Journal of Black Poetry* 1 (Spring 1969): 13–15. Poem.

"Our Detroit Conference." *The Afro-American Woman Magazine* 1 (March/April 1969): 22. Poem, later included in *Black Feeling, Black Talk.*

"Poems (For Dudley Randall)." *The Afro-American Woman Magazine* 1 (March/April 1969): 22. Poem, later included in *Black Feeling, Black Talk.*

"Response to A Letter from Ron Welburn." *Negro Digest* 18 (May 1969): 97–98. "I'm not a cultural nationalist. . . . I'm a Black woman; that embodies a larger responsibility."

"Black Poems, Poseurs, and Power." *Negro Digest* 18 (June 1969): 30–34. Essay, later incorporated into *Gemini.*

"two untitled poems from barbados." *Negro Digest* 18 (September 1969): 72. Later included in *Re: Creation.*

"I Fell Off the Roof One Day (A View of the Black University)." In *The Black Woman: An Anthology*, edited by Toni Cade, 132–36. New York: New American Library, 1970.

"The Library." In *Brothers and Sisters*, edited by Arnold Adoff, 141–46. New York: Macmillan, 1970. Reprinted in *Reading Rooms*, edited by Susan Allen Toth and John Couglan. New York: Doubleday, 1991.

"Poem of Angela Yvonne Davis." 1970. A privately printed broadside. Rpt. in *Black Works* (Spring 1971): 29–31.

"A Very Special Christmas." *Essence* 1 (December 1970): 50. Essay.

"Convalescence—Compared to What." In *Black Review*, edited by Mel Watkins, 117–28. New York: Morrow, 1971. Satirical essay criticizing some aspects of "the revolution."

"What I Would Like To Have Happen In 1971." *Contact* 2 (January 1971): 10. Essay.

"Soul Impressions." *Image* 8 (January 1971): 12–13. An essay on the television program, *Soul!*

"A Poem Too Late For You." *Black Creation* 2 (April 1971): 29. Poem.

"For Gwen Brooks From Nikki Giovanni." *Essence* 1 (April 1971): 26. A tribute to Brooks.

"Conversation With Ida Lewis." *Essence* 1 (May 1971): 30–33, 95.

"For Saundra." *Black Works* (Spring 1971): 31. Included in *Black Judgement.*

"Atrocities." *Black Creation* 2 (Summer 1971): 17. Poem, later included in *My House.*

Foreword to *Blackspirits: A Festival of New Black Poets in America*, edited by Woodie King. New York: Random, 1972.

"Poet to Poet." *Encore* 1 (Spring 1972): 42–48. A conversation with the Russian poet Yevgeny Yevtushenko.

"Interview: A Conversation with Lewis Michaux, Chester Himes, and Nikki Giovanni." *Encore* 1 (September 1972): 46–51.

"How Will We Raise Our Children in the Year 2000?" *Saturday Review of Education*, 10 February 1973, 30–31. Short essay.

"Interview with Roy Wilkins." *Encore* 2 (May, 1973): 58–60.

"Preventive Maintenance." *Encore* 2 (July 1973): 33. Essay in Giovanni's feature column, The Root of the Matter.

"Mankind Had Better Shape Up." *Encore* 2 (August 1973): 60. Essay in Giovanni's feature column, The Root of the Matter.

"Kapo." *Encore* 9 (September 1973): 56. Essay on the Jamaican artist.

"A Lesson in Human Relationships." *Encore* 2 (October 1973): 47. Essay in Giovanni's feature column, The Root of the Matter. Observations about Watergate.

"Number, Pu-leeze." *Encore* 2 (November 1973): 27. Essay in Giovanni's feature column, The Root of the Matter.

"Last Word." *Viva: The International Magazine for Women* 1 (December 1973): 140.

"Lois Lane Knows." *Encore* 3 (January 1974): 22. Essay in Giovanni's feature column, The Root of the Matter. Criticism of the Nixon administration.

"Martin Luther King, Jr.: A Different Drummer." *Encore* 3 (February 1974): 34–35.

"We Must Do It Ourselves." *Encore* 3 (March 1974): 27. Essay in Giovanni's feature column, The Root of the Matter.

"A Poetic Equation." *Encore* 3 (April 1974): 32–35. An excerpt from Giovanni's book of conversations with Margaret Walker.

"The Whole Point Is To Share." *International Educational and Cultural Exchange* 10 (Summer 1974): 20–22. Discussion of her 1973 lecture-tour of Africa.

"Before and Beyond Nixon: An Interview with James MacGregor Burns." *Encore* 3 (June 1974): 40–42.

Untitled. *Literary Cavalcade* 27 (October 1974): 16–17. Essay for young people on identity.

"No Business Like Snow Business." *Encore* 3 (November 1974): 21. Essay in Giovanni's feature column, The Root of the Matter. On politics as business.

Afterword to *A Singer In the Dawn: Reinterpretations of Paul Laurence Dunbar*, edited by Jay Martin. New York: Dodd, Mead, 1975.

"Why Weren't Our 'Sisters in Liberation' in Boston?" *Encore American & Worldwide News* 4 (6 January 1975): 20. Essay in Giovanni's feature column, The Root of the Matter. On the women's movement as a white women's movement.

"Rev. Ike—'You Can't Lose With the Stuff I Use.'" *Encore American & Worldwide News* 4 (17 March 1975): 21–25. Essay focuses on Reverend Frederick J. Eikerenkoetter II and on the role of the black preacher in the black community.

"Leave It to Cleaver." *Encore American & Worldwide News* 4 (19 May 1975): 26. Essay in Giovanni's feature column, The Root of the Matter. Explores the reasons for Eldridge Cleaver's apparent special status—a kind of immunity—with the federal government.

"The Silent Revolution of the Domestic Worker." *Encore American & Worldwide News* 4 (23 June 1975): 36. Essay in Giovanni's feature column, The Root of the Matter. The changing role of the domestic worker, mostly black and female, in our society.

"Feeling: Mankind's Last Frontier." *San Francisco Examiner*, 14 July 1975.

"Ego Tripping." *New York Times*, 18 August 1975. One of many reprints of this poem.

"Why Landlords Get Relief." *Encore American & Worldwide News* 4 (18 August 1975): 32. Essay in Giovanni's feature column, The Root of the Matter. Problems of rent in New York City.

"Aftra: A Rip-Off." *Encore American & Worldwide News* 4 (8 September 1975): 28–29. Essay in Giovanni's feature column, The Root of the Matter. The evils of unions, especially the American Federation of Television and Radio Announcers.

"Are Unions Good for the Schools?" *Encore American & Worldwide News* 4 (20 October 1975): 48. Essay in Giovanni's feature column, The Root of the Matter. The role of the American Federation of Teachers in the deterioration of public schools.

"The Great Stonewaller." *Encore American & Worldwide News* 5 (22 March 1976): 36. Essay in Giovanni's feature column, The Root of the Matter. Denunciation of Nixon's being allowed to visit China.

"Campaign 1976: Hubert Humphrey." *Encore American & Worldwide News* 5 (3 May 1976): 18. Argument against nominating Humphrey for the presidential election.

"Kennedy: Is Congress A Conspirator?" *Encore American & Worldwide News* 6 (6 June 1977): 8. The failure of Congress to pursue the investigations into Kennedy's assassination.

"Same Old Voices, Same Old (Smoke-filled) Rooms." *Encore American & Worldwide News* 5 (21 June 1976): 48. Essay in Giovanni's feature column, The Root of the Matter. On the need for President Carter to turn to new black leaders.

"Celebrating the Human Species." *Encore American & Worldwide News* 7 (18 December 1978): 20–23. On our responsibilities to children.

"An Emotional View of Lorraine Hansberry." *Freedomways* 19 (1979): 281–82. An essay that is later used in the poem "Lorraine Hansberry: An Emotional View," published in *Those Who Ride The Night Winds*.

"Decoding Carter's Message." *Encore American & Worldwide News* 8 (19 March 1979): 13. Essay in Giovanni's feature column, The Root of the Matter. "Carter's message" is that "Blacks may as well not exist."

"A Message from Phyllis Hyman's Lifetime." *Eagle and Swan* 4 (September 1979): 22–25.

"Why We Are Brokers At The Table of Peace." *Encore American & Worldwide News* 8 (15 October 1979): 8–9. Role of black Americans in foreign affairs, particularly the Middle East.

"Martin Luther King's Letter From Birmingham Jail." *Encore American & Worldwide News* 8 (19 November 1979): 19.

"a song for new-ark." *New Jersey Monthly* 6 (November 1981): 60. Later included in *Those Who Ride The Night Winds.*

"An Answer to Some Questions on How I Write: In Three Parts." In *Black Women Writers (1950–1980): A Critical Evaluation*, edited by Mari Evans, 205–10. New York: Anchor/Doubleday, 1984. Later included in *Sacred Cows.*

"Writing and Being." *Career Insights* (1984): 98–99. "I consider writing to be the ultimate existential situation; for me, it's something I need to do in order to be."

"Mother-to-Mother." *Essence* 15 (September 1984): 154, 175. Later incorporated into "In Sympathy With Another Motherless Child."

"In Sympathy With Another Motherless Child (One View of the Profession of Writing)." Vol. 6, *Contemporary Authors: Autobiography Series*, 151–64. Detroit: Gale Research Co., 1984. Later included in *Sacred Cows.*

Introduction to *Intro to Fine*, by Adele Stephanie Sebastian. San Francisco: WIM Publications, 1985.

"My Own Style." *Essence* 16 (May 1985): 60, 62.

"The Poet's Mind: A Positive Look Toward the Year 2000." *Spelman Magazine* 101 (Winter 1985): 10–11. Excerpted from a convocation address delivered 22 September 1983.

"Pioneers: A View of Home." *Artemis* 11 (1988): 3.

Introduction to *Wailing the Dead to Sleep*, by Lucinda Roy. London: Bogle-L'Ouverture Publication Ltd., 1988.

"Episodes." *Catalyst*, Summer 1988, 35.

"A Letter from Nikki." *Catalyst*, Winter 1988, 9.

Foreword to *The Abandoned Baobab: The Autobiography of a Senegalese Woman*, by Ken Bugul. New York: Lawrence Hill Books, 1991.

"My Road to Virginia." *Ohioana Quarterly* 34 (Spring 1991): 2–7. Essay on academe.

"Campus Racism 101." *Essence* 22 (August 1991): 71–72.

Reviews (a chronological listing)

Review of *Hog Butcher*, by Ronald Fari. *Elan: A Journal of Review and Opinion* 1 (November–December 1966): 7–8. *Elan* was "an independent, intervarsity journal of review, opinion, and Black Arts," of which she was the managing editor.

Review of *Zeely*, by Virginia Hamilton. *Negro Digest* 16 (August 1967): 93.

Review of *The Flagellants*, by Carlene Hatcher Polite. *Negro Digest* 17 (January 1968): 97–98.

Review of *Curling*, by Robert Boles. *Negro Digest* 17 (August 1968): 86–88.

Review of *The Clarion People*, by Audrey Lee. *Negro Digest* 17 (September–October 1968): 14–15.

Review of *The Speeches of Malcolm X at Harvard* by Archie Epps. *Negro Digest* 18 (November 1968): 51–52.

Review of *Tear Down These Walls!* by Dorothy Sterling. *Negro Digest* 18 (January 1969): 51–52, 70.

Review of *Howard Street*, by Calvin C. Heard. *Negro Digest* 18 (February 1969): 71–73.

"And What About Laurie?" Review of *Uptight. Black Dialogue* 4 (Spring 1969): 14–16.

Review of *The Raw Pearl*, by Pearl Bailey. *Negro Digest* 18 (April 1969): 85–86.

Review of *Seeds Beneath the Snow*, by Arthenia Bates. *Negro Digest* 18 (August 1969): 94.

Review of *Revolution*, by Ebon. *Negro Digest* 18 (August 1969): 95.

Review of *The Rocks Cry Out*, by Beatrice M. Murphy and Nancy L. Arnez. *Negro Digest* 18 (August 1969): 97–98. Life is "not about waiting for Godot, being a tool of the fates, what white folks haven't and have done. It's about taking control, deciding our own direction, being our own fine Black selves."

Review of *Cities Burning*, by Dudley Randall. *Negro Digest* 18 (September 1969): 96.

Review of *Pisstain Stairs and The Monkey Man's Wares*, by Jayne Cortez. *Negro Digest* 19 (December 1969): 97.

Review of *Malcolm X—The Man and His Times*, edited by John Henrik Clarke. *Freedomways* 10 (1970): 84–87. "Malcolm was maybe an oral Bible for Black folks—each can dig on the chapter he wishes."

Review of *The Chosen Place, The Timeless People*, by Paule Marshall. *Negro Digest* 19 (January 1970): 51–52, 84.

Review of *Daddy Was A Number Runner*, by Louise Meriwether. *Black World* 19 (July 1970): 85–86.

Review of *Blue Blackness*, by John Chenault. *Black World* 19 (August 1970): 91–93.

Review of *Third World Poets Speak the Truth*, edited by M. A. Mahadi. *Black World* 20 (March 1971): 89–90.

Review of *Poems By Nikki*, by Nikki Grimes. *Black World* 20 (March 1971): 87–88.

Review of *We A BaddDDD People*, by Sonia Sanchez. *Black World* 20 (September 1971): 88–89.

Review of *The Planet of Junior Brown*, by Virginia Hamilton. *Black World* 21 (March 1972): 70–71.

Review of *No Name in the Street*, by James Baldwin. *Encore* 1 (Summer 1972): 76.

Review of *Buck and the Preacher. Encore* 1 (Summer 1972): 59.

Review of *The Washington Pay-Off*, by Robert N. Winter-Berger. *Encore* 1 (October 1972): 70.

Review of *The Star Spangled Hustle*, by Robert Lee Grant. *Encore* 1 (October 1972): 64.

Review of *The Harder They Come. Encore* 2 (May 1973): 14.

Review of *Bessie*, by Chris Albertson. *Encore* 2 (June 1973): 59.

Review of *In Love and Trouble*, by Alice Walker. *The Washington Post Book World*, 18 November 1973, 1.

Review of *The Autobiography of Miss Jane Pittman. Encore* 3 (April 1974): 46. Review of the film.

Review of *Exploring Black America*, by Marcella Thum. *Encore American & Worldwide News* 4 (4 August 1975): 39.

Review of *The Junior Bachelor Society*, by John A. Williams. *Encore American & Worldwide News* 5 (6 July 1976): 43.

Review of *Love, Black Love*, by George Davis. *Encore American & Worldwide News* 7 (3 April 1978): 41.

"A Poet's Reflections." Review of *the heart as ever green*, by Carolyn Rodgers. *Encore American & Worldwide News* 7 (18 September 1978): 39.

Review of *Just Above My Head*, by James Baldwin. *Encore American & Worldwide News* 9 (January 1980): 46.

Review of *Those the Sun Has Loved*, by Rose Jourdain. *Encore American & Worldwide News* 9 (January 1980): 45.

Review of *Stark Raving Elvis*, by William McCranor Henderson. *New York Times Book Review*, 9 December 1984, 26.

Interviews (a chronological listing)

Anon. "Nikki Giovanni: On Race, Age, & Sex." *The Black Collegian* 1 (December–January 1970–71): 30–34. Some of Giovanni's earliest opinions on a range of topics, especially interesting for her antagonism toward the women's movement, "a movement for white women."

Editors. "Nikki Giovanni: La Poesie-Conscience." *Jeune Afrique*, 25 March 1972, 42–43. "Au fond, je suis comme les autres femmes, je veux vieillir at mourir dans mon lit entourée de mes petits-enfants." ("Basically, I am like other women, I want to grow old and to die of natural causes, surrounded by my grandchildren.")

Terrell, Angela. "Nikki Giovanni: 'Vision and Space.'" *The Washington Post*, 23 July 1972. Giovanni comments on literary critics and the black aesthetic.

Cohen, Toba. "Do You Know *Why* You Like A Particular Novel, Painting, or Symphony?" *Today's Health* 52 (May 1974): 28–33, 65. An interview/panel discussion with Giovanni, Peter Farb, and Rudolf Schramm about the purpose of art.

Elder, Arlene. "A *MELUS* Interview: Nikki Giovanni." *MELUS* 9 (Winter

1982): 61–75. The first major interview with the mature Giovanni; important comments about the role of the writer.

Tate, Claudia. *Black Women Writers At Work*, 60–78. New York: Continuum, 1983. An important interview in which Giovanni talks extensively about her own development as a writer.

Bonner, Carrington. "An Interview with Nikki Giovanni." *Black American Literature Forum* 18 (Spring 1984): 29–30. Deals with the South Africa issue.

Reynolds, Barbara. "Inquiry." *USA Today*, 19 September 1985. Giovanni's denial of the accusations that she performed in South Africa.

Rigney, Barbara Hill. "An Interview with Nikki Giovanni." *Ohio Journal* 9 (Spring 1986): 24–26. Giovanni speaks about her career as well as about the South Africa issue.

Reynolds, Barbara. "Interview with Nikki Giovanni." In *And Still I Rise: Interviews With 50 Black Role Models*, 93–96. Washington: Gannett New Media Services, 1988. Giovanni looks back on her career; responds to questions about South Africa.

Anon. "An Interview with Nikki Giovanni." *Reflections: The National Student Poetry Magazine for All Ages* 7 (1989): 14–15.

Anon. "An Interview with Nikki Giovanni." *Jordan Creek Anthology* 3 (1990): 59–71. Giovanni comments on writing and teaching.

SECONDARY SOURCES

Critical Books and Articles: Background

Barbour, Floyd B., ed. *The Black Seventies*. Boston: Porter Sargent Publisher, 1970. Contains 20 essays, most never previously published, projecting goals for the 1970s.

Barksdale, Richard K. "Humanistic Protest in Recent Black Poetry." In Gibson, *Modern Black Poets*, 157–64. Historical outline of literary protest in the black literary tradition.

Bell, Bernard W. "New Black Poetry: A Double-Edged Sword." *CLA Journal* 15 (1971): 37–43. Argues that the new black poets use hatred as a rhetorical strategy and that "on a deeper level" their "poetry is rooted in a love of black people and an affirmation of life."

Davis, Arthur P. "The New Poetry of Black Hate." In Gibson, *Modern Black Poets*, 147–56. (First published in *CLA Journal* 13 [June 1970]: 382–91.) Argues that the "hatred" in the poetry of black hate is perhaps primarily an artistic convention or device.

Fabio, Sarah Webster. "Who Speaks Negro? What Is Black?" *Negro Digest* 7

(September/October 1968): 33–37. Distinguishes between the concepts of *Negro* and *Black* in American culture.

Fuller, Hoyt W. "The New Black Literature: Protest or Affirmation." In Gayle, *The Black Aesthetic*, 346–69. Examines the dismissal, by white literary critics, of Afro-American literature as "protest," and therefore "on the far periphery of art."

———. "Towards A Black Aesthetic." In Gayle, *The Black Aesthetic*, 3–12. Situates the conflict between black writers and white critics within the larger context of race relations in America.

Gayle, Addison, Jr., ed. *Black Expression: Essays By and About Black Americans in the Creative Arts*. New York: Weybright and Talley, 1969. This generically arranged collection of 40 essays, most previously published, usefully brings together classic statements about Afro-American literature.

———. *The Black Aesthetic*. Garden City, N.Y.: Doubleday, 1971. More than 30 essays, most previously published, on the need for and possibility of a black aesthetic in understanding black music and literature.

Gerald, Carolyn F. "The Black Writer and His Role." In Gayle, *The Black Aesthetic*, 370–78. Argues that the black writer provides necessary racial images to black people and is "the myth-maker of his people."

Gibson, Donald B., ed. *Modern Black Poets: A Collection of Critical Essays*. Englewood Cliffs, N.J.: Prentice-Hall, 1973. Twelve previously published essays on poetry, from the Harlem Renaissance to the 1960s.

Jackson, Kathryn. "LeRoi Jones and the New Black Writers of the Sixties." *Freedomways* 9 (1969): 232–46. A useful summary of the goals and literary strategies of Jones and other Black Arts writers.

Jeffers, Lance. "The Death of the Defensive Posture: Toward Grandeur in Afro-American Letters." In Barbour, *The Black Seventies*, 253–63. An excellent essay that analyzes the influence of racism on earlier black writers, who felt obliged "to be a defender of Blacks." One result of the Black Arts Movement will be that the writer "will cast aside his traditional defensive posture."

Johnson, Abby Arthur, and Ronald Maberry Johnson. *Propaganda and Aesthetics: The Literary Politics of Afro-American Magazines in the Twentieth Century*. Amherst: University of Massachusetts Press, 1979. A valuable historical study of the reflection of politics in the underlying aesthetics of literary magazines.

Karenga, Ron. "Black Cultural Nationalism." In Gayle, *The Black Aesthetic*, 32–38. This essay provides a representative sampling of the positions taken by Karenga, who was among the more radical and visible of the black cultural nationalists. "The real function of art is to make revolution."

Kgositsile, William Keorapetse. "Paths to the Future." In Gayle, *The Black Aesthetic*, 248–60. Essay on the political goals of black writers in the 1960s.

Lee, Don L. "Black Poetry: Which Direction?" *Negro Digest* 17 (September/October 1968): 27–32. "Black poets will live their poems; they, themselves, will be poems."

———. "Toward A Definition: Black Poetry of the Sixties (After LeRoi Jones)." In Gayle, *The Black Aesthetic*, 235–47. Identifies the defining features of the new black poetry.

Neal, Larry. *Visions of A Liberated Future: Black Arts Movement Writings*. New York: Thunder's Mouth Press, 1989. A posthumous collection of Neal's essays; also includes commentary by Amiri Baraka, Stanley Crouch, Charles Fuller, and Jayne Cortez.

———. "And Shine Swam On." In *Black Fire: An Anthology of Afro-American Writing*, edited by LeRoi Jones and Larry Neal, 638–56. New York: William Morrow, 1968. Reprinted in Neal, *Visions of A Liberated Future*. An important essay on the relationship between the black writer in America and the problem of "double consciousness" for black Americans.

———. "The Black Arts Movement." In Gayle, *The Black Aesthetic*, 272–90. Valuable essay on the history and aesthetics of the Black Arts Movement.

Perkins, Eugene. "The Black Arts Movement: Its Challenge and Responsibility." In Barbour, *The Black Seventies*, 85–97. Argues that art must serve the revolution.

Snead, James A. "Repetition As A Figure of Black Culture." In *Black Literature and Literary Theory*, edited by Henry Louis Gates, Jr., 59–79. New York: Methuen, 1984. Extremely useful essay on the forms of repetition in black music and language, which are exploited in black literature.

Critical Books and Articles: General Appraisals

Brooks, A. Russell. "The Motif of Dynamic Change in Black Revolutionary Poetry." *CLA Journal* 15 (1971): 7–17. Unlike the poetry of Don Lee, Giovanni's poetry offers no vision of a new future.

Christian, Barbara T. "Images of Black Women in Afro-American Literature: From Stereotype to Character." Chapter 1 in *Black Feminist Criticism: Perspectives On Black Women Writers*. New York: Pergamon, 1985. Examines the oral quality of Giovanni's poetry; argues that her poetry "peaks" at the juncture of race and gender.

Cook, Martha. "Nikki Giovanni: Place and Sense of Place in Her Poetry." In *Southern Women Writers: The New Generation*, edited by Tonette Bond Inge, 279–300. Tuscaloosa: The University of Alabama Press, 1990. Provides a useful overview of Giovanni's poetry and of critical responses to it; focuses especially on place in the poetry.

Fox-Genovese, Elizabeth. "My Statue, My Self: Autobiographical Writings of Afro-American Women." In *The Private Self: Theory and Practice of Women's Autobiographical Writings*, edited by Shari Benstock, 63–89. Chapel Hill: University of North Carolina Press, 1988. Places Giovanni within the larger context of autobiographical writings by Afro-American women.

One of the few critics to offer serious and objective analysis of Giovanni's prose works.

Georgoudaki, Ekaterini. *Race, Gender, and Class Perspectives in the Works of Maya Angelou, Gwendolyn Brooks, Rita Dove, Nikki Giovanni, and Audre Lorde.* Thessaloniki, Greece: Aristotle University of Thessaloniki, 1991. Interesting for the perspective of a non-American looking at Giovanni's poetry, the book also offers one of the few examinations of Giovanni's poetry for children.

Giddings, Paula. "Nikki Giovanni: Taking A Chance On Feeling." In *Black Women Writers (1950–1980): A Critical Evaluation*, edited by Mari Evans, 211–17. New York: Anchor/Doubleday, 1984. In this overview of Giovanni's work, Giddings often bases critical judgments of Giovanni's poetry on personality traits of Giovanni. Condescending at the beginning, the essay becomes openly hostile by the end. Offers little insight into Giovanni's work.

Harris, William J. "Sweet Soft Essence of Possibility: The Poetry of Nikki Giovanni." In *Black Women Writers (1950–1980): A Critical Evaluation*, edited by Mari Evans, 218–28. New York: Anchor/Doubleday, 1984. Offers a useful analysis of Giovanni as a good popular poet who "is also a serious artist because she tries to examine her life honestly."

Henderson, Stephen. *Understanding the New Black Poetry: Black Speech and Black Music as Poetic References*. New York: William Morrow, 1973. Henderson's now classic study usefully discusses the influence of black music and speech on the new black poetry in general and on Giovanni's poetry in particular.

Jones, Dawn Renee. "Nikki Giovanni: A Poetry of Revolutionary Love." *The Loft* 13 (June 1991): 1, 14. An interesting reflection of Giovanni's impact on younger writers.

Juhasz, Suzanne. "'A Sweet Inspiration . . . of My People': The Poetry of Gwendolyn Brooks and Nikki Giovanni." Chapter 7 in *Naked and Fiery Forms: Modern American Poetry by Women, A New Tradition*. New York: Octagon/Farrar, Straus and Giroux, 1976. One of the best essays on Giovanni's work up through *My House*.

McDowell, Margaret B. "Groundwork for a More Comprehensive Criticism of Nikki Giovanni." In *Belief vs. Theory in Black American Literary Criticism*, edited by Joe Weixlmann and Chester J. Fontenot, 135–60. Studies in Black American Literature, vol. 2. Greenwood, Fla.: Penkevill Publishing Co., 1986. An excellent essay on the early critical reception of Giovanni's work; early reviews were based on personal and ideological differences rather than on the work itself, and yet their influence on subsequent reception has been profound.

Noble, Jeanne. "Speak the Truth to the People." Chapter 7 in *Beautiful Also Are the Souls of My Black Sisters: A History of the Black Woman in America.* Englewood Cliffs, N.J.: Prentice-Hall, 1978. Connects Giovanni to earlier black women poets, and offers a positive appraisal of her work through 1978.

Palmer, R. Roderick. "The Poetry of Three Revolutionists: Don L. Lee, Sonia Sanchez, and Nikki Giovanni." In Gibson, *Modern Black Poets*, 135–46. (First published in *CLA Journal* 15 [1971]: 25–36.) This now classic essay argues that Giovanni is "the most polemic, the most incendiary" of the three poets considered.

Redmond, Eugene B. *Drumvoices: The Mission of Afro-American Poetry*. New York: Anchor/Doubleday, 1976. Places Giovanni rather unflatteringly within the historical context of Afro-American poetry.

Reid, Margaret A. "A Rhetorical Analysis of Black Protest Poetry of the Revolutionary Sixties." *Middle Atlantic Writers Association Review* 1 (1982): 50–55. Highly technical analysis of the rhetorical features of the early poetry.

Robinson, Anna T. *Nikki Giovanni: From Revolution to Revelation.* Columbus: State Library of Ohio, 1979. A balanced overview of Giovanni's work through *Cotton Candy.*

Sheffey, Ruthe. "Wit and Irony in Militant Black Poetry." *Black World* 22 (June 1973): 14–21. Discusses the use, by Giovanni and others, of irony and satire as a means of retreating "from the abyss of despair . . . into a saving grace of laughter."

Williams, Sherley A. "The Blue Roots of Contemporary Afro-American Poetry." *Massachusetts Review* 18 (1977): 542–54. Excellent essay on the features of the blues that are appropriated by Afro-American poets, including Giovanni.

Critical Articles and Reviews: Individual Volumes

Brooks, A. Russell. "Power and Morality as Imperatives for Nikki Giovanni and James Baldwin: A View of *A Dialogue*." In *James Baldwin: A Critical Evaluation*, edited by Therman B. O'Daniel, 205–9. Washington, D.C.: Howard University Press, 1977. Argues that *Re: Creation* signals "an abrupt change" in Giovanni's values, and that *My House* "moves still further from revolution."

Bryant, Jerry H. Review of *Gemini. Saturday Review*, 15 January 1972, 34. This largely negative assessment of Giovanni's autobiography chides the poet for not revealing her private self and for adopting a "pose of childlike defiance."

Duffy, Martha. Review of *Gemini. Time*, 17 January 1972, 63–64. A balanced review of *Gemini*.

Fabio, Sarah Webster. Review of *Black Feeling, Black Talk/Black Judgement. Black World* 19 (December 1970): 102–4. A thoughtful and detailed review that finds the volume successful in "conjuring up the spirit of time, and, to a lesser degree, place."

Giddings, Paula. Review of *Gemini. Black World* 21 (August 1972): 51–52. Argues that Giovanni's autobiography resembles "Black literature of the past," meaning that "it is written from a personal as well as a personalist view."

Golden, Marita. Review of *Sacred Cows . . . And Other Edibles. The Washington Post*, 14 February 1988, 3. Criticizes Giovanni's handling of the essay form.

Guenther, Charles. Review of *Sacred Cows . . . And Other Edibles. St. Louis Post-Dispatch*, 27 February 1988. Highly favorable review which finds the book "typically American" and "sometimes . . . universal."

Jordan, June. Review of *Gemini. New York Times Book Review*, 13 February 1972. Important for its notice of "a transition taking place inside the artist."

Kent, George E. "The 1975 Literary Scene: Significant Developments." *Phylon* 37 (1976): 100–12. Favorable review of *My House*, which gives us "varied voices from the poet."

Llorens, David. Review of *Black Judgement. Negro Digest* 18 (April 1969): 82–84. A positive review, interesting for the aesthetic it invokes; it gives the reader a good sense of the intellectual climate in which Giovanni was writing.

McClain, Ruth. Review of *Re: Creation. Black World* 20 (February 1971): 62–64. Registers disappointment in Giovanni's transformation into "an almost declawed, tamed Panther with bad teeth."

Prescott, Peter S. "Truth in Black and White." *Newsweek*, 31 January 1972, 80–81. Considers *Gemini* along with works by other writers. Finds Giovanni honest and not "as evil as she wants to be."

Salaam, Kalamu Ya. [Val Ferdinand]. Review of *My House* and *Like A Ripple On A Pond. Black World* 23 (July 1974): 64–70. An example of the personal and ideological criticism to which Giovanni was subject early in her career.

Critical Articles: Biographical

Anon. "Princess of Black Poetry: Nikki Giovanni." *Soul Sounds & Stars*, 15 August 1971. Valuable for Giovanni's comments on her relationship to an oral tradition.

Bailey, Peter. "Nikki Giovanni: 'I Am Black, Female, Polite . . .'" *Ebony*, February 1972. Major article on Giovanni's career up through the release of *Truth*.

Barnes, S. Brandi. "Nikki Giovanni." *Seanna: For Women of Color in Today's World*, February 1985. Touches on the South Africa episode; contains inaccuracies.

Batman, Alex. "Nikki Giovanni." In *American Poets Since World War II*. Dictionary of Literary Biography, vol. 5, part 1. Detroit: Gale Research Co., 1980. A balanced overview of Giovanni's life and work, through *Cotton Candy*.

Coffin, Patricia. "Nikki Giovanni: Princess of Black Poetry." *Single*, December

1973. Well-researched biographical essay on Giovanni's life in the early 1970s.

Dusky, Lorraine. "Fascinating Woman." *Ingenue*, February 1973. Detailed information about Giovanni's publication of her first two volumes.

Gould, Jean. *Modern American Women Poets.* New York: Dodd, Mead, 1984. A sympathetic but frequently speculative and inaccurate overview of Giovanni's life and career.

Lang, Tony. "Nikki." *Cincinnati Enquirer Magazine*, 8 July 1973. A good overview of Giovanni's life and early career; also contains statements by the poet about writing.

Litterine, Lynn. "Nikki Giovanni: 'If Revolution Kills Old Women, Then I Don't Want the Revolution.'" *The Record* (of Bergen County, N.J.), 13 September 1973. Giovanni's public denunciation of violence; "the revolutionaries have to be better than the existing order and they're not."

Loercher, Diana. "Nikki Giovanni's Poems . . . Radiate Black Pride, Woman Pride." *The Black American* 15 (1973): 24. Based on an interview after Giovanni's July 1972 performance at Alice Tully Hall, the article contains comments by Giovanni about changes in her poetry and about feminism.

Mitchell, Mozella G. "Nikki Giovanni." In *Afro-American Poets Since 1955.* Dictionary of Literary Biography, vol. 41. Detroit: Gale Research, 1985. Balanced, accurate overview of Giovanni's life and work, through *Night Winds.*

Murphy, Frederick D. "Nikki." *Encore American & Worldwide News* 4 (5 May 1975): 30–34. Provides information, some anecdotal, unavailable elsewhere about Giovanni's career.

Rosenthal, Lois. "Writing As Breathing: Nikki Giovanni." *Writer's Digest*, February 1989, 30–34. Relatively recent comments by Giovanni about writing and the writer.

Stokes, Stephanie J. "'My House': Nikki Giovanni." *Essence*, August 1981. Giovanni's life after she moved from New York back to Cincinnati.

Tucker, Michael A. "Nikki Giovanni: The Poet From Lincoln Heights." *Tristate: The Cincinnati Enquirer Magazine*, 20 April 1986, 4–8. Based on interview with Giovanni about the controversy over South Africa. Contains information unavailable elsewhere.

Index

The Author

Virginia Fowler was educated at the University of Kentucky and the University of Pittsburgh. She began teaching at Virginia Polytechnic Institute and State University in 1977, where she is an Associate Professor of English.

Professor Fowler's earlier work was primarily on Henry James; her book, *Henry James's American Girl: The Embroidery on the Canvas*, was published by the University of Wisconsin Press in 1984.

More recently, Professor Fowler has worked in the area of curriculum development. She helped initiate a Women's Studies Program at Virginia Tech and received grants to work toward the development of a curriculum that is inclusive of women and minorities. Her teaching and research interests are primarily in the area of Afro-American literature, particularly Afro-American women writers. She is also engaged in efforts aimed at the recruitment and retention of Afro-American students.

Professor Fowler's interest in Nikki Giovanni dates back to the early 1970s, when she first began reading the poet's work. A number of years later, she recruited the poet to Virginia Tech under the auspices of a state program aimed at attracting Afro-American writers and scholars to Virginia's colleges and universities.

The Editor

Frank Day is a professor of English at Clemson University. He is the author of *Sir William Empson: An Annotated Bibliography* and *Arthur Koestler: A Guide to Research*. He was a Fulbright Lecturer in American Literature in Romania (1980–81) and in Bangladesh (1986–87).